ASHA KAUSHIK has been teaching in the Department of Political Science, University of Rajasthan, Jaipur since 1973. She had meritorious academic performance and was awarded the Ph.D. degree (1986) on *Political Criticism in Post-Independence Indo-Anglian Novel* by the University of Rajasthan, Jaipur. She has published over two dozen research papers in national and international journals and was recently awarded Senior Fellowship by the ICSSR on Symbols of Political Activism. Her forthcoming publication is : *M.N. Roy: Quest for Alternative Paradigms*.

POLITICS, AESTHETICS AND CULTURE
A Study of Indo-Anglian Political Novel

POLITICS, AESTHETICS AND CULTURE

A Study of Indo-Anglian Political Novel

ASHA KAUSHIK

MANOHAR

1988

The Indian Council of Social Science Research gave the financial support towards the publication of this work. However, the responsibility for the contents of the book—facts, opinions, etc. are entirely that of the author and not of the ICSSR.

ISBN-81-85054-49-7

First Published 1988

Published by
Ramesh Jain
for Manohar Publications,
1 Ansari Road, Daryaganj,
New Delhi 110002

Printed by
Patel Enterprises
at Sunil Printers
1067, Naraina,
New Delhi-110028

For

Ashlesha

Preface

Relationship between politics and literature has been a subject of growing interest in recent years all over the world. The subject, however, remains largely unexplored. The present study was undertaken primarily as an academic adventure motivated more by inquisitiveness than any special claims to insight into the vast and challenging field.

The study assumes that literature is a recorded form of culture as creative activity. Culture also forms part of the process of domination of one segment of society over another. It is an inclusive form of power-relationships in a complex interlocking of political, cultural and social forces. Creative literature, therefore, is a legitimate source of studying interaction of politics and culture in a given society. Employment of literary perspective as a cultural mode of political enquiry provides an opportunity for comprehending a political system on its own terms, that is, in an indigenous spectrum of values, goals, ideals and norms.

Selection of Indian novel in English as a specific datum for the present study, is defensible for two reasons. Firstly, in India since creative writing in English grew and evolved in the characteristic historic-political milieu of the nineteenth century, the political motif was discernibly the dominant one during the initial stages of its evolution. And, as the study brings out, it has since then, constantly occupied a central place in the Indo-Anglian imagination. Secondly, irrespective of partisan claims to the contrary, English continues to be the virtual *lingua franca* in India, more specifically, for intellectual communication, creative as well as critical.

An interdisciplinary study of this kind is faced with the challenge of interweaving relevant aspects of both literature and political science, without transgression into the autonomy and identity of either. How far I have succeeded is for the readers to judge but I can say that I have sincerely tried to keep the objective in view.

The study as a Ph.D. dissertation owed its initiation to my supervisor and teacher, Professor Iqbal Narain. a persistent advocate of interdisciplinary orientation in political science in India. The subject had been his concern for a number of years. When he suggested it to me, I gratefully accepted the challenging prospects. And I must say that the study has not been without its own academic rewards. For counsel, encouragement and guidance at each step of the work, I owe a sense of deep gratitude to him.

I am also profoundly indebted to Professor William Mulder, former Director, American Studies Research Centre (ASRC) Hyderabad, who worked for promotion of interdisciplinary research in India in several ways. His academic guidance, at the initial stages of my work, was immensely valuable.

The study might not have sustained its critical vigour but for the genuine critical comments on my preliminary draft by professor G.S. Amur, Department of English, Marathwada University, Aurangabad, Dr. Meenakshi Mukherjee, Department of English, Central University, Hyderabad, and Dr. D.B. Mathur, Department of Political Science, University of Rajasthan, Jaipur.

It is not often that a researcher gets the privilege to sit before a great mind and learn. I am grateful for the long and fascinating interview granted to me by Raja Rao on 7 June, 1981, at the Central Institute of English and Foreign Languages (CIE&FL), Hyderabad. It was an experience, as it were, for a life time.

Welcome financial assistance for the project was provided by the U.G.C. during 1982-83 and by the ASRC during 1980-82. The ICSSR granted a subsidy for publication of the work. I am grateful to all the three institutions and their authorities.

I cherish happy and grateful memories of the library staff of the ASRC and the CIE&FL, Hyderabad and the Central Library, University of Rajasthan, Jaipur. I am particularly grateful to Ms. Sreenidhi Iyengar, Librarian, ASRC, for her unfailing personal interest in obtaining rare books for my project from other libraries on loan.

It is to the Department of Political Science, University of Rajasthan, Jaipur that I owe my academic roots. My thanks are due to the colleagues, teachers and students there, for their constant concern, appreciation and criticism.

The ultimate credit for the study goes to my husband, Dr. Surendra Nath Kaushik, and to our darling daughter, Ashlesha. My brother, Arun too deserves special appreciation.

Finally, I am thankful to Mr. Ramesh Jain for expeditious publication of the work.

Jaipur, 1987   ASHA KAUSHIK

Contents

1

Introduction

Those who are awake have a world in common, but every
sleeper has a world of his own.

—Heraclitus

The study seeks to enquire into the nature, extent and
possibilities of interaction between politics and literature both
at theoretical and applied levels. The nexus of study is the
Indian novel in English in post-independence India. The
assumption is that politics and aesthetics are not exclusive or
antagonistic spheres. On the contrary, they reinforce each
other simultaneously conditioning and being conditioned,
characterized by a dialectical interrelationship, manifest in a
variety of forms. It would, therefore, be counter-productive to
advocate disengagement of art from socio-political concerns.
This is further vindicated, when one perceives the growing
incidence of cultural and personal schizophrenia, genocide,
perpetual want, misery and deprivation on the one hand, and
persistence of socio-political repression and persecution on the
other, in spite of considerable advancement of human
knowledge.

The collaboration between political science and literature,
or for that matter, between social sciences and humanities in
general, is possible without damaging the autonomy of either
of the disciplines, resistance to such collaboration being mainly
the consequence of lack of intellectual democracy on both
sides.[1] For instance, James Davidson, in his presidential address
to the American Political Science Association, more than two

decades back, pointed out that reasonable loyalty to the
term 'Political Science', in no way excludes consideration of
fictional writing on politics. On the contrary, "the compulsion
toward a science of politics has in the recent past, led to a
concentration on methods, inappropriate to or insufficient for,
the production of significant meaning. Efforts towards a more
exact knowledge of politics through a reinforcement of technique are to be encouraged but they must also be challenged
to produce conclusions meaningful to experienced observers".[2]
Conceding that fictional form is deceptive, Davidson has
argued that "so in their own ways are the theoretical models
of Political Science". If attention to political fiction did nothing
more than remind us of the extent to which we fictionalize in
all analysis or restore the critical role of the writer or give
greater vitality to the language in which we discuss politics, it
would still be justified. Finally, Davidson suggests: "The
subject is politics. The end is communicable understanding.
The means ought to be any that contribute. We need experience, insight and correction, wherever we can get them".[3]
That, in sum, is the *raison d'etre* of the present study.

The issue of the interaction between political science and
literature is part of the larger issue of collaboration between
social sciences and humanities. "How different things would
have been", Nisbet wonders, "if social sciences at the time of
their systematic formation in the nineteenth century had taken
the arts in the same degree they took the physical sciences as
models".[4]

Social sciences cannot and need, of course, not be written in
a literary form. Nevertheless, while analysing the consciousness of men and the functioning of social institutions, "the
sort of typification which would best serve the social investi-
gator would be that which sought the objectivity and imper-
sonality of the literary artist".[5] The literary artists have also
been provided with "terrifying occasions" for "agonizing
about the purpose and meaning of their creativity",[6] by the
prevailing socio-political order.

Like social science, literature cannot be adequately grasped
in isolation of the socio-political milieu, in which it has been
created. At the same time, literature cannot be fully merged
with the milieu without surrendering a vital part of itself. As

Harry Levin has aptly suggested that it is possible to resolve the issue of the supposed dichotomy of facts and fiction, if literature is accepted as an 'institution'. "Once we have grasped this fact, we begin to perceive how art may belong to society and yet be autonomous within its own limits; and are no longer puzzled by the apparent polarity of social and formal criticism".[7]

Whereas the artist's major preoccupation is the concrete, emotive presentation of the subjective, existential, evaluative truth, that is, knowledge of the 'feel' of things; the social scientist's prime interest is the abstract, referential presentation of external, objective, non-evaluative truth, that is, knowledge of the 'look' of things.[8] A possible collaboration of these two segmented 'preoccupations', characterized by Henry Murray as subjective-objective, existential-external, evaluative-non-evaluative, might pave the way for an organic approach, interpreting human experience both as a 'totality' and a part thereof.

Those who polarize fiction and social science and wish to establish superiority of one or the other should, as Morroe Berger suggests, address themselves to another question : "Superior for what purpose?"[9] In discussions of relationship between the two, the element of "purpose", as the vital part of living reality, is the common ground where the social scientist and the artist may meet, time and again, and explore possibilities of cooperation, however small the area of such cooperation may be. As Borenstein states, "in the desire to know the world, there is the dream of transforming it and in the desire to transform the world, there is the dream of knowing it. These desires and dreams give life to one another. They are the dreams and desires of both, writers and of social scientists. The social sciences are rooted in the humanities, yet a preoccupation with ideology or methodology draws them ever further from their real source".[10]

The necessary relationship of fiction and facts is explained by Frank Kermode in slightly different terms. Quoting Ortega, he states, "man is impossible without imagination, without the capacity to invent for himself a conception of life, to 'ideate' the character he is going to be". To be free means "to be lacking in constitutive identity, not to have subscribed to a determined being, to be able to be other than what one was".[11] The denial of the freedom to be the architect of one's own destiny is "the sin of social science".

Of the social scientist, who according to Borenstein, confines 'reality' to outer life and thinks of feeling and images as epiphenomena of sociological place, it might be said, as Kierkegaard remarked of Hegel, that "his work is full of syntheses, but life is full of choices".[12]

Truly enough as Marx said, the periods of artistic upsurge do not necessarily coincide with social progress in other fields.[13] Definite connections between the two are, however, possible to discern. 'Aesthetic', in this sense, is both an existential and a social category. Social or political sensibility is not brought to bear on art from outside as imposed sensibility; on the contrary, it belongs to art in its 'aesthetic' form as such, as Herbert Marcuse would put it. In subverting the dominant consciousness, art both protests and transcends the given socio-political reality.[14] Arguing the same point from a different angle, Jean Paul Sartre categorically states that it is not possible to choose between politics and writing. The adventure of writing, in his view, challenges the whole of mankind, for writing cannot be critical without calling everything into question. It is the highest form of the basic need to communicate and, therefore, the most powerful instrument of social transformation.[15]

The problem of the correlation between politics and art was resolved in idealist aesthetics by the proposition that art and politics were completely different by nature and fulfilled completely different functions. They were projected as mutually incompatible. For instance, R.G. Collingwood, the renowned British aesthetician, a follower of Benedetto Croce, and known for his staunch advocacy of 'Pure Art', argued that any aspiration on the part of an artist to evoke definite political emotions among his audience, can at best be 'serviceable' to politics but not to artistic creation.[16]

This kind of denial of link between politics and literature, however, appears outmoded when centrality of politics in social life has come to be established beyond doubt. Denial of links does not sever those that already exist. In fact, instead of avoiding political facts, aesthetics needs to contest and confront them.

On a conceptual level, the problem of relationship of politics and art, has claims to a long, rich and variegated intellectual history. On the applied level also, a substantial number of aestheticians and political analysts have addressed themselves to the problem in a variety of ways in the recent past.[17]

The growing interest in political fiction, of an increasing number of critics as well as artists, confirms the growing role of politics in the ordinary life of contemporary man. The prospects of political fiction are certainly bright. Growingly, private life can no longer be isolated from the central problems of politics. Literary texts, on the other hand, are not simply created or enacted. They are, as Eagleton argues, "constituted" in the normative sense, communicating certain valued meanings. We will certainly make little headway, to recall Eagleton again, if "politics and literature" are conceived merely in terms of a new set of textual interpretations. The fundamental question for political criticism is to ascertain the political significance of literature.[18]

In order to ascertain the political significance of literature, the argument regarding the relationship of politics and literature needs to be pursued—not on Platonic level alone, as it is often done—but in relation to a given society under study. The relationship of politics and literature varies with each society, depending on the historical and cultural uniqueness, the nature of polity, levels of economic development and socio-political awareness and scores of other situational variables. Despite elements of universalism, characteristic of all good art, political fiction, its content, utility and vitality, is best understood as a culture-specific phenomenon.

Political criticism, transmitted through the prism of artistic imagination, offers critical imagination to politics and responsible involvement to artists. Aesthetic political criticism thus exposes the limitations of both 'pure aesthetics' and 'pure politics', usually defined as absolutely separate vocations. It reminds one of an apt remark by Bernard Crick : "Karl Marx was right, as was Schiller before him, to protest that excessive division of labour is alienating".[19]

A work of literature may be designated as "political" by several criteria : by the explicit intention of the author, by selection of characters who move in a political setting or by a description and projection of political events. Works of art can also be used as socio-political data conducive to explain the broader phenomena of acceptability, currency or rejection of socio-politico-cultural ideas, conventions and processes.[20] Political fiction here is defined as a corpus of novels which offer a direct treatment of political process, inclusive of political antecedents and traditions, institutions, practices and formations of change. It is pertinent here to distinguish a political novel from a historical novel, although both share several common indices. A historical novel can be designated as 'political', when it specifically and directly deals with political history. In comparison to a historical novel, a political novel is narrower in one sense and broader in another. It is narrower since it is constricted to political aspects of history, whereas a historical novel extends beyond the political terrain, to social, cultural, moral and economic aspects of history. The political novel attains broader dimensions than a historical novel, as it moves beyond history and addresses itself to living political problems, ideas and ideologies.

A political novelist consciously chooses politics as a legitimate subject matter for his artistic imagination. Politics thus gets incorporated into the artistic fabric of a political novel. Political meaning does not precede or follow the artistic meaning. In order to offer genuine aesthetic political criticism, political fiction must strike a balance between artistic integrity and social responsibility. Sincere efforts of this kind alone are capable of acquiring the level of "political resonance", to use Ernest Hemingway's phrase, and prove directly relevant for the understanding of politics.

The expression "aesthetic political criticism" is employed here to refer to the entire rubric of political criticism—inclusive of the various levels of awareness, such as cognitive, affective and evaluative—available in works of art, selected here, under the definition of 'political fiction'. Further, as proposed in the "Theoretical Formulations' in Chapter two of this study, literature (and political fiction in particular) as recorded culture and aesthetic political consciousness as socio-cultural consciousness, are accepted as a form of cultural approach to politics and have, therefore, been directly treated as relevant to political inquiry as a possible source of information, interpretation and insight. Viewed thus, aesthetic political criticism contributes to comprehending aspects of political culture in society.

The present study confines itself to works originally written in English by Indians, under the term 'Indo-Anglian', as explained by Meenakshi Mukherjee.[21] Such of these works, as deal with the political theme in a substantial manner, and are amenable to critical consideration, within the confines of the theoretical framework proposed in Chapter two, will be taken up for analysis in detail. The fiction of Mulk Raj Anand, Raja Rao, Bhabani Bhattacharya, Nayantara Sahgal and Salaman Rushdie, for instance, is directly relevant for a study like the present one. Relevant facets of the politico-historical fiction of Khushwant Singh, Manohar Malgonkar, Chaman Nahal, Kamla Markandaya and B. Rajan, have also been included. Some other major writers like R.K. Narayan, Anita Desai and Arun Joshi, have however, been left out of the study (except for R.K. Narayan's *Waiting for the Mahatma*), owing to the constraints already identified.

Within the aforesaid limits the study attempts a politico-literary analysis of select Indo-Anglian novels in post-independence India.[22] This has been done with a view to ascertaining certain marked perceptual trends, relevant for comprehending aspects of politics in India. The underlying assumption is that these novels are representative of the major political strands available in Indo-Anglian novel in post-independence India.

References

1. Most critics still believe that "the majority of marriages contracted between the political and artistic avantgardes have resulted in crippled offspring and rapid divorce." David Caute, *The Illusion: An Essay On Politics, Theatre and the Novel* (New York, Harper and Row, 1972), p. 31. Also see: Bruce Waters, "Politics And Literature", *The Prarie Schooner*, 25 (Winter, 1951), 347.
2. James F. Davidson, "Political Science and Political Fiction", *The American Political Science Review*, LV, 4 (December 1961), 860.
3. *n.* 2.

4. Robert A. Nisbet, *Sociology as an art Form* (Oxford, Oxford University Press, 1976), p. 16.

5. G.H. Bantock, "Literature and the Social Sciences", *Critical Quarterly*, 17, 2, (Summer 1975), 126-7.

6. Audrey Borenstein, *Redeeming the Sin: Social Sciences and Literature* (New York; Columbia University Press, 1978), p. 178. Also see: T.S. Eliot, *To Criticize the Critic and other Writings* (London, Faber & Faber, 1965), pp. 141 & 144.

7. Harry Levin, "Literature as an Institution", *Accent*, 6, 3, (Spring 1966), 146.

8. Henry Murry, "Foreword", in Robert N. Wilson, *Man Made Plain* (Cleveland, Howard Allen, 1958), p. xx.

9. Morroe Berger, *Real and Imagined Worlds: The Novel and Social Science* (Cambridge, Mass., Harvard University Press, 1977), p. 171. Also see: Joyce Cary, *Art and Reality* (London, Cambridge, 1957), pp. 5, 9-10.

10. Borenstein, *n.* 6, pp. xii-iii.

11. Frank Kermode, *The Sense of an Ending: Studies in the Theory of Fiction* (Oxford, Oxford University Press, 1967), pp. 140-41.

12. Borenstein, *n.* 6, p. 33. Also see: Maxim Gorky, *On Literature* (Seatle, University of Washington Press, 1973), p. 124, and Leo Lowenthal, *Literature and the Image of Man* (Boston, Beacon, 1957), p. 3.

13. Karl Marx and Frederick Engels, *On Literature And Art* (Moscow, Progress, 1976), p. 82.

14. Herbert Marcuse, *The Aesthetic Dimension—Toward a Crituque of Marxist Aesthetics* (Boston, Beacon, 1977), p. ix.

15. Jean Paul Sartre, *Between Existentialism and Marxism* (New York, William Morrow and Co., 1974), pp. 26-31.

16. R.G. Collingwood, *The Principles of Art* (Oxford; Oxford University Press, 1947), pp. 279-80.

17. See for instance:
    (i) Bernard Crick, "Writers and Politics", *Critical Quarterly*, 22, 2 (Summer 1980), 63-73.
    (ii) David Spitz, "Politics and the Critical Imagination", *The Review of Politics*, 324 (October 1970), 419-435.
    (iii) Henry M. Holland, Jr. (ed.), *Politics Through Literature*, (New Jersey, Prentice Hall, Inc., 1968), 2.
    (iv) Hilde Hein, "Aesthetic Consciousness: The Ground of Political Experienee", *Journal of Aesthetics and Art Criticism*, XXXV, 2, (Winter 1976), 143-152.
    (v) R.D. Reck, *The Politics of Literature*, *PMLA*, 85 (May 1970), 429-432.
    (vi) J.E. Vacha, "It Could Happen Here: The Rise of the Political Scenario Novel", *American Quarterly*, XXIX (Summer 1977), 194-206.

18. Terry Eagleton, "Literature and Politics Now" *Critical Quarterly*, 20, 3 (Autumn 1978), 66-68.
19. Bernard Crick, "Writers and Politics", *n.* 17, 73.
20. See for instance:
 (i) Irwing Howe, *Politics and the Novel* (New York, Horizon Press, 1957), pp. 22-24.
(ii) Morris Edmund Speare, *The Political Novel* (New York, Russell and (iii) Russell, 1966), IX. Joseph L. Blotner, *The Political Novel* (New York, Doubley and Co., Inc., 1966).
21. Meenakshi Mukherjee, *The Twice Born Fiction*, (Delhi, Arnold Heinemann, 1971), pp. 14-15. Thus, R.P. Jhabvala and V.S. Naipaul are not included among 'Indo-Anglian' authors.
22. Relevant references to pre-independence novels are made wherever required, especially in Chapter 3. In Chapter 5, Mulk Raj Anand's pre-independence publications are discussed in detail for their contemporary political significance.

2

Aesthetic Political Criticism: A Theoretical Formulation of Politics, Aesthetics and Culture

The opinion that art should have nothing to do with politics is
itself a political attitude.

—*George Orwell*

Aesthetic consciousness is a form of socal consciousness. In interdependence with other forms of social consciousness, it attains both artistic excellence and social relevance. To sever these links is to strip art of its cognitive significance, ideological import, ethical projection and socio-economic orientation, leaving it just as an idealized "pure form". Art, however, cannot be made auxiliary to other forms of social consciousness. Through self-contained unity and speciality of form, art acquires the status of an aesthetic value. Just as art cannot perform its social role if it is not true to life, so also the truth of life is unattainable in art, if life is not fashioned according to the laws of art itself. An aware and conscious work of art, by its very nature, responds to the hopes and despair, aspirations and problems of real human beings—thinking, feeling, suffering—in concrete life situations. Art works, while alive to genuine human problems, can also become powerful vehicles of socio-political concerns. The political, the aesthetic and the social, thus, do not remain incompatible in conscious works of art.

Some Theoretical Premises

Aesthetic political criticism assumes that like all human experience, aesthetic experience is at once self-determining and self-transcending, for "the absorption *of* self in aesthetic consciousness is not *in* self but in an objective externality . . . marked by the capacity to hold oneself apart from and yet enter into intensive emotional and intellectual interaction with an object and this same capacity is presupposed by cognitive activity and by political awareness".[1]

The supposition of interaction of "cognitive activity" and "political awareness" is rooted in a long history, represented through the metaphor of "reflection", enunciated in a variety of ways by several radically different theories. Interpretation of reality in terms of "real objects as they are"—separable and identifiable—, or as essential forces and processes underlying the objects, has been an important point of distinction between realism and naturalism; the former identified as dynamic and the latter as static. The idea of reflection has been re-stated in terms of "typification" by socialist realists such as Lukacs; in terms of "homology" by structuralists such as Althusser; and in terms of the notion of "correspondence" by critical theorists such as Benjamin. The concept of "mediation" and "dialectical image" proposed by the Frankfurt School is another re-statement, though of a different nature. The point of emphasis in a 'dialectical image' is that social reality does not get directly reflected in art, it necessarily passes through process of 'mediation', in which its original content gets changed. A dialectical image is a genuine form of such mediation, in which the social condition represents itself.[2] These variants of reflection theory, although rather abstract, still remain the seminal source of perception and exposition of the relationship between art and society.

In the process, art has sometimes been reduced to "particularistic" representation and ideology and sometimes been celebrated as 'universal' in an undifferentiated manner bordering on a metaphysical eulogy. There has also been a differentiated analysis of creativity as a specific aesthetic activity within the general socio-historical process. The contribution of humanistic Marxist tradition of aesthetics is of special significance in this regard. Raymond Williams, for instance, has pointed out that "Writing is often a new articulation and in effect a new formation, extending beyond its own modes. But to separate this as art, which in practice includes, always partly, sometimes wholly, elements elsewhere in the continuum, is to lose contact with the substantive creative process and then to idealize it; to put it above or below the social, when it is in fact the social in one of its most distinctive, durable and total forms".[3]

However, the confining of the variable and multiple relationship of art and society to the metaphor of 'reflection' has the danger of converting a living process into a cause-effect, or a passive relationship. In order to become an innovative and progressive consciousness, aesthetic criticism, therefore, needs to move beyond both "reductions" and "dichotomies" imposed by formal modes of analysis. It is imperative for an innovative art work to transcend, on the one hand, the historically specified legacy of a situation in order to 'evolve'; and, on the other, to surpass the reduction of the creative to the 'subjective', in order to be 'relevant'. These reductions, epistemologically speaking, are based on the separation of 'mind' and 'world' in idealist philosophy, converted into separation of 'individual' and 'society' by conservative as well as liberal schools of thought. These distinctions have resulted into false dichotomies and deformations, for instance, of fcats and fiction, imagination and the imaginary, information and interpretation, which are analytically pejorative and practically detrimental to the evolution of innovative aesthetics. To confine and compartmentalize creativity in terms of either kind of reduction — 'subjectivist' or 'objectivist' — is to interpret art in a very narrow sense and regulate the possibilities of genuine innovative consciousness through art.

Aesthetic political criticism, thus, does not stop at the levels of perception and reflection. The interaction between politics and literature is not a case of simple cause and effect relationship. It is at once specific and organic and in essence variable and dialectical. At the applied level, it is, therefore, unjustified to expect in political fiction either the factual accuracy of newspaper journalism or complete objectivity, solidly documented references or extensive expositions of political theory as in a scholarly presentation. The prime concern of aesthetic political criticism is not merely to record facts, as in a chronicle, but to interconnect facts and present them as a sequel of socio-historic forces in relation to a given political process. It is the 'socio-political concern', more than political facts or events, that is of fundamental importance in distinguishing political fiction from the other varieties—social, psychological, philosophical and science fiction. As Williams says, in another context, recognition of all the levels of sociability is necessary for a composite socio-political analysis. Specification and selection, for instance, of 'the political' in political fiction is, however, inevitable, in view of the multiplicity of levels and range of what is amorphously called, 'social reality'.

Specification and selection immediately introduces the problematic proposition of 'point of view' in aesthetic political criticism—variously interpreted as 'alignment', 'commitment', 'ideology', or 'message', against the claims of 'objectivity', 'neutrality' or 'fidelity to truth', proposed by advocates of 'pure aesthetics'. Arguing against the notions of 'pure art', Sartre states that art works, when they are serious, are always forms (however concealed) of social commitment and when they are trivial, are simply evasions. Writers necessarily involved with meanings, according to him "reveal, demonstrate, represent; after that people can look at each other face to face, and act as they want".[4] Literature, explains Sartre, "wilts if it is reduced to innocence, or to songs. If a written sentence does not reverberate at every level of man and society, then it makes no sense. What is the literature of the epoch but the epoch appropriated by its literature".[5] It is in this sense, he argues, that it is impossible to "choose between politics and writing".[6] Sartre's argument stresses the need of recognizing the fact of the centrality of politics in contemporary social organization. In any art work it is possible to discover the realities of socio-political relations and in this way also its alignment. Moreover, socio-political relations are not only 'received', they are also challenged, questioned and transformed. Interpreting these changes inevitably implies 'commitment' in the Sartrian sense. 'Point of view', then, is the choice of perception or even of position, which it is not possible or necessary to escape. Commitment as Williams defines it, "is conscious alignment or conscious change of alignment".[7] And, in this sense, it is a matter of choice for the writer.

The areas of possibility and range of ideas, analysis and propositions of aesthetic political criticism are, thus, immense. Without being over-ambitious or imperious, aesthetic political criticism dispels the myth of compartmentalizing art and politics as exclusive, antagonistic or incompatible spheres of human thinking and activity. In one sense, therefore, Aesthetic political criticism agrees with what George Orwell says, namely that "the opinion, that art should have nothing to do with politics is itself a political attitude".[8] However aesthetic political criticism is not necessarily an advocacy of an overt and a specific kind of commitment. On the contrary, it is an aspiration for a conscious and responsible exposition of the prevailing unfreedom and repression in society and enunciation of an innovative consciousness, rooted in, yet transcending, the society of which it is a product. Aesthetic political criticism thus, is the inherent political potential of a work of art, in 'art form as such', as Marcuse would say.[9] It is also a specification of what Mao called the "historical relativity" of art in political revolution.[10]

Since there are no fixed formulae for either political correctness or artistic excellence, the fundamental challenge before any aesthetic political critic lies in the precarious balance of awareness and pleasure, of artistic integrity and social responsibility. Aesthetic political criticism, therefore, ultimately becomes relevant as socio-cultural criticism as well.

II

Search for a Perspective: The Intellectual Roots

The treatment of aesthetic political criticism as socio-cultural criticism is not an entirely new proposition. The intellectual roots of socio-political approach to literature, in fact, go back to the times when humanities and social sciences had not yet developed as distinct disciplines of study. Plato's ideal polity, for instance, is very importantly concerned with the fundamental question of the place of art in society. Being a proponent of the "theory of ideas", Plato perceives art to be 'mimesis' understood as falsification of a pre-existing reality and proposes censorship of poets in Book X of *The Republic*.[11] Aristotle accepts the idea of 'mimesis,' but develops it, contrary to Plato, from a general conception of learning to its highest form in that it shows through its universal statements, the permanent and the necessary.[12] The immense intellectual tradition which flowed from Plato and Aristotle came to include not only these two opposing valuations, but an extraordinary series of modifications and developments. In the excitement of Renaissance theory, as Williams points out, the idea of imitation was replaced by the idea of 'creation'. Tasso, for instance, said, 'Nature is God's Creation, art is man's creation'.[13]

However, till the beginning of the 17th century, literature had rarely been treated in material terms and it was not until the collapse of the material world with its static social structures and all-pervasive religious values that men became really aware of society and its institutions as secular forces.[14] It was with Vico's *New Science* (1725), one of the first genuine works of social science, that the social world, including social institutions and art, began to be analysed in material terms.[15] The empirical, anti-metaphysical 'mechanical materialism'[16] was brought to its logical summation in the writings of Herder and Madame de Stael. This was a reaction to the *a priori* aesthetics of Immanuel Kant who had stated that a sense of beauty could result only from a purely disinterested judgment. Both Herder and de Stael argued that each work of literature was rooted in a certain social and geographical environment, where it performed specific functions. Literary history, they proposed, could be understood only as cultural history. The analysis attempted by them, however, remained mechanistic, vague and generalized.[17] The mechanical materialism which resulted in commercialization, on the one hand, and in artistic fragmentation, on the other, was staunchly opposed by Schiller and Hegel. They visualized art as providing the civilizing component, reuniting man with nature and intellect with sense and thereby returning the 'wholeness' of man to him.[18] This was the commencement of organic, instead of mechanical, approach to both history and art.

Hyppolyte Taine's *History of English Literature* (1871), proved to be a trend-setting work in many ways for subsequent socio-political approach to art. For Taine, art was the collective expression of society. He distinguished three concepts: race, moment and milieu, as the material foundations of literature. He defined 'race' as innate and involving hereditary characteristics; 'moment' as the epoch, the spirit of the time or as literary tradition; and, 'milieu' as environment, emphasizing climate and geography. Taine's positivism, however, did not succeed in going beyond crude cause-effect analysis of literature as a response to specific external conditions,[19] since it failed to take cognizance of 'consciousness' as an important variable in socio-political analysis of literature. Even so his analytical categories were stimulating.

In contrast to Taine's positivism and the preceding theories of mechanical materialism, idealism and subjectivism from which subsequent liberal literary criticism was to draw substantially in the twentieth century,[20] Marx's theory of dialectical materialism revolutionized the world of ideas, art and action. As Stephen Morawski states, although the aesthetic ideas of Marx and Engels do not comprise a full-blown theory of aesthetics, to dismiss them, however, as fortuitous and incidental speculations, or as utterances of sheer taste and preference would be to miss their historical and theoretical importance.[21]

Art, in Marx's framework, is one of the forms of social consciousness. It, therefore, follows that the reasons for its changes should be sought in the social existence of men. Marx does not qualify art as a passive product of the economic system, as is often misunderstood. Despite assuming art to be subordinate to the general laws of social development, Marx concedes the "relative independence" of art as its distinctive feature.[22] Marx is aware of the enduring significance of genuine art works outliving the social structures with which they are historically connected. He explains the gap between upsurge of art and progress in other fields with reference to the spiritual culture which he views as determined, not only by the level of material production, but also by the character of social relations peculiar to that period. It is a dialectical feature of art, Marx asserts in the specific context of capitalism, to exhibit and enhance consciousness of contradictions between humanistic ideals and the inhuman reality.[23] However, stressing the phenomenon of great writers being pressurized, in a class society, by the ruling classes into making serious concessions in their works, Marx proposes his key aesthetic argument that the essence, origin, development and social role of art could be fully understood only through analysis of the social system as a whole.[24] The point of emphasis in Marx's statement is often mistaken for inflexibility by both the determinist school of Marxists and anti-Marxists.

Subsequent development of the aesthetic political criticism in later nineteenth and twentieth centuries presents a rich and interesting variety of interpretations, although there are critics like Sidney Hook, who have characterized Marxist legacy as "ambiguous".[25] Such views notwithstanding, Marx, along with Freud, remains the most powerful influence in all intellectual thinking, including aesthetics, in the present century.

This is evidenced by the varied and complex transition that has taken place from Marx to Marxism. This transition incorporates a rich variety of schools of thought such as classical realism (of artists like Pushkin, Gogol, Tolstoy, Dostoyevsky and Chekhov); expressionism (Toller, Kaiser, Kraus, the early Brecht, and most importantly Ernst Bloch), socialist realism (Gorky, Mayakovsky, Alexi Tolstoy, Sholokhov, Barbusse, Aragon, Becher, Brecht and Isaac Dunayevsky), the critical theory of Frankfurt School (Horkheimer, Adorno, Benjamin, Fromm and Marcuse), and revival of critical realism of Balzac (propounded by English writers such as Aldington, Graham Greene, the Italian, Alberto Moravia, American writers such as Hemingway and Steinbeck and the French writers such as Romain Rolland and Roger Martin du Gard). Besides these recognized schools, with their specific contributions, there have also been several intermediary forms of criticism getting across the so-called boundaries of these schools, which will be taken up later for discussion.

Just as it is not possible to discuss all the postulates of the schools of criticism mentioned above, it is also exacting to reduce their contribution to a common denominator. All of them, however, have one basic point of agreement that the source of their basic parameters relates to the writings of Marx, the difference of emphasis, whether on *Economic and Philosophic Manuscripts* or on *German Ideology*, notwithstanding.

Several other ideas which also form the principal areas of agreement and as such, are relevant for us may be mentioned here. In the first instance, all of them proceed, with minor variations, from an 'ideo-artistic' conception of aesthetics, which views art as a response to the concerns, hopes and aspirations of real men; suffering from either material deprivation or from social alienation, repression and disintegration of personality or from both. Art is regarded as a legitimate forum for agonizing over the problems of man and society as well as reflecting, representing and recreating the world through creative imagination. Thus, art may contest reality as Albert Camus says but does not avoid it.[26]

Realists of all these various schools realized the difficulties of the proposition of 'reconstructing' the world which appear much more precarious than building it anew. This leads to a consideration of the external problem of "art and action", taken up for resolution by several artists. In these attempts, Marxist realism has also developed and renewed its form, both in combat and in interaction with other literary movements. Contemporary realism, for instance, has sometimes borrowed from current modernist or post-modernist movements in portrayal of human experience as estrangement or in emphasizing the role of dreams and visions, for instance. This, however, does not signify the integration of realism and modernism, although, it does not prove the case of "realism without bounds".[27]

In fact, the boundaries within realism are flexible precisely because reality itself is not static. The seminal fact about the twentieth century is that it differs radically in more ways than one from the nineteenth or the earlier centuries. This aspect, the influence of our age on changes in perceptions, including realism, in all possible manifestations, however, for want of adequate investigation, would not warrant any conclusions.

The 'mobility of boundaries' among the various schools gets significantly vindicated through efforts of intellectual bridge-builders, such as Lukacs, Brecht, Goldmann, Sartre, Marcuse, Caudwell and Raymond Williams. These aestheticians propose to see 'realism in artworks' instead of realism as a fixed formula of aesthetic criticism. Such perception, they argue, specifically aims at a dialectical understanding of art works as 'socio-aesthetic' constructs. The writings of Marx are regarded as a guide not as an end, as a method not as ultimate explanation. It is proposed that a dialectical understanding of Marx's ideas is needed rather than an undialectical acceptance of these ideas as 'received truths.' Aesthetic criticism, thus, turns out to be a persistent open-ended critique of culture and society, from which it originates in the hands of these innovators. This fundamental proposition, in fact, forms the central tenet of twentieth century aesthetics and is also a seminal contribution to subsequent progressive aesthetics, and, therefore, deserves elaboration.

One could begin with Georg Lukacs, the most controversial of all Marxist theoreticians, who has been denounced by Soviet and Hungarian Communists as a 'philosophical idealist' and a "political revisionist",[28] and by Western Marxists as a "formalist".[29] Realizing the Hegelian roots of Marxism, Lukacs proposed that the ultimate significance of artistic creation was ontological, in the sense that art disclosed the true nature of man as a 'species being'. The anthropo-centric standpoint of Lukacs was based on Marx's central idea of "totality", through which he related the individual creations to 'types' or genres corresponding to particular historical stages in the gradual emancipation of man.[30] However, when Lukacs exhibited indifference to the effects of technological innovations on art and insensitivity to achievements of modern art rejecting such innovations as mere 'bourgeoisie apologetics'; his aesthetics turned into dogmatism which was subsequently denounced by Brecht.

Lucian Goldmann, in France, attempted to integrate Lukacs' concepts of "totality" and "world vision" with his own "intermediary link of the collective consciousness". He pointed to the fact that "there survives in Market societies a radical modification of the status of the individual and collective consciousness and, implicitly, relations between the infrastructure and the super-structure".[31] This idea of Goldmann later recurred in Marcuse and Williams with different emphases.

Viewing art as a cultural construct, Trotsky, however, had warned against too much of scienticizing of literature. The methods of formal analysis were necessary but insufficient.

Trotsky opposed the superimposed contradiction between the 'art's unique methods' and its determination by 'social being'.[32]

The need for preserving the autonomy of art, despite its essentially historical character, felt by Trotsky, was staunchly defended by Bertolt Brecht and Walter Benjamin. Brecht stressed the indispensable need for experiment—and the necessary freedom of the artist for such experimentation. Perhaps no other Marxist aesthetician has been as forceful on this subject as Brecht.[33]

Brecht's theatre of the thirties was consciously concerned with cultural innovation. Cultural heritage was as central to Brechtian thinking as for Lukacs: 'one isn't proud of other people's property', was his favourite aphorism. Brecht's discovery of the principle of 'moderation' epitomised in an optimistic attitude towards the revolutionary potential of popular art and technological innovation, was also shared by Walter Benjamin. Benjamin, however, expressed his optimism through the notion of "aura" (the special sense of "here and now" giving authenticity to an art work), which expressed the "unique phenomenon of a distance, however close it might be".[34] This uniqueness of a work of art was inseparable from the fact of its rootedness in tradition. Thus cultural heritage, as a nexus of uniqueness, was appreciated by Benjamin in slightly different terms from Lukacs and Brecht. Emphasis on cultural heritage was also subsequently discernible in the intellectual ethos of the Frankfurt school, despite the fact that the critical theory of the Frankfurt school exhibited clear dislike for the formalistic aesthetic postulates of Lukacs and Brecht and those ideas of Benjamin which displayed the impact of Brecht.

The critical theory developed by the Frankfurt School primarily aimed at a searching re-examination of the fundamental Marxist assumptions in the changed context of the twentieth century. The critical theory proved to be a major landmark in the direction of "a dialectical social science" that would avoid absolutes or identity theories and yet preserve the right of the observer to go beyond the givens of his experience. What distinguished the Frankfurt school's theory of art from its more orthodox Marxist counterparts was its refusal to reduce cultural phenomena to an ideological reflex of class interests. In Adorno's view, the task of "criticism must be not so much to search for the particular interest groups to which cultural phenomena are to be assigned, but rather to decipher the general social tendencies which are expressed in these phenomena and through which the most powerful interests realize themselves. Cultural Criticism must become social physiognomy".[36] Not only was art an expression and reflection of existing social tendencies (and here it diverged most sharply from Leninist criticism and from Lukacs as well) but also genuine art acted as the last preserve of human yearnings for that "other" society beyond the present one. True art was an expression of man's legitimate interest in his future happiness. Thus, although false in one sense, the claims of culture to transcend society were true in another.[36]

In accordance with distrust of any positive representation of the reconciliation of contradictions as displayed in critical theory the harmonies it most admired always contained a recognition that a solely aesthetic reconciliation was insignificant. In other words, until social contradictions were reconciled in reality, the utopian harmony of art must always maintain an element of protest, a protest "of the humane, against the pressure of domineering institutions" as Adorno would say. Thus the aesthetic sphere was inevitably political as well. Herbert Marcuse, of all the critical theorists, consistently emphasized this point.[37]

Art, like all cultural phenomena, was neither fully reflective nor fully autonomous. Art, however, like theory must go beyond the prevailing consciousness of the masses. In the present, as Marcuse pointed out, the greatest threat came from cultural tendencies that implied the premature reconciliation of contradictions at the level of popular consciousness. Assuming art to be something more than derivative reflection of observed reality, without dismissing appearances as totally insubstantial (a popular fallacy in philosophical phenomenology), and always 'mindful of the duality of the moments", to use Adorno's phrase, Frankfurt school's aesthetic criticism maintained a determined stress on the importance of mediation and non-identity. No facet of social reality could be understood by the observer as final or complete in itself. There were no social "facets", as the positivists believed, which were the substratum of a social theory. Instead, there was a constant interplay of the particular and the universal of "moment" (phase or aspect of a cumulative dialectical process)[38] and totality. Thus, as Lukacs said, the category of mediation was a "lever with which to overcome the mere immediacy of the empirical world".[39] The emphasis on the totality of dialectical mediations also resulted in rejection of the dogma of fetishization.

It is important to note that all over the world, in Europe, America and also in India, the nineteen thirties exhibited an apparent drive towards political commitment and the left-wing preoccupations of the literary intellectuals. Neal Wood, for instance, highlighted the disintegration of liberalism as a dynamic faith in modern industrial society.[40] Communism appeared an attractive alternative to the prevalent ideological instability, socio-economic depression and revulsion from political action.[41] In 1936, the Left Book Club was formed in England. Escapist movements were also popular in both Europe and America. Literary intellectuals expressed their disquiet through their writings. D.H. Lawrence, T.S. Eliot, Bertrand Russell, Christopher Caudwell, George Orwell and Mulk Raj Anand represent some of the major contemporary perspectives amongst intellectuals, concerned with what may be termed questions about "quality of life". Williams points out that Lawrence's humanism is close to the socialism of William Morris and Eliot's concept of 'culture as a whole way of life' has its roots in the literary tradition of Carlyle and Coleridge.[42] Caudwell, however, argued that the ideology of the society's whole culture was the ideology of the ruling class[43], an assertion adumbrating the general basis of the theory of hegemony being developed by Gramsci around the same time.

Caudwell enunciated ideas resembling those of Sartre, though from a less high pedestal. Caudwell proposed the familiar Marxist assumption that literature and society exist in a dialectical unity, but emphasized that not only does social existence determine literature but literature also influences society and therefore has a "conscious social purpose". Art is "an affective experimenting with selected pieces of external reality".[44] Anticipating Sartre as it were, Caudwell realized the significance of works of art, not merely as aesthetic creations but as social process. However, whereas Sartre visualized a literature of "praxis" for the future, Caudwell proposed the idea of "directed feeling". Just as 'directed thinking' is controlled by reason and acknowledges the social criterion of truth; so 'directed feeling' is controlled by heart and acknowledges the social criterion of beauty and goodness. This reality of "directed feeling" on the part of the artist gives him the social status of a "producer". Art, through an illusion, changes men and the changed men transform the world to make that illusion a reality.[45] Caudwell's work did provide some insights, in terms of Marxist cultural analysis, into the cultural critique which Williams also set out to establish in the 1950s. In a similar vein George Orwell, working through the tensions of commitment to politics and to writing, advocated a humanized socialism and proclaimed the virtues of bringing art to the people, a position he perceived as defying both contemporary socialists and the English literary tradition.

As in America, in Europe also, the 1950s and 1960s were characterized by affluence and consumerism, hegemonic grasp of the ruling class, and the cold war which formed the background to the writings of the New Left, which brought forth a moral critique of industrial capitalism and was committed to a humanistic socialism. It, however, failed to develop a rigorous social theory based on analysis of structural bases of societies under analysis. That critique of culture and society should not remain confined to a moral critique in the humanist literary tradition (of the 19th century) but address itself to structural bases of society, became the central concern of Marxists like Raymond Williams in the 1970s, devoted to rectify the weaknesses and limitations of Marxist cultural analysis, particularly of the New Left.

With Raymond Williams' framework of 'cultural materialism', European progressive aesthetics attained new heights of scholastic analysis and meaningful insights. Eagleton points out that Williams was initially influenced by F.R. Leavis, the renowned 'anti-ideology' editor of *Scrutiny*. However, Williams did not accept the political implications of "empirical" social writings of Leavis. The latter did, however, provide Williams the basis for a cultural critique of society when he could turn to very little in the tradition of English thought.[46] Following Matthew Arnold, Leavis ascribed a universal character to literature, viewing it as fundamental for the sustenance of moral

values. By reviving the idea of the central position of literature
and literacy criticism, Leavis visualized the revival of a shared
system of beliefs and values or what he called 'common
culture'.[47] Leavis also rejected the idea that culture was always
dependent on society for its well-being, an idea rejected in turn,
by Williams. Before coming to Williams, it is important to remember the structural intervention as well, represented by
Althusser. Eagleton, though a student of Williams, has been
influenced by Louis Althusser's search for a scientific basis of
literary criticism, within the Marxist tradition and the consequent rejection of humanist literary tradition for its neglect of
structural bases of society. Eagleton, following Althusser, de-
clares the humanist literary tradition as an affirmation of
bourgeois approach to the individual and the society.[48]

Raymond Williams remains fundamentally opposed to a
materialist reduction of art. Though he rejects all ideological
notions of literary production, he continues to seek to establish
the social value of art or creative activity as defined fairly
broadly. The central thrust of his argument concerning reality
as a social phenomenon is to show that art forms part of our
attempt to categorize and communicate experience. As an
individual creative act, he says art is part of the general process
which creates conventions and institutions, through which the
ways of seeing the meanings that are valued by the community
are shared and made active. It is possible, Williams suggests,
to reconcile, culture as "creative activity" and culture as a
"whole way of life", if the various meanings of culture—the
lived culture, the recorded culture and the culture of the selective tradition—and the fundamental relation between the
meanings, are grasped to a satisfactory extent.[49] Williams seeks
to resolve the tension among various commitments through his
conceptual ideal of common culture.

As Williams explains, a common culture is the inherited
culture, it has to be made and remade by the people themselves;
it cannot be achieved in any final sense. Common culture, as
"the detailed practice of revolution", also typifies the struggle
"to create public meanings which are authentic forums", to
create a society whose values are at once commonly created
and criticized, and where the discussions and exclusions of class

may be replaced by the reality of common and equal member-ship.[50]

Thus, despite being indebted for his humanistic concerns to literary intellectuals like Matthew Arnold, William Morris and F.R. Leavis, Williams rejects any suggestion of hierarchical vision of society in his writings on culture. He redefines 'culture' in terms of patterns learned and created in the mind and the means of communication within a social group; scrupulously rejecting "modern preoccuption with individual and creative self-realization".[51]

In the late 1960s, Williams specifically turned to the task of exploring as well as formulating a Marxist cultural and literary theory, accepting Marxism itself as a historical development, with highly variable and even alternative positions. Williams began his cultural-literary analysis, (not with classical categories of Marxist analysis, such as exploitation, dictatorship of the proletariat, etc.) but with revising the fundamental Marxist assumption of 'a determining base' and a 'determined super-structure'. He pointed out that "the base to which it is habitual to *refer* variations, is itself a dynamic and internally contradictory process". For in practice, "determination is never only the setting of limits, it is also the exertion of pressures". The social and political order, which maintains a capitalist market, like the social and political struggles which created it, is necessarily material production, not a set of super-structural activities.[52] Williams, like Marcuse, stressed that this kind of specialized materialism has also failed to grasp "the material character of the production of a cultural order".[53]

The concept of 'hegemony' derived from Gramsci, acquired special significance in Williams' inquiry into the way in which culture forms part of the process of domination of one class over another, just as much as the basis of communication within a social group. An important aspect of the 'effective dominative culture', is the the 'selective culture', which is represented as the tradition, 'the significant past'.[54] Through this selective tradition or culture, our relationship with history, society and knowledge is defined for us. Thus, through his concepts of hegemony and emergent, residual and selective culture,[55] Williams moved away from his attempts to reconcile the different levels of meaning in the term 'culture'—which

was his prime concern in conceptualizing common culture—
to a consideration of culture in its relationship to the structure
of society and to a recognition of the importance of focussing
on the relationship between ideas and the social structures
in which they are embedded.

Thus, Williams' analysis provides a basis for understanding
constant shifts, contradictions and conflicts in the relationship
and interaction of culture and society. The issue of 'social
control' becomes as relevant here as that of social change.
Williams mentions institutions such as family, education,
religion and media as means of 'incorporation' and the foundation of the hegemonic process. Hence, his emphasis, like that of
his Marxist predecessors, on taking up of creative expression
as a serious activity and making education 'critical' of all
cultural work becomes meaningful.[56] As for Frankfurt theorists
for Williams also an art work is simultaneously material and
imaginative. Art, as reflection not merely of objects, but of
real and verifiable social and historical processes, becomes at
once a cultural programme and a critical school.

It is, thus, important to remember that the socio-political
approach to art has a long history and a rich intellectual tradition, variously interpreted and employed, spanning over several
centuries, revealing its potential to accommodate both radical
and liberal theories of aesthetics, within its broad rubric.[57]

The tradition appears fairly unsteady as is inherent,
probably, in its very nature. The essential concern, however,
which has sustained it over the centuries is the retention of
creativity as an indispensable preserve of the artist, responding
to and transcending the current historical phenomenon at a
given point of time and context. The intellectual roots of
studying art, culture and politics further reveal that the question
of form and method would remain for ever subjects of debate,
as they have been in the past. This turbulence, however, is
not a sign of impatience or exhaustion, but of a constant
search for a perspective, which is not likely to prove inconsequential in the long run. Aesthetic political criticism through
this perspective, therefore, emerges as an organic, creative
forum, where the political and the artistic dialectically intersect,
mediated by socio-cultural totality.

III

The Proposed Framework: A Politico-Cultural Perspective

The study proposes that political fiction, like all literature, is a recorded form of culture. Further, aesthetic political criticism is relevant to political analysis as a mode of cultural interpretation. As a cultural approach to politics—highlighting the uniqueness of a system's cultural values, beliefs, loyalty-structures and their changing connotations in the political world—it is expected to contribute, in whatever small measure, to the need and the possibility of building up an indigenous framework of enquiry.[58] This is to take cognizance of the fact that each political system evolves in the context of a peculiar historical and cultural experience which cannot be divorced from its current political context. The additional relevance of studying politics in its cultural aspects in India (and the rest of the third world), lies in the fact that the goals of rapid political, economic and socio-cultural transformation have been pursued here, notwithstanding the most diverse historical and cultural traditions, thus presenting politics and culture as related processes of change and continuity, rather than as isolated fragments. Political fiction, in terms of aesthetic political criticism, is taken up in this study as a specific datum of politico-cultural perspective.

Interaction of politics and culture has been a subject of study for a long time in anthropology, sociology and political science in such vague concepts as national character, public opinion, ideology and political style. The term 'political culture' was also used sporadically for years before a serious attempt was made to discuss and develop it as a specific concept in the social sciences. Although, sometimes employed by Lenin, the first use of the term was made by Sidney and Beatrice Webb in the mid-thirties.[59]

The earliest attempts to theorize politics in cultural terms were anthropological in approach, for instance by Nathan Leites.[60] The idea of 'political culture' was enunciated by Gabriel Almond, as a reaction against anthropological 'psycho-cultural' approach, which appeared ambiguous as well as

simplistic in the sense of being a reproduction of family experiences. Sensitive to the ambiguities in the anthropological use of
the term 'Culture,' Almond specifically limited 'political
culture' to one of its many meanings, "the psychological
orientation toward political objects".[61]

The concept was further developed by Almond in his later
works, in terms of specific political orientations—attitudes
towards the political system and its various parts and attitudes
toward the role of the 'self' in the system. The subsequent
decades witnessed a large number of political scientists, sociologists and economists coming forward with their own enunciations of political culture, accepting, modifying or denouncing
the initial frameworks of Parsons, Shils, Leites and Almond.

Treating political culture as one of the four variables
crucial to the analysis of a political system, Samuel Beer, for
instance, defined it as "Certain aspects of the general culture
of a society", which are "concerned with *how* government
ought to be conducted and *what* it should try to do".[62] Thus,
the principal components of political culture, according to
Beer, were values, beliefs and emotional attitudes.[63] Robert
Dahl, on the other hand, singled out political culture as a
factor, which explains the varying patterns of political opposition in terms of orientations to problem-solving, to collective
action, to the political system in general, and to fellow citizens. Such orientations in Dahl's view may be pragmatic or
rationalistic, cooperative or non-cooperative, allegiant or
apathetic, trustful or mistrustful.[64] Lucian Pye perceived political culture as intimately related to political development in a
given political system, including fundamental concerns such as
the scope of politics, the relationship of ends and means, the
standards or criteria for evaluation of political action and
values that are salient for political action.[65] Roy C. Macridis
highlighted the existence of the multiplicity of interest and
pressure groups and sub-culture variations in a political system
and interpreted political culture as "the commonly shared goals
and commonly accepted rules".[66]

Whereas David McClelland emphasized economic aspects in
studying political culture[67] (as very few political scientists have
done), Danial Lerner, proposed a psychological perspective
with modernization as the focal point of transformation of a

traditional society.[68] S.E. Finer and Harry Eckstein, though highlighting different contexts, concentrated on authority relations in democratic and non-democratic systems and analysed the interrelationship of political institutions and non-political attitudes, in terms of the degree of harmony between a nation's governmental and social structures.[69] Political culture as an instrument reducing strains and bringing about appropriate expectations for future roles was viewed as highly significant for maintaining stable democracy by Harry Eckstein.[70]

The behavioural argument regarding political culture[71] would not be complete without reference to Gabriel Almond's framework, which is a seminal contribution, despite serious methodological and ideological limitations. Almond assumes that every political system is embedded in particular patterns of orientations, defined as predispositions to action. These orientations are distinguishable as political culture when addressed specifically to political objects.[72]

Adapting from the sociological theory of Parsons and Shils,[73] Almond and Verba propose three types of political orientations—cognitive, affective and evaluative. These orientations are necessarily addressed to political objects, which are again divided into three broad categories—roles, structures and policies as components of the political system. The 'political objects' also incorporate the political system in "general" terms and "self" as political actor or observer. On this basis, Almond and Verba construct an ideal typology of political culture, identifiable as the parochial, the subject and the participant political cultures, on the basis of availability or absence of specialized roles and of expectations among individuals of responsiveness of the political system to their needs.[74] This typology is a cumulative extension of orientations. Almond and Verba, however, realize that dimensions of political cultures in empirical reality are inevitably a "mix", resulting in either 'parochial-subject' or 'subject-participant' or 'parochial-participant' variety of political cultures. The persistence of the "mix" involves inevitable strains on interaction between culture and sub-cultures, which leads to a characteristic tendency of structural instability. These strains further result in more articulate orientations of alienation, apathy or allegiance vis-a-vis the political system.[75] These articulated orientations explain the extent of congruence or otherwise between political culture and political system. The civic culture, notwithstanding all its contradictions in political attitudes, is seen as "particularly appropriate for democratic political systems",[76] for it sustains the balance between governmental power and responsiveness, consensus and cleavages, citizen influence and passivity.

True, Almond and Verba's framework of civic culture has the distinction of being the pioneering enunciation and application of the concept of political culture. However, it is inhibited by serious methodological limitations and ideological presumptions, when viewed in the third world context. Almond's civic culture model, like other behaviouralist frameworks, assumes a unilinear framework of development. It is, therefore, intrinsically an ideological justification for the western type of stable democracies.[77] As a consequence, the 'other' kinds of democratic experiments elsewhere, as that of India, suffer from ambience—not approximating to the ideals of 'civic culture'— or even from prejudice as being "un-civic". The concept initially conceived as a flexible tool of explaining political reality of different societies *on their own terms*, gets converted into a closed framework, when narrowly identified and idealized in terms such as Civic Culture or stable democracy.

A more dangerous presumption, advocating the maintenance of distribution of parochial, subject and participant orientations among the population amounts to a rationalization of apathy and non-participation of the majority as well as of deprivations and social gaps. "The parochials are assumed to be uninvolved not because of the cumulative deprivations— poverty, lack of education, low media exposure—which may deny them effective political capital nor because they may be systematically prevented from gaining political access, but because they are regarded as fundamentally satisfied with the system: if they were not satisfied, they would be "pounding at the door".[78] Parochials, in fact, are not born parochials, they are the products of a particular pattern of the hegemonic process in society. In developing countries like India, this segment, designated as parochial, is disproportionately poor, uneducated, unexposed, yet in electoral politics it is the most significant by virtue of its numbers. Treatment of apathy as functional to democracy is embedded in the pluralist notion of democracy as 'moderation', 'accommodation' and 'bargain', which tends to undermine the conflict-potential of underlying sub-cultural entities and allows only marginal shifts in the assumed wider interests of the system.

The behaviouralist argument further assumes that people act in ways that can be variously categorized because they have "internalized" certain orientations of action. This is to circumscribe the concept of political culture in a conservative fashion as something 'received' as a finished product. However, there is no justification to exclude newly learned ideas and attitudes. Indeed, as Bluhm points out, the understanding of the revolutionary political culture involves precisely an awareness of how new ideas and attitudes are inculcated and old ones modified, although many revolutions carry forward old ideas. A political culture, therefore, may be a complex entity of discontinuous parts. During periods of change, this is usually the case.[79]

An overall emphasis on aspects of "congruence" would also amount to complete disregard of the reality of "incongruence', which happens to be the predominant reality in non-western societies of Africa and Asia. 'Congruence' between the political structure and the individual is, more often than not, an 'ideal' condition for societies undergoing rapid transformation. In order to avert the crisis of confidence, a certain degree of congruence may be accepted as an imperative condition, though incongruence cannot be ruled out altogether in the process of development. Incongruence also plays a positive role in clearing up issues and revealing contradictions. Contrary to the behaviouralist assumption, incongruence—within a consensus on fundamentals—is a healthy symptom of an aware citizenry and a progressive socio-political order.

The behaviouralist intellectual attempts at theorization of political culture resulting in disguised ideological justifications of some sort or the other (for idealized Western democracy in most cases) have led some critics to reject the concept[80] and others to doubt its adequacy.[81] Political culture, in fact, is much else and much more than the American behaviouralist attempts at theorization in terms of civic culture, stable democracy and pluralism by Almond, Verba, Eckstein, Lispet, Dahl and others, who have intertwined it with theories of political development, modernization and systems analysis, thus, undermining the utility of the framework in explaining political reality of specific societies *on their own terms*.

In the present study, it is assumed that creative literature as a source of studying interaction of politics and culture provides an opportunity for understanding a given political system *on its own terms*. Accepting political system, in general terms, (without identifying with behaviouralist rhetoric) as a network of political institutions and patterns of political behaviour in a given state, and employing political culture as a short-hand expression for the interaction of politics and culture, in a broad sense, this study specifies the interactive role of aesthetic political criticism in the above-mentioned context. This may be explained with the help of two paradigms of interaction as on the next page.

Thus, as evidenced by the proposed paradigms of interaction, there is a triangular interaction among politics, literature and culture, mediated by the social totality. This interaction necessarily involves reciprocity and variability, going beyond the conventional cause-effect oriented categories of 'reflections' or 'representation'. The interaction also defies the crude equation of propaganda and politics, resulting in a simplistic interpretation of both, politics and art. Finally, the interaction does not reduce culture to fixed social forms, but accepts it as a complex entity providing both a rich heritage and stimulating opportunities for change to a given social unit. Art, in this sense, does not have to be political ideology with an artistic veneer in order to convey a political meaning. Political meaning is inherent in the artistic fabric of an 'aware' art work. It does not necessarily precede the creation of that fabric, nor does it have a separate life of its own. The political meaning gets converged through the responsible presentation of the 'selected' issues in an art work. The political novel, thus, faces the challenge of integrating aesthetics and politics in such a manner that it neither indulges in distortion of politics nor in damage to aesthetics.

The 'political', as any other aspect of social reality, does not get documented or factually reproduced in political fiction. Creative practice operates through 'selection' in order to be meaningful. The phenomenon of selection explains the levels of

PARADIGMS OF INTERACTION

Figure I

LITERATURE, POLITICS & CULTURE MEDIATED BY SOCIAL TOTALITY

Figure II

POLITICAL CULTURE & AESTHETIC POLITICAL CRITICISM IN A POLITICAL SYSTEM

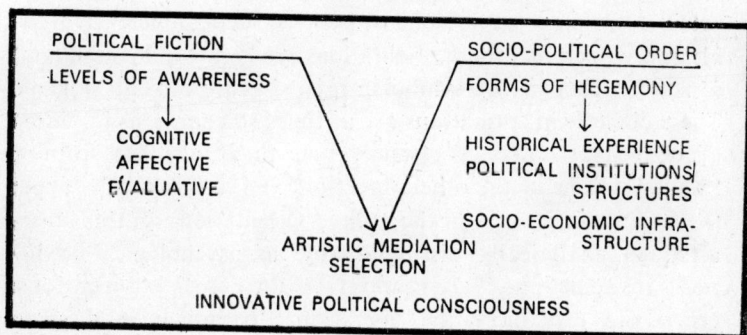

awareness exhibited by an artist in his artwork. Parsons and Almond, as seen earlier, propose that political orientations operate at three levels: *cognitive* (general perceptions about the system), *affective* (emotional dispositions toward the system) and *evaluative* (judgment about the system). These levels of orientations interpreted here as levels of awareness, are relevant in creative practice, as constitutive parts of what Williams calls 'practical consciousness' in a given society, capable of relating to each other and constantly interacting.

An art work, while simply projecting a very general image of the political system or certain aspects of politics recognizable in common parlance, exhibits a 'cognitive' level of awareness. An 'affective' level of awareness brings forth emotional dispositions toward the political structure. Though these two levels may not be critical they cannot be excluded from the realm of the 'political' in its inclusive sense. Symbols and myths play an important role in developing cognitive and affective orientations to politics. These orientations are not only 'subjective' as Almond has interpreted them, but also 'socio-historic' in operational terms, rooted in socio-historic experience and as 'responses' to socio-historic changes, thus, inseparably related to the socio-political structure at a given time. Cognitive and affective orientations are, therefore, unorganized, inarticulate, yet not formless perceptions of politics. Being inherently flexible and vulnerable, these orientations are highly influenced and sometimes changed by symbols, myths and political slogans. These changes in formations are at times so enormous in terms of quantity, if not in essence, that they take the form of "waves" in one or the other direction and substantially affect the hegemonic process in the polity. Orientations, in this sense, although analytically distinguishable as psychological predispositions to actions,[82] are however, in their social dimensions, crucial in explaining the operational paradigm in a given polity.

It is to be further remembered that all orientations do not reach levels of articulation. The range of such orientations is rather expansive.[83] It is the average man's world of diffuse and amorphous ideas identified as 'latent ideology' by Lane,[84] of emotional dispositions, conceptualized as 'structures of feeling'

by Williams';[85] and of subjective perceptions, theorized as 'senti-
ment' by Leighton.[86] Thus the levels of orientations or awareness may be cognitive or affective in any or all of these
senses.

Aesthetic political criticism is not merely adaptive, extensive
or incorporative; it is also critical. Evaluation is a conscious
and critical orientation and exhibits the highest level of awareness. When an artist chooses to confront vital issues of politics
and moves beyond the constraints of contemporaneity and
visualizes transcedence of the prevailing unfreedom, repression
and alienation in society, he contributes to the creation of what
may be termed, *innovative political consciousness.* Such an art
work, formulated and projected through required information
and description, arrives at an interpretation, if not judgment.
Commitment to an ideology or an idea is not ruled out in conscious artistic evaluation. It is, in fact, in the politico-aesthetic
vision that the true indispensability of political fiction lies.

Aesthetic political criticism, thus incorporates several levels
of awareness discerned in art works, broadly categorized here as
cognitive, affective and evaluative, for methodological specificity.
In creative practice (as in political behaviour), they are over-
lapping rather than exclusive categories. However, points of
distinction as seen above, are possible to identify in specific
works of art.

Aesthetic political consciousness, inclusive of all the levels
of awareness, addresses itself to the process of political culture
as operating in a given socio-political order. The socio-political
order is not a network of static, unchanging institutions. The
socio-political order in operation is an ever-going hegemonic
process, to use Gramsci's expression. It is an inclusive form of
power relationships, in a complex interlocking of political,
social and cultural forces. Hegemony, in other words, is specific distribution of power and influence in society. To say that
men define and shape their own destiny is true as an abstrac-
tion. In actual practice, there are always gaps and inequalities
in resources and, therefore, in the capacity to realize this goal.
Hegemony is the necessary recognition of the actuality of
domination and subordination in any society, not necessarily
confined to formal institutions, although institutions are the
most powerful instruments.[87] The process of hegemony is

always in formation. It is, therefore, continually to be renewed, defended and modified, on the one hand, and resisted, challenged and limited, on the other. In democratic political structure, the process has also to be responsive to the alternatives which threaten its dominance.

Works of art, by their general character, are capable of projecting this complex process, signifying their role as important sources of evidence of such a process. In practice, hegemonic process operates through various forums in various forms. The present study specifies three forums for elucidation: historical experience, political institutions and structures and the socio-economic infrastructure.

The socio-political order, perceived as a living process of hegemony, provides the broadest possible range of operational multiplicity of levels of political culture. The context of political culture, confined by behaviouralists to political objects such as the political system or the self, gets operated, modified or altered through historical experience, political institutions and the socio-economic infrastructure. In interaction with the socio-political order, orientations remain neither static nor homogenous. Being always in formation, the objective constraints significantly influence the relationship of individual or group orientations to the macro-political structure, displaying a potential for both conflict and congruence, continuity and change. In this tension of interaction, however, lies the vitality of political culture. Political culture, in this sense, need not be undermined as 'subjective' in a pejorative sense. If at all, it is to be qualified as subjective, it would be justifiable in the Platonic sense of 'self in society', identifying the 'subjective' with the 'objective', in an inclusive sense, assuming their dialectical interaction.

The final and decisive dimension of interaction between aesthetics, culture and politics is the artistic mediation and selection. The artist in using his prerogative of 'selection' of specific aspects of the socio-political order, as themes for interpretation, gives a 'specific orientation' to the political phenomenon under consideration. Involvement with culture (in the sense of literature, arts and, in general, the finer developments of human possibility) is no reason for political non-commitment; in fact, it is often taken to carry with it special political

obligations.[88] In exploring areas of tension and exposing paradoxes prevalent in the existing context, the artist also strikes at
the roots of prevailing hegemonic consciousness and process
whether directly or as a metaphor.[89] An aware artist averts
premature reconciliations; instead, he protests and rebels
against the dominant consciousness through responsible
criticism.

Whether or not the artist succeeds in transcending the given
context, he does have a creative role in creating a cultural consciousness against unfreedom and injustice in a given society.
Since purely cultural solutions are likely to prove insufficient,
cultural protest needs to be integrated with political protest.
Aesthetic political criticism may prove to be just this kind of an
integrating forum. Between an unquestioning ideological soli-
darity and wilful independence, the artist, like the political
analyst, faces the challenge of carving his own path, though
maintaining a critical distance. The critical edge sharpens,
when the artist idealizes identification with popular forces in an
effort to be 'relevant'. Political involvement of artists may, at
worst result in sentimental nostalgia, at best in valuable responsible critique of the epoch. History of aesthetic political
criticism (as discussed earlier), however, brings out numerous
instances when artists have successfully combined artistic
integrity with social responsibility.

In the ultimate analysis, aesthetic political criticism as a
cultural mode of political inquiry may contribute in regaining
to whatever extent, due esteem for values, beliefs and norms, on
which a political system is founded.

The restoration of this esteem may further explain legitimacy
of a given polity *on its own terms*, that is, in the context of the
goals and ideals and norms of conduct, valued in a society
under study at a given point of time. Such approach also brings
home the need of reviving the historical perspective and the
tradition of critical inquiry in political analysis. Politico-aesthetic criticism, thus, has several points in common with other
forms of enquiry, reaffirming the perennial relevance of
'dialogue' among these seemingly separate spheres of understanding. These objectives may be much more ambitious for
individual artists than for political analysts, their unrealized

existence, however, being valuable as milestones in the unending creative process.

References

1. Stephen Spender, "Writers and Politics", *Partisan Review*, 34 (Summer 1967), 372.
2. Theodore Adorno, "Reconciliation under Duress", in Ronald Taylor, (translation editor), *Aesthetics And Politics* (London, NLB, 1977), pp. 159-160.
3. Raymond Williams, *Marxism and Literature* (London, Oxford University Press, 1977), pp. 211-12.
4. Jean Paul Sartre, *Between Existentialism and Marxism* (New York, William Morrow and Co., 1974), p. 13.
5. *n.* 4, p. 14.
6. *n.* 4, p. 25.
7. Williams, *n.* 3, p. 204. Also see: T. Adorno, "Commitment" in R. Taylore *Aesthetics and Politics*, *n.* 2, pp. 177-195.
8. George Orwell, *A Collection of Essays*, (Garden City, Doubley and Co., 1957), p. 316.
9. Herbert Marcuse, *The Aesthetic Dimension* (Boston, Beacon, 1977), pp. ix-x.
10. See Fredrick Jameson, *Marxism And Form—Twentieth Century Dialectical Theories of Literature* (New Jersey, Princeton, 1971), p. 305.
11. T.S. Dorsch (Trans.), *Classical Literary Criticism* (Harmondsworth, Penguin Books, 1965), p. 12. R.W. Hall, in his paper "Plato's Theory of Art: A Reassessment", disagrees with this interpretation and proposes that Book X of *The Republic* must be read along with Book II and III, in order to grasp fully Plato's normative theory of art. *Journal of Aesthetics and Art Criticism*, 33, 1 (1974), 75-82. (Hereafter referred as *JAAS*).
12. T.S. Dorsch, *n.* 9, pp. 15-18.
13. Raymond Williams, *The Long Revolution* (Harmondsworth, Penguine Books, 1965), p. 22. Also see: C.D. Narasimhaiah's observation: "For after Aristotle and Longinus the western world had to wait for over 1500 years before it witnessed anything resembling criticism. What are usually called the Dark Ages of Europe happened to be the most creative period of Indian history. Consider the great names in literary criticism in India in the first millenium after Christ: Bharata, Bhamaha, Dandin, Vamana, Ananda Vardhana, Kuntaka and Abhinavagupta and their amazing contributions of *Rasa*, *Alankara*, *Riti*, *Dhvani* and *Vakrokti* to Sanskrit Poetics". C.D. Narasimhaiah (ed.), *Literary Criticism: European and Indian Traditions* (Mysore, University of Mysore, n.d.), p. 7.

14. Diana T. Lawrenson and Allan Swingewood, *The Sociology of Literature* (New York, Schocker Books, 1972), p. 24.

15. Rene Wellek, *The Rise of English Literary History* (Chapel Hill, University of North Carolina Press, 1941), pp. 33-34.

16. 'Mechanical' in the sense that it implied a simple 'one to one' relation between culture and the material base of society and thus underrated the active functions of human consciousness.

17. Rene Wellek, *The Later Eighteenth Century* (London, Jonathan Cape, 1955), pp. 5-11 and 181-200.

18. *n.* 17, pp. 232-55. Also see: Gary Shapiro, "Hegel's Dialectic of Artistic Meaning", *JAAC* XXXV, 1, (Fall 1976), 23-35.

19. See Rene Wellek, *The Later Nineteenth Century* (London; Jonathan Cape 1966), pp. 27-57.

20. See Lionel Trilling, *The Liberal Imagination—Essays on Literature and Society* (New York, The Viking Press, 1951), pp. 281-303. Also Edward Zwick (ed) *Literature and Liberalism* (Washington, D.C., The New Republic Book Co., 1970), pp. xi-xxiv.

21. Stephen Morawski, "The Aesthetic Views of Marx and Engels", *JAAC*, 3 (Spring 1970), 313-14.

22. Karl Marx and Frederick Engels, *On Literature and Art* (Moscow, Progress, 1976), pp. 17 and 84.

23. *n.* 22, pp. 20 and 141.

24. Karl Marx, *Economic and Philosophic Manuscripts of 1844.* (Moscow, Progress, 1974), pp. 83-124. For a valuable critical assessment see: S.S. Prawer, *Karl Marx and World Literature* (London; Oxford University Press, 1978), pp. 399-425.

25. Sidney Hook, *Marx And the Marxists—The Ambiguous Legacy* (N.J.D. Van Nostrand Co. Inc., 1955), pp. 11-12. Two notable studies on the theme, from the contrary view point, are: Fredrick Jameson, *Marxism And Form* (New Jersey, Princeton Univ. Press, 1971), and Cliff Slaughter, *Marxism, Ideology and Literature* (London, Macmillan, 1980).

26. Albert Camus, *The Rebel* (Harmondsworth, Penguine Books, 1977), p. 224.

27. See Fredrick Jameson, "Reflections in Conclusion", in R. Taylor (ed), *Aesthetics and Politics*, *n.* 2, pp. 196-212.

28. See Irwing Howe, Preface to the American Edition "A Word about George Lukacs", G. Lukacs, *The Historical Novel* (Boston, Beacon, 1963), p. 7.

29. B. Brecht, "On the Formalistic Character of Theory of Realism", in Roland Taylor (ed), *Aesthetics and Politics*, *n.* 2, pp. 70-76.

30. Georg Lukacs, *The Meaning of Contemporary Realism* (London, Merlin Press, 1963), pp. 55-57 and 60. For an interesting comparison see: George Plekhanov, *Art and Social Life* (London, Lawrence and Wishart, 1953), pp. 20, 108-9 and 164.

31. Lucian Goldmann, *Towards a Sociology of the Novel* (Trans. A. Sheridan) (London, Tavistock, 1975), pp. 9-11.

32. Leon Trotsky, *Literature and Revolution* (Ann Arbor, University of Michigan Press, 1960), pp. 16-18, 178 and 180.

33. R. Taylor (ed), *Aesthetics and Politics*, n. 2, pp. 66-67.

34. Walter Benjamin, *Illuminations: Essays and Reflections* (ed. with an Introduction by Hannah Arendt, Trans, Harry Zohn), (London, Jonathan Cape, 1970), pp. 223-25. Also see: W. Benjamin, *Understanding Brecht* (London, New Left Books, 1973), p. 102.

35. Theodore Adorno, *Prisms*, p. 30, cited by Martin Jay, *The Dialectical Imagination,* (Boston; Little Brown and Co., 1973), p. 178.

36. Martin Jay, *The Dialectical Imagination*, p. 179.

37. Herbert Marcuse, *Negations: Essays in Critical Theory* (trans. J.J. Spino), (Boston, Beacon, 1968), pp. 115-117, and, *An Essay on Liberation* (Boston, Beacon, 1969), pp. 31-54.

38. Martin Jay, *n.* 36, p. 54.

39. G. Lukacs, *Studies in European Realism* (New York; Grosset and Dunlop, 1964), pp. 115-6.

40. Neal Wood, *Communism and British Intellectuals* (New York, Columbia University Press, 1959), p. 80. Also see: David Madden (ed.), *Proletarian Writers of the Thirties* (Southern Illinois Univ. Press, 1968), pp. xvi-xviii.

41. See Mulk Raj Anand, *Apology for Heroism* (New Delhi, Arnold Heinemann, 1975), pp. 125-126.

42. Roymond Williams, *Culture and Society* (London, Harper and Row, 1958), p. 209 and 229.

43. C. Caudwell, *Studies and Further Studies in a Dying Culture*, (New York, Monthly Review Press, 1971), p. 44.

44. C. Caudwell, *Illusion and Reality: A Study of the Sources of Poetry* (London, Lawrence and Wishart, 1946), pp. 192 and 267.

45. *n.* 44. For elucidation also see: David N. Margolies, *The Function of Literature—A Study of Christopher Caudwell's Aesthetics* (New York, International Publishers, 1969), p. 125.

46. Terry Eagleton, *Criticism and Ideology* (London, New Left Books, 1976), pp. 24-26.

47. F.R. Leavis and Denys Thompson, *Culture and Environment*, (London, Chatto and Windus, 1960), p. 5.

48. T. Eagleton, *n.* 46, pp. 26-38.

49. R. Williams, *The Long Revolution*, *n.* 13, pp. 55 and 66.

50. R. Williams, "Culture And Revolution: A Response", in Terry Eagleton and Brian Wicker (eds), *From Culture to Revolution* (London, Sheed and Ward, 1968), p. 308.

51. See Evan Watkins, *The Critical Act—Criticism and Community* (New Haven, Yale University Press, 1978), p. 141.

52. Raymond Williams, *n.* 3, pp. 82 and 94.

53. Herbert Marcuse also developed an identical argument in *Eros and Civilization* (New York, Random House, 1955), p. 144.

54. *n.* 3, pp. 115-117, 194.

55. *n.* 3, pp. 108-114 and 121-135.

56. R. Williams, *Communications* (Harmondsworth, Penguine, 1971), pp. 127-37.

57. It is relevant to note here that India has a rich heritage in Sanskrit aesthetics. Two valuable discussions on the theme are: S.K. De, *Studies in the History of Sanskrit Poetics* (London, Luzac and Co., 1923) and *The Journal of Aesthetics and Art Criticism* (Special issue on Oriental Aesthetics) Fall (1965). The reason for not including ancient Indian aesthetics in the present discussion is absence of notable impact of this tradition on modern socio-political aesthetics in India. There is, however, a renaissance of interest in them currently. See, for instance, C.D. Narasimhaiah (ed), *Literary Criticism: European and Indian Traditions, n.* 13, and C.P. Verghese, *Essays on Indian Writing in English* (New Delhi, V.N. Publications, 1975), pp. 113-144.

58. For an stimulating proposition see P.C. Mathur, "Indigenization of pre-existing Intellectual Disciplines: An Enquiry Into The Problems and Preconditions of the Development of Indian Political Science", *Political Science Review*, 18.2 (January-March, April-June 1979), pp. 89-106.

59. Archie Brown and Jack Gray (eds), *Political Culture and Political Change in Communist States* (London, Macmillan, 1977), p. 2.

60. Nathan Leites, "Psycho-Cultural Hypotheses about Political Acts", *World Politics*, 1 (1948), 102-11. Also see: Alfred L. Kroeber and Clyde Klukhohn, *Culture: A Critical Review of Concepts and Definitions* (New York, Vintage Books, 1963).

61. G. Almond, "Comparative Political Systems", *Journal of Politics*, 18 (1956), 391-409. Also see: David Easton, *A Systems Analysis of Political Life*, (New York, John Wiley and Sons, 1965), pp. 100-116.

62. Samuel Beer and Adam Ulam (eds), *Patterns of Government* (New York, Random House, 1958), p. 12.

63. *n.* 62.

64. Robert Dahl, *Political Oppositions in Western Democracies* (New Haven, Yale University Press, 1966), pp. 352-355.

65. Lucian Pye, *Politics, Personality and Nation Building* (New Haven, Yale University Press, 1962), pp. 122-124.

66. Roy C. Macridis, "Interest Groups in Comparative Analysis", *Journal of Politics*, xviii, (1961), 40.

67. See, David McClelland, "National Character and Economic Growth in Turkey and Iran", in L.W. Pye (ed), *Communications And Political Development* (New Delhi, Radha Krishna Prakashan), 1972, pp. 152-187.

68. Daniel Learner, *The Passing of Traditional Society* (Glencoe, III, The Free Prees, 1958).

69. S.E. Finer, *The Man on Horseback: The Role of the Military in Politics* (London, Pall Mall Press, 1962).

70. H. Eckstein, *A Theory of Stable Democracy* (Princeton, Centre of International Studies, 1961).

71. For valuable discussion of some of the conceptual and methodological issues raised by behaviouralists on political culture, see Dennis Kavanagh, *Political Culture* (London, Macmillan, 1972) and, Young. C. Kim, "The Concept of Political Culture", *Journal of Politics*, 26, 2(May 1964), pp. 313-336.

72. Gabriel A. Almond and Sidney Verba, *The Civil Culture* (Princeton, Princeton University Press, 1963), pp. 13-14.

73. Talcott Parsons and Edward Shils, *Toward A General Theory of Action* (Cambridge, Harvard University Press, 1951), pp. 58-60.

74. *n. 72*, pp. 17-19.

75. *n. 72*, pp. 20-23.

76. *n. 72*, p. 476.

77. For an incisive critique, see Brian Barry, *Sociologists, Economists and Democracy* (London, Collier-Macmillan, 1970), pp. 47-74.

78. James A. Bill and Robert L. Hardgrave Jr., *Comparative Politics— The Quest for Theory* (Columbus, Ohio, Charles E. Merill, 1973), p. 91. Also see Guiseppe Di Palma, *Apathy and Participation: Mass Politics in Western Societies*, (New York; Free Press, 1970).

79. W.T. Bluhm, *Ideologies and Attitudes: Modern Political Culture* (New Jersey, Prentice Hall, Inc., 1974), p. 11.

80. See Barrington Moore Jr., *Social Origins of Dictatorship and Democracy: Lord and Peasant in the Making of the Modern World*, (Harmondsworth, Penguine ed., 1969), pp. 483-87. Frank Parkin, *Class Inequality and Political Order: Social Stratification in Capitalist and Communist Societies*, (London, MacGibbon and Kee, 1971), pp. 80-82.

81. Brian M. Barry, *n. 77*, pp. 47-74.

82. Robert C. Tucker takes the opposite view and advocates inclusion of both beliefs and actions. See "Culture, Political Culture and Communist Society", *Political Science Quarterly*, 88, 2 (June 1971), 173-90.

83. See Kenneth Sherill, "The Attitudes of Modernity", *Comparative Politics*, 1 (January 1969), 184-210.

84. Robert E. Lane, *Political Ideology* (New Work, Free Press, 1962), 16.

85. *Marxism and Literature, n. 3*, 128-135.

86. Alexander Leighton, *My Name is Legion: Foundations for a Theory of Man in Relation to Culture*, (New York, Basic Books, 1959), pp. 241-53 and 369.

87. Sidney Hook's distinction of the *origin* of any cultural fact and its *acceptance*, is useful to some extent, in explaining the role of political institutions as a selective agency. See S. Hook, *Towards an Understanding of Karl Marx*, (New York, John Day, 1933), p. 160.

88. For a stimulating discussion on the subject, see the inter-disciplinary symposium, Richard Church (et al.) "Claims of Politics", *Scrutiny*, 8, 2 (September 1939), 130-167.
89. For an interesting interpretation of politics as metaphor, see: Garrett Epps, "Politics as Metaphor", *The Virginia Quarterly Review* (Winter 1979), 79-98.

3

Political History and the Indo-Anglian Novel: The Legacy of the Nationalist Movement

The present and the future inevitably grow out of the past and bear its stamp, and to forget this is to build without foundations and to cut off roots of national growth.

—*Jawaharlal Nehru*

Political fiction is in part historical self-discovery. As a useful index of history as 'lived experience' of the past, it possesses significant inter-linkages with the present. History, thus depicted, may, however, be less scientific, less sequential, less objective, yet more interpretative. From the large mass of material available in history, a political novelist has a big range of choices extending from studying a single individual, such as Gandhi, to an entire epoch. The historical value of political fiction is, in fact, proportionate to the depth with which it captures the 'essence' of the socio-political order, in the specific era under consideration, in terms of the underlying historical forces that have decidedly influenced the hegemonic process, one way or the other. At another level, through crystallization of the 'particular' and then its extension to the 'general', political fiction also unfolds the historical links existing between the two, often, through myths, symbols, images and icons. Thus history as legacy is an inescapable omnipresence. It is both compelling and challenging for a political novelist to assimilate critically the legacy in terms of the norms, reflected as reference points for the present as well as to re-interpret and "re-enact past experience" as Collingwood would say,[1] and formulate his own reflections regarding the central political values of a society.

The present chapter examines select Indo-Anglian novels against the backdrop of major aspects of India's political history.

I

National Heritage : A Politico-Cultural Syndrome

Modern India, as a political entity, is a product of a variety of influences, strands and traditions, spread over thousands of years and of alternating experiences of glory and degeneration, achievements and frustrations, freedom and subjugation. The legacy of India's past is in essence, a mixed heritage of positive and negative elements. In positive terms, it provides a durable core to which the artist may turn for foundation, firmness and faith. The negative aspects have tended to grow out of the pluralistic, heterogeneous character of Indian society, resulting into divisive trends and sub-nationalistic loyalties. The legacy, its ambivalence notwithstanding, showed itself sometimes as an asset and at others as a liability. However, it has been both inspiring and instructive for the political analyst and the novelist.

Indian history witnessed an evolution through a variety of political forms and styles of rule, ranging from monarchical, republican and feudal to the imperial. However, the overall structure of society remained, by and large, 'apolitical' till the advent of the British. Ashis Nandy has aptly pointed out: "when the first impact of the raj started bringing parts of an apolitical social order within the compass of politics toward the end of the eighteenth century, it initiated the first stage of India's politicization".[2]

It is a point of dispute whether the British policies were intended to initiate politicization. The fact, however, remains that these attempts 'resulted'—by accident or design—in spreading political awareness in India on a national scale. Politicization in India was not an event identifiable with a

specific moment in time. It was a long and gradual process
preceded, accompanied and substantially shaped by the cultural
renaissance, heralded by Ram Mohan Roy in the beginning of
the nineteenth century and later advanced by Ranade, Naoroji,
Madhusudan Dutt and R.C. Dutt in modern liberal idiom, and
by Dayanand, Vivekanand, Tilak and Aurobindo in terms of
robust revivalism. The cultural awakening was at once a
redefinition of India's national identity in terms of its past
glory and a re-examination of traditional social structure. This
incorporated an enquiry into factors responsible for the
degeneration that had gradually taken over during preceding
centuries. A questioning of this kind also involved a fresh
look at the fundamental notions of governance with dignity
and justice as guiding principles. Cultural renaissance, thus,
subsequently became the foundation of political nationalism,
inspiring both the liberal and the radical traditions of political
protest.

The nationalist movement, as it evolved, inevitably acquired
a predominantly political character, though it was extended as
a parallel struggle on socio-cultural fronts as well. This
attitudinal transformation from some sort of a receptive perception in the eighteenth century to political resentment by the
middle of the nineteenth century, however, remained confined
to the upper middle classes of educated India.[3] It was a strange
situation, where prevalence of mass illiteracy and ignorance
were only aggravated by the British policy of non-intervention
in society, despite introduction of English education in
pockets. If, on the one hand, western contact resulted in some
sort of resistance against change and sustenance of traditional
primacies, on the other, a new spirit was in evidence which
took considerable inspiration from the west. Nevertheless,
both the revivalists and the modernists, the liberals and
the militants, projected 'Indianness' as a defensive cultural
posture for political nationalism till the beginning of the
twentieth century.[4]

It was in 1920s, with the emergence of Gandhi, that the
politico-cultural integration of these two strands of cultural
consciousness and traditions of political protest was substantially achieved, although voices of dissent continued to
persist.[5] Western norms of nationalism were synthesized with

India's Sanskritic identity by invoking traditional symbols and myths and thus reinterpreting traditions with reference to the present. Nationalism, thus became a creed which could serve as the crystallizing centre for the growing unrest among the youth, unite the divided communities[6] and also offer a programme of action in which the people themselves would act as the principal actors, reminiscent of the 'philosophy of action' of the *Gita*.[7] The people lost their religious attachment to the rulers, as B.C. Shafer points out, and believed that they, not the king, were supreme. As the king lost his divinity, the nation acquired it.[8]

As people fought, suffered and exalted the nation as 'mother', it became a kind of "organic, planetary work of art", as Burke would say, and an object of 'worship', as the source of everything they cherished. Although not possessed of supernatural bliss, the concept of nation unleashed a missionary zeal and a new form of morality like *anasakti*, *aparigraha*, *ahimsa* and *brahmcharya* and rewards and punishments and idealized martyrdom.[9] Protest became ethical and politics assumed an imperative perspective. Intellectuals, artists and scholars had their own role to play in this creation of a common past of custom, literature, art and political life. Thus, on attitudinal plane, nationalism offered an opportunity of involvement in, and commitment to, a "great cause" for some and an outlet for human sentiments like love, hate and anger, for others. Gandhi, of all the Indian leaders, not only contributed to the attitudinal transformation but also effectively employed it for practical political purposes.

However, the idealization of traditional Indian values of harmony, unity, reconciliation and tolerance of dissent[10] by Gandhi as guiding political norms also led to far-reaching consequences which, according to some analysts, were responsible for the miscalculations in the 1940s and an ambiguous legacy after independence.[11] The transient harmony of the communities during the 1920s and the thirties had given way to strong communal biases in the 1940s, which demanded a firmer, more cautious and realistic approach, whereas Gandhi's open politics was idealized by ethical principles.[12]

The fruition of the unarmed revolution brought about by

Gandhi through non-violence and satyagraha in the face of the might and repression of the British empire is now part of history. These very ideals, however, were betrayed when it came to resolving the domestic crisis and the 'partition' of India was accepted. The concept of 'nation' and its realization had come about through more than a century of toil, trials and errors. The changing international politico-economic realities and the transforming attitudes of the younger generations, impatient for concrete results, also demanded a more dynamic and less idealistic political outlook. Jawaharlal Nehru and Sardar Patel sought to fulfil this need without abandoning the fundamental humanist concerns of Gandhian philosophy. The deviance was apparent in so far as systemic operational requirements had to be countered and alternatives devised for free India, aspiring to become a modern state. In any case, maturing through the national movement, India's leadership faced the challenge of directing efforts towards nation-building and development.

Ideologically speaking, the success of the Bolshevik Revolution in Russia in 1917, and the consequent popularity of Marxist Socialism in Europe in the 1920s and the 1930s, also attracted young nationalists, intellectuals and artists in India; for instance, M.N. Roy, Jawaharlal Nehru, Mulk Raj Anand and Yashpal, to name only a few. Scientific socialism thus became a contending ideology with Gandhian idealism and substantially affected the course of cultural, intellectual and political development in a number of ways. The subsequent developments bearing upon democratic socialist strand in India's politics and of social realism in aesthetics, may be traced to this phenomenon.

The preceding two hundred years of political history thus witnessed India's emergence as a 'nation' in a pervasive sense, inheriting a legacy of mixed acquisitions, notable attainments and missed opportunities, soaring idealism and realism, inclusive of conservative, liberal and radical strands of protest, though qualified by a universal appreciation of the inevitability of national independence.

II

Major Indo-Anglian Novels: Themes and Issues

In India, where literature in regional languages already existed before the advent of the British, creative writing in English language was a unique consequence of historical and political circumstances of the nineteenth century, particularly the introduction of English in India. The introduction was as much the result of the imperial policies as of Ram Mohan Roy's persistent efforts from 1823 to 1835 for a liberal and enlightened system of education, embracing Mathematics, Natural Philosophy, Chemistry and Anatomy, along with other useful sciences. Lord Macaulay and William Bentinck played their own role for different (now well known) reasons. Although there were isolated instances of writing in English in India even before 1835 (for example of Henry Derozio and K.P. Ghose), notable impact of the West was felt on literary efforts after the formal introduction of western education on a national scale. It is generally conceded that exposure to western education heightened inquisitive enquiry and expedited interaction with new ideals, processes and institutions. "Indian writing in English was but one manifestation of the new creative urge in India—what is often referred to as the literary renaissance in India . . . Bengali led the way, but the others were not slow to follow. And Indo-Anglian literature had the same origin as the other modern Indian literatures. . . ."[13] The birth of Indian novel in English was, thus, intimately related to the evolution of the nationalist history in India. As such the political motif was not only prominent but inherent in its very genesis.

It is an interesting fact that the first novel written in India, *A Journal of Forty-Eight Hours of the Year 1945* by Kylash Chunder Dutt in 1835, was written in English, not in any indigenous language. Also, it was a political novel, anticipating the movement for independence, one hundred and ten years in advance of the actual occurrence. Another Indo-Anglian novel, *The Republic of Orissa: Annals from the Pages of the Twentieth Century* (1845), by Sochee Chunder Dutt, was also a political novel, again anticipating the events of the first two decades of the twentieth century.[14] The trend of socio-political awareness and inquisitive enquiry, along with softened criticism, was sustained in 19th century Indo-Anglian fiction. Some notable examples are: Lal Behari Day's *Govind Samanta* (1874), S.C. Dutt's *The Young Zamindar* (1885) and *Shunkur: A Tale of the Indian Mutiny of 1857* (1885), Krupabai Satthianandhan's *Kamla* (1894) and *Saguna* (1895), and Shivantibai Nikambe's *Ratnabai* (1895). However, it was Bankim Chandra Chatterjee's Bengali novel, *Anandmath* (1882) that surpassed all the Indo-Anglian attempts through its powerful indictment of the British hegemony and enunciation of the nationalist creed of determined protest. As it is well known, the impact of *Anandmath*, as of no other novel, was felt during the subsequent decades.

By the beginning of the twentieth century and during the first two decades, one comes across considerable tilt towards revivalism, in terms of nostalgia for the grandeur of the past. In this context, one could cite some novels, such as K.K. Sinha's *Sanjogita* (1903), T. Ramakrishna's *Padmini* (1903), Jogender Singh's *Nur Jahan* (1909), S.K. Ghose's *The Prince of Destiny* (1909) and S.M. Mitra's *Hindupore* (1909). It is not before the 1920s that the Indo-Anglian novel, prominently political in content, makes a "diffident appearance" and gets "established in the next two decades".[15] "Some fifty years later", William Walsh observes, "it is clear that this was a form peculiarly suited to the Indian sensibility, and one to which Indian writers have made a distinct and significant contribution".[16]

Gandhi's emergence in the 1920s revolutionized not only politics but also aesthetics in India.[17] Although in linguistic terms, Gandhi proposed bilingualism, in the tradition of Ram Mohan Roy, Tilak and Aurobindo, writing in English also continued to flourish along with other Indian languages. Gandhi extolled virtues of clarity, directness and brevity rather than eloquence, ornamentation and exuberance, both in politics and in writing. However, this should not be taken to mean that Gandhi's priorities were followed scrupulously.

Indo-Anglian fiction of the 1920s, 1930s and also early 1940s was evidently inspired by the new content of ethical imperatives of Gandhian politics symbolised by his action theory of *Satya*, *Abhay* and *Ahimsa*. Political freedom acquired a new form and literature acquired a new content as Gandhi's experiments with truth unfolded new vistas of the grand alternative.[18] Responding and reacting in varying degrees and different ways to such determinants, Indo-Anglian fiction gradually evolved to discernible maturity. Some of the notable contributions to Indo-Anglian fiction, epitomizing this phase of India's political history are: Dhangopal Mukherjee's *My Brother's Face* (1925), K.S. Venkatramani's *Murugan, The Tiller* (1927), F.H. Das' *Into The Sun* (1933), Hasan Ali's *The Changeling* (1933), D.F. Karaka's *There Lay the City* (1942) and *We Never Die* (1944), K.A. Abbas', *Defeat for Death* (1944), K. Nagarajan's *Athawar House* (1939), and, perhaps one of the most important works, K.S. Venkatramani's *Kandan, The Patriot* (1932). One might trace the beginnings of modern political novel in English in India to these works. It is, however, with Raja Rao's *Kanthapura* (1938) that the Indo-Anglian "Gandhi-fiction" achieves a breakthrough.

The general trend of adoration, admiration and glorification of Gandhi as a "phenomenon", unprecedented and unparalleled in Indian and world history as presented in these novels, may be traced partly to ideological orientations of these novelists. Also, one would not ignore the fact that they were in close proximity to the events and, hence, could not escape or belittle the pervasive impact of Gandhi. Such involvement, if not direct participation, was inherent in the situational context.

In the works of Mulk Raj Anand, especially, *Untouchable* (1935), *Coolie* (1936), *The Village* (1939), *Across the Black Waters* (1940) and *The Sword and the Sickle* (1942), one could also identify a parallel progressive movement in Indian literature. Mulk Raj Anand's perception of the contemporary milieu in India could be seen to have taken a hue different from that of other fellow novelists during the mid-thirties, when Gandhi was at the zenith of his popularity. To a considerable extent, this was fashioned by his exposure to Marxist sensitivity, visualized by him as a possible corrective to Gandhian idealism. Anand's *Untouchable* is rightly credited with heralding revolutionary consciousness and political maturity in the Indo-Anglian novel. K.A. Abbas, Bhabani Bhattacharya and Nayantara Sahgal (with differing political preferences) have further enriched the tradition of political protest and innovative consciousness in Indo-Anglian novel in post-independence India initiated by Anand in the nineteen thirties.

It is, however, important to bear in mind that the ideals of political freedom, social justice and national dignity are perceptible in all political novelists of the era, whether inspired by Gandhi or by Marx. Nationalism was both a precondition and a supreme value. Whereas the former school of Indo-Anglian novel, by and large, justified Gandhi's spiritualized politics of tolerance, non-violence and gradual social reform, the latter, upholding progressive and radical postures, romanticized revolution and projected the ideal of non-repressive, "liberated" society. Both the schools claimed to be realists. However, both could also be taken to be romanticists in a way, as they did not entirely succeed in freeing themselves from pervasive idealism, perhaps understandable in an epoch of crises.[19] At that time as Anand explains, "life was politics and politics life".[20] Nationalism encompassed both.

With the attainment of independence, accompanied by the trauma of partition, contemporary politics of nationalism all of a sudden got converted into a kind of "history" that remained with us owing both to its proximity and intensity of impact. To interpret such recent history as "legacy", owning its negative and positive attributes and re-enact it in terms of experience, norms and ideals in keeping with contextual priorities, was a challenging task both for the literary historian and for the social scientist. Publication of a large number of novels (the process continues) reflecting upon phases of the nationalist struggle is an indication that the Indo-Anglian novelist, like his counterpart in regional literatures, has not diminished the importance of history. On the contrary, if the Indo-Anglian novel seems intimately conscious of history, in a purposive way, it reflects a sustained quest for identity, both individual and national. It also explains the urge to re-interpret what was significant in the past, primarily to lend meaning to the legacy, or, one might present it all as a creative escape from the mediocrity of the 'present' in the name of aesthetic preference. Whatever be the genesis, the output exhibits a 'sense of history' and is significantly relevant in terms of interpretations of vital issues, events and epochs.

It took more than a decade after independence, for the

Indo-Anglian novelist, generally speaking, to get out of the euphoric mood of Gandhian nationalism, despite the fact that Gandhian alternative had not succeeded in ensuring the nation's integrated form in geographical terms. A sense of disillusionment was perceptible among the youth and radical sections of society. Although novelists like Bhabani Bhattacharya and K.A. Abbas, in the footsteps of Mulk Raj Anand, were attempting critical appreciation of the epoch, the majority of the novelists persisted with idealized re-enactment of the nationalist struggle, more or less eulogizing Gandhi. Novelists like Venu Chetale (*In Transit*, 1950), Zeenut Futehally (*Zohra*, 1951), Nayantara Sahgal (*A Time to be Happy*, 1958), S.M. Marath (*The Wound of Spring*, 1960), Aamir Ali (*Conflict*, 1947), Kamla Markandaya (*Some Inner Fury*, 1957), K. Nagarajan (*Chronicles of Kedaram*, 1961), R.K. Narayan (*Waiting for the Mahatma*, 1955), B. Rajan (*The Dark Dancer*, 1959) and Chaman Nahal (*The Crown and the Loincloth*, 1982) went back to the twenties, thirties and forties, in order probably to search for the forgotten ideals of communal harmony, social progressivism and dedication to the nation, and inadvertently eulogized Gandhi as the beacon-light.

None of the post-independence novels, however, is comparable to the intensity of emotional attachment of Venkataramani's *Kandan, The Patriot* and depth of comprehension of Raja Rao's *Kanthapura*. Whereas *Kandan. The Patriot* is an involved portrayal of compelling abnegation, sacrifice and resolution for the supreme ideal of national freedom as practised by Gandhi,[21] *Kanthapura* is a personification of Gandhism as renaissance, penetrating the hitherto neglected segments of society, in quest of regeneration as well as freedom. Gandhism, for Raja Rao as for no other novelist, is an architectonic framework, perceived as an integrated totality in terms of both an 'ideal' and 'ideology' and aimed at basic transformation of outlook in Indian society. As an aesthetic compendium of renaissant India, *Kanthapura* is taken up here in some detail.

The loftiness of Gandhi, as Raja Rao sees him—"Like the Sahyadri mountains . . . high and yet seeable, firm and yet blue with dust",[22] lies in Gandhi's proximity to the commonman. Capturing the spirit of Gandhian appeal, for instance, through symbols of modernized *harikathas*, *bhajans* and

community feasts, spinning, weaving and wearing *Khaḍi*, the
novelist presents it as a living philosophy of action. By choosing
an old grandmother as the narrator of the story in ancient
Indian style, Raja Rao mingles "fact and fiction in an effective
manner".[23] The novelist does not stop with emotional dispositions. His evaluative perspective also highlights contemporary social practices.

Moorthy, the local Gandhi of *Kanthapura* is more than
symbolic of the youth-force in the Congress. He represents the
political resentment and discontent among the youth, when the
Civil Disobedience movement is suspended by Gandhi (p. 256).
Here, along with Gandhi's charisma, Raja Rao does not fail to
register the nuances of change and projects Nehru as a potential initiator of innovation. Drawing attention to the socio-
ethical and economic concerns of Gandhi, C.D. Narasimhaiah
remarks that *Kanthapura* is no political novel any more than is
Gandhi's movement a mere political movement.[24] Accepting
socio-econo-ethical concerns as central to the Gandhian
scheme of change, his movement for independence had to be
fundamentally, 'not merely', political in the sense that political
freedom as a precondition for other freedoms was the first and
foremost goal. Gandhi reiterated it time and again. *Kanthapura*
in this sense, could be treated fundamentally as a serious
political novel of resurgent India.

As an epitomization of India in transition, *Kanthapura*
imbibes history and legend as living experience,[25] mingling it
with the turbulent present. It also highlights the diverse social
and religious customs,[26] caught in the throes of obscurantism
and superstition, also coming to terms with tentative realisa-
tion of consciousness, dynamism and aspiration through a
dialectic of aquiescence and protest. Being a "singular fusion
of poetry and politics" to use K.R.S. Iyengar's expression,
Kanthapura could well be described as the foremost Gandhian
classic, visualizing transcendence of unfreedom by collective
human effort : "A cock does not make a morning nor a single
man revolution, but we'll build a thousand pillared temple. . . .
India then will live in a temple of our making" (p. 170). The
novel, thus, exudes an aura of optimism, faith and dedication to
the national cause in a vivid, authentic and spontaneous ethos.

Moving from the passionate ethos of pre-independence to

the post-independence response to Gandhian politics is an experience in terms of spatial and perspectival change, ranging from adoration and ritualization to informed criticism and intellectual analysis. R.K. Narayan's *Waiting for the Mahatma* (1955) could be taken here for detailed analysis, as more or less representing the trend of faith in Gandhian charisma. In this novel, R.K. Narayan overcomes the charac-teristic generally attributed to him of being "placidly un-responsive" to contemporary political issues[27] and presents parts of Gandhian struggle in the forties, through an average Indian's perception. The average Indian may not necessarily be ideologically committed, intellectually accomplished or selflessly involved like the memorable characters in Raja Rao, Mulk Raj Anand and Bhabani Bhattacharya. Yet, this "average" is positive[28] in the sense that it is 'genuine' even in its limitations, 'unpretencious' in its efforts and 'seminal' for the society, for it comprises the majority. Sriram, the prota-gonist in *Waiting for the Mahatma*, is one such average young Indian, who does want to belong to the political com-munity of freedom fighters. His political concepts, however, are blurred though he has an urge to do something useful for his nation. His conception of priorities is also confused. Like scores of his type, Sriram initially comes to Gandhi, not for selfless national service, but for some 'other motive', namely, to realize his love for one of the disciples of Gandhi, Bharati, who has identified herself with the Mahatma. During the course of events, however, Sriram gets involved in the movement in several ways. While working for the Gandhian movement under Bharati's guidance, Sriram, actually, has no comprehension of the fall-out of colonial exploitation, social injustice or economic deprivation against which the struggle was aimed. He simply adores Gandhi as 'Bapu' and accepts whatever he does as 'right', because Bharati also thinks likewise. This kind of affective orientation to politics was shared by millions like Sriram, then as now.

At the instance of Bharati, Sriram becomes an active pro-testant, pasting notices decrying the war and distributing nationalist literature in the mountain villages. However, in the absence of the sobering counsel of Bharati, Sriram comes under the spell of a terrorist, Jagadish, who tells him : "Britain will leave India with a *Salam*, if we crush the backbone of her administration . . . and it lies in the courts and schools and railway lines, from these she draws the strength for her survival".[29]

Sriram is impressed and gets engaged in clandestine terrorist activities, setting fire to the records in a dozen law courts, derailing trains, exploding a bomb outside an agricultural research station and paralysiing work in schools. He, later, repents for these activities. His remorse is heightened when he is released from prison and meets his terrorist friend. Jagadish, who takes both pride and credit for the hard work done for independence and produces supportive photographs (processed in his own studio) to prove his claim. Sriram is told how independence had already been celebrated, while he was in prison. Feeling sad and cheated, he goes to Bharati and Bapu, seeks the Mahatma's forgiveness as well as permission to marry Bharati.

As a contrast to the confused political world of Sriram, Narayan portrays the sincere dedicated, clear-headed character of Bharati, who is the central consciousness in the novel, genuinely representing Gandhian spirit. Opportunistic postures of patriotism adopted by officials like the municipal chairman and the timber merchants, medieval social orthodoxy exhibited by the Malgudi crowd at Sriram's granny's funeral, levels of political sincerity, as shown in Gandhi's camps, all contribute to crystallize varied glimpses of the socio-political world, inhabited by diverse people. Without condemnation, one way or the other, Narayan treats nationalists "with the same comic irony deployed against cheats, bohemians, bossy wives, indulgent grand parents and the vanishing British".[30] The novel, therefore, is not "pointless", as is alleged,[31] for it successfully exposes diverse forces of reaction, retrogression and repression. Probably by portraying a "muddle of the Gandhian principle"[32] as is done by several practitioners, Narayan seems to be achieving his aim of "exposing" them, though vicariously. William Walsh justifiably appreciates the "attentive tolerance and ironic gentleness", with which Narayan treats such characters.[33]

Compared to Nagarajan, Chetale, Nahal and others, R.K. Narayan is not a historical novelist. Thus, *Waiting For The*

Mahatma is basically neither a historical narrative as *The Crown and the Loincloth* is, nor a reform novel as *In Transit*. It is not also meant to be an ethical statement of Gandhism as one perceives in *Chronicles of Kedaram*, although as a novel depicting the forties, it could not have ignored all these aspects totally. The novel is politically relevant, not as much for theoretical, ideological or historical comprehension of the freedom struggle and Gandhian politics, as for its lucid portrayal of a large variety of socio-political attitudes, ranging from ignorance, cognition and involvement to pragmatism, opportunism and apathy. For all his non-ideological pretensions, Narayan, like Salman Rushdie later displays conviction in the potential of the average man, the man on the periphery, who, if, provided opportunity and direction, may vindicate purposive partnership in the national political process.

If *Waiting For The Mahatma* is an ideal portrayal of the average Indian's amorphous political world, B. Rajan's *The Dark Dancer* (1959) is a comprehensive intellectual delineation of particular objects in it without damaging its wholeness.[34] Whereas the former is manifestly simple, the latter is profound and complex. The two might usefully explain the contrasts of a society in transition coming to terms with itself.

The Dark Dancer portrays the attitudinal, emotional and bureaucratic environment surcharged with the "expectancy of freedom," inevitably accompanied by the tragedy of the partition. V.S. Krishnan is an intellectual, returning to India after a long sojourn in England. The crisis of identity that Krishnan faces on his return, in several ways, mirrors in microcosm the crisis of colonized India's identity. The personal and the political, thus, get suffused at every level, unfolding the dialectics of tension symbolised through the images of *Natraja*, *Karna* and *Gopuram*.

Rajan's attempt at using myth as the central icon of political interpretation is interestingly comparable to Raja Rao's attempt in *Kanthapura*, where he uses the Rama-Sita-Ravana parables and *harikathas*, for similar purposes. Nataraja is the central icon in *The Dark Dancer*, suggestive of the ever-present reality of the unity of opposites: "Creation, destruction. Two concepts but one dance, the trampling leg, the outthrust arms, asserting the law of invincibility . . . for something to be born, something must die." (p. 29). This metaphysical awareness of the impending 'destructive force' is implicit throughout the narrative, portraying vividly the mood of uncertainty, alienation and hypersensitiveness of young intellectuals at that moment in India's history.

To counter the schizophrenic drives of the alienated intellectual (the imagery of Kunti's son, Karna) the novelist presents the resilient, firm and 'believing' character of Kamala, whom Krishnan marries in the traditional manner, probably in keeping with his quest for 'belonging.' "Nothing ever dies. It says so in the Gita" (p. 29), she tells Krishnan. For her, Gandhi's non-violence vindicates true Indian values: "When a country is poor, it must build its strength on its poverty. Non-violence is like water falling, forever falling, each little drop of protest doesn't matter, but just going on eternally, unceasingly, wearing away the very stones of conscience." (p. 50). Krishnan, exposed to the ethos of the west, initially finds this moral, apolitical, defence of non-violence unconvincing and unacceptable. However, during the course of events in subsequent months, culminating in both freedom and partition, he gets convinced of non-violence as the right strategy for the freedom movement.

The existentialist consciousness of Krishnan matures into realistic perceptions of the situation, through instances of participation in a demonstration, and later, exposure to the facts of carnage in Hindu-Muslim riots during the partition. As the novel proceeds he comes to believe in Gandhi's non-violence. At one place, he tells Cynthia, his Cambridge-friend (with whom he gets infatuated only to be disillusioned): "We owe our independence to non-violence applied persistently over thirty years. That calls not only for discipline, but for stamina and certain inbred qualities" (p. 127). That perhaps was expected of an England-educated bureaucrat. However, Cynthia disagreeing with such eulogization, describes non-violence as an escape-route for frustrations and as philosophy of resignation and acquiescence (not pacificism). With ongoing debates regarding alternative strategies of the nationalist movement," as freedom actually comes, resulting in the birth... of two nations, the cataclysms without a historical parallel" (p. 149), even the well-trained cadres of bureaucracy, (a unique legacy of British India, to which Krishnan also belongs) find it difficult to cope with the crisis. For the bewildered nation, freedom was nothing more than "the red line upon the trembling map, established by deadlock, defended by the law's guns, ripped at and eroded by the violence of fear" (p. 149).

Whereas later, Malgonkar (*A Bend in the Ganges*) attributes partition to communalism as cultural aberration, Rajan, in *The Dark Dancer*, primarily holds the British responsible for the catastrophe. For instance, Krishnan points out to Cynthia: "You made this awful thing grow. For a whole generation, you British have stirred up the trouble. It's you who made the religious divisions take priority over our political interests. Communal electorates, communal representation in the civil service, communal this and communal that. Even the cricket matches are communally organized" (p. 163). The fall-out of the communal carnage described in the concluding sections of the novel only confirms Krishnan's apprehensions. The hallucination of the "day train to disaster," comparable to sections from Khushwant Singh's *Train to Pakistan*, are revealing as well as revolting. A Sikh, for instance, justifies the murder of Muslims: "You think we haven't paid for being Indian, the thousands that are dead and the millions that are homeless. The rich land abandoned and the lives we've left behind. That has been our sacrifice for making India" (pp. 203-4). The Muslims argued likewise. Such arguments neither explained the carnage nor justified it.

Summing up the situation of anarchy and violence, the novelist explains that the strategies employed to handle the riots were lacking in flexibility, "which indeed could be held true of all tactics that ended in defeat . . . The point was not to avoid disaster. . . but to confront it with dignity and in the appropriate dress." (p. 266). Kamala, Krishnan's wife, in sacrificing her life to save a Muslim girl, truly confronts the disaster with dignity and that also, in conformity with her conviction in Gandhian ideals of non-violence and communal amity. Through her death for a purpose, Kamala lives up to the philosophical ideal of action of the *Gita*. On the other hand, one cannot help marking the intellectual's hesitation for action when Krishnan falters. Though not strictly in the political sense, the portrayal of these two different modes of sensibility explains the socio-ethical implications of Gandhism in a full view representing different segments of Indian society.

In political terms, *The Dark Dancer*, on the one hand, defies the tendency of euphoric nostalgia and blind adoration of Gandhi and, on the other, justifies the relevance of Gandhism as a suitable strategy for freedom movement. Through constant awareness of the presence of the "trampling foot," signifying the Hindu view of 'destruction—creation continuum, the novelist rejects absolutist conceptions of life and history, including politics. Thus, the intellectual analysis in the novel is sometimes jargonized,[35] and at others mythicized.[36] Nevertheless, it is always profound and insightful, as it unfolds the tensions of politics and society during those times. B. Rajan, barring several faltering enunciations in the initial stage, seriously enquires into the adequacy or otherwise of the Gandhian alternative in keeping with the changing political scene in the forties, as is done by Bhattacharya, Malgonkar and Nahal in differing degrees, in the footsteps of Mulk Raj Anand, as it were.

We now turn to novelists, who provide a critical rather than an adorative presentation of Gandhian politics, along with other strands. Bhabani Bhattacharya's *So Many Hungers* is a critical depiction of the impact of the Second World War, imposed on unwilling Indians (like the first world war, discussed in M.R. Anand's trilogy), and concerns the socio-economic life in Bengal. The story evolves through two parallel streams, the urban political India (currently involved in the Quit India Movement of 1942) and the simultaneous tragedy of famine in Bengal in 1943, exposing the callousness of imperialist authoritarianism and the complicity of Indian capitalists. Davesh Basu an old Gandhian, venerated as 'Devata,' is presented as the symbol of synthesis of the rural-urban configurations, artificially created by the imperial forces.

Samrendra Basu, an industrialist, in complete contrast to his father Davesh Basu, aligns himself with the blackmarketeers and uses war as "the most enriching industry."[37] His sons, Rahoul and Kunal, however, turn out to be nationalists. Staggered political consciousness through three generations, thus, highlights the inherent dialectics of protest. Commenting on the retrogressive attitude of his father, Rahoul, the young

England-returned scientist who later turned into a nationalist, says: "It was his kind, bred in the decadence that overtakes a race at certain periods in its history, yet it was his kind that had made possible England's long drawn occupation of India" (p. 30). The novelist brings out the powerful hold of this class in alliance with the imperialist forces in India. He, therefore, presents Rahoul and Kunal, belonging to this class, as forces of negation and confrontation, instead of presenting a utopian reconciliation. It is in the hazards of this confrontation that Bhattacharya, like Anand, projects revolutionary consciousness. Whereas Kunal joins the army to prove India's manhood, as against the ignonymous myth of "Bengal effeminacy," spread by Macauley in the 19th century,[38] Rahoul, the scientist, works to support the national movement in a different way.

Although venerating Gandhi for his humanistic ideals and dedication to the cause of national independence, Rahoul represents that section of the Indian youth, within and outside the Congress, which questioned Gandhi's sudden cooperative postures towards the British. For instance, questioning the Congress decision to cooperate in the war effort, Rahoul resentingly asks, "how could people step out into a war said to be waged for democratic freedom, so long as that very freedom was denied them?" (p. 12) Again, "Alien leadership perched proudly on the debris of a dead country would not win the war only to lose empire" (p. 65). Gandhi's nationalism is, thus, projected as having "more morality than strategy" (p. 51), which was resented even within the Congress. The subsequent Quit India Resolution was, therefore, glorified as an opportunity for action, rejuvenating larger social segments, especially the youth. Nehru's defiant statement during Gorakhpur trial proved to be a stirring call to the youth and students to join the Quit India movement. There was no alternative to freedom. It was treated as an imperative.

The imperial government's suppression was total as witnessed during the famine of 1943 in Bengal. It was man-made scarcity, for the harvest had been fair and, even if the army had bought up big stocks, with rationing at the right level, there should have been adequate food for all. But there was no rationing. Forty thousand country boats were wantonly destroyed. Many villages were evacuated. The uprooted people were pauperized, and inflated currency gave a fiendish finishing touch to the human tragedy (p. 105). There were isolated instances of emergence of revolutionaries, as the family of Kajoli (the adopted grand-daughter of Davesh Basu) depicted in the novel or symbolized by the young revolutionary Kishore, who married Kajoli and thereby identified himself with the peasants and coined the slogan: "Unite, Workers: What have you to lose but your begging-bowls?" (p. 89). The Indian peasants, however, would not rise in revolt, inhibited as they were by antique moral tradition: "They would fight and die over a moral issue. But hunger was their fate, an expiation of the sins of past lives . . . The rice-robbers were safe from peril because of the peasants' tradition." (p. 108). Nationalism had not penetrated deep down enough.

Bhattacharya's portrayal of Bengal economy is grim, though entirely true. The nightmare of hunger and deprivation that runs through the pages of the book is a comprehensive indictment of British apathy as much as it is a tribute to the empathy of the novelist. Instances, like that of a dead body of a destitute woman lying on railway platform, with a suckling baby, or of the unequal contest between men and animals for peels and rotten vegetables in the rubbish can, succinctly expose the extent of human degradation. One gets a disturbing exposure of the time when human sensitivity and dignity were subjected to conscious erosion. In view of the two-fold impact of the Bengal tragedy and the Quit India resolution, Bhattacharya, through his intellectual hero, Rahoul, highlights the urgency for independence : "You have done us some good along with much evil. For the good you've been paid in full. The accounts have been settled. Now, for God's sake quit" (p. 202). The logic of events culminates in the realization that there is no alternative to freedom : it is a dialectical necessity as prophesied by Tagore "the more they tighten the chains, the more the chains loosen". (p. 205).

For Bhattacharya, as also for Anand political freedom is the stepping stone for other freedoms. *So Many Hungers* is one of the most revealing portrayals of "an impeachment of man's inhumanity to man"[39] and of freedom as a categorical imperative.

True, freedom was imperative but at what cost? Manohar

Malgonkar, of all the Indo-Anglian novelists, addressed himself to this question most seriously in *A Bend in the Ganges*
(1964). The earlier novels concerning the partition, such as
Khushwant Singh's *Train to Pakistan* (1955) and Attia
Hosain's *Sunlight on a Broken Column* (1961), among others,
had highlighted the artistic need for a critical evaluation of
India's nationalism with reference to points of omissions and
errors, culminating into the partition along with the achievement
of freedom. Malgonkar's *A Bend in the Ganges*, thus, came as
a refreshing aesthetic interpretation.

Malgonkar, unlike Raja Rao, treats Gandhism not as
Renaissance, but as one of prevailing strategies to obtain independence and as an explicit ideology of non-violence. This
is comparable to Anand's analysis in the *Sword and the Sickle*
in analytical (not ideological) terms. By projecting militant and
communalist forces, both equally defiant as contending schemes
to Gandhian nationalism, Malgonkar places the latter in a
comparative perspective.

The canvas of the novel is broad enough to cover the major
historical events beginning from the Civil Disobedience movement till independence, as well as the 'spirit' of the times,
thoroughly documented and artistically rendered. The story
progresses mainly through the dialectics of perceptions, responses and actions such as the committed allegiance of freedom
fighters like Debi Dayal, the Machiavellian pragmatism of
opportunists like Gian Talwar, and the loyalism of industria-
lists like Dewan Bahadur Tekchand. On the social level, a
suggestive contrast is presented between the affluent, sophisti-
cated and westernized culture (which was epitomised as the
Linen bush-shirt and sun-glasses set of Bombay) and the
culture of the poor, aggressive, fatalistic folk. Politically
speaking, the former was apathetic to the national revolution
and the latter was ignorant and alienated. Neither had a vital
role to play in the freedom struggle. Another segment of
aristocratic class in India, represented in the novel by Dewan
Bahadur Tekchand Kerwad of Duriabad, typifies the persistent
conservative values of *status quoism* and self-preservation.
Preoccupied with concerns of economic security and social
stability, this class was convinced that there was no alternative
to the British.[40] The price for the transfer of power was chaos,

too heavy to be paid. All revolution was suspect and retrogressive for this class.

One finds, nevertheless, that revolutionary consciousness was already in the offing. As in *So Many Hungers*, antagonisms inevitably emerge within this class as illustrated through the rejection of aristocratic comforts by Dewan Bahadur's own children, for political conviction (by Debi Dayal) and moral considerations (by Sundari). For Dewan Bahadur "the Americans who fought to win independence were heroes but that our own fighters are sedititionists." (p. 112). Both, Sundari and Debi Dayal, condemn such colonial consciousness and act in their own independent ways. Whereas Sundari admires Gandhian ideals, Debi Dayal opts for terrorist methods.

The central configuration of political orientations is between Gian Talwar and Debi Dayal, the former symbolizing faith in Gandhian non-violence and the latter personifying militant nationalism. The presentation, however, is uneven. Whereas Gian Talwar is portrayed as only *believing* in Gandhian creed, not directly participating in the movement; Debi Dayal is actively involved in terrorist activities, convinced of his ideals and actions. The hiatus between these two levels of perception and action, thus, unfolds the dialectics of protest in India and brings out the contradictions resulting from a situation in which communalism emerged as the most pernicious phenomenon. Communalism is represented in the novel by a Muslim Leaguer, Hafiz, and later by Shafi Usman, who was won over by Hafiz from terrorism to communalism. Malgonkar, thus, provides a parallel critique of Gandhian non-violence through militant and communal points of view.

For Gian Talwar, Gandhian non-violence is a political creed to be used at convenience, not sacrosanct as a philosophy of life. He, therefore, has no qualms in renouncing it as and when demanded by the situation. He seems to be impressed by the charisma of Gandhi rather than Gandhian ideology. An almost magnetic attraction of Gandhi for millions is sought to be explained by the novelist, through a detailed portrayal of the rural middle class ethos of Gian Talwar and his family. The nature of identity, an average Indian seemed to be subconsciously searching for, appeared to be attainable through the image of simplicity, humanity and fearlessness that Gandhi epitomized in his person. His syncretic politics seemed to agree with the centrist tenets of popular expectations. The average Indian might at times be perceived to be inadequately equipped to comprehend the dialectics of the national movement. At times, it also seemed that the nuances of the liberal, constitutional protest or militant agitative methods were not clearly perceived by the commonman. Thus, when Gandhi synthesized the spirit of Gokhale's liberalism and Tilak's radicalism in his own improvisation of non-violent revolution as an alternative, he seems to have taken a conscious decision to propound the message and call of action in the language of the common man. That explains, at least in part, Gandhi's acceptance by the people.

Militant nationalism, particularly popular with radical sections of the youth in urban centres, thought of Gandhian non-violence as "the philosophy of sheep, a creed for cowards . . . the greatest danger to this country." (p. 18) "You could not have both freedom and Orthodoxy." (p. 18) Religious differences, Malgonkar explains, among the races of India were the root cause of the country's slavery and the British had learnt to take the fullest advantage of these differences, playing the Hindus against the Muslims and the Sikhs against both. "The only saving grace of the nationalist movement has gone, it is no longer united, no longer secular" (p. 73), the militants retorted in the forties. In spite of a sense of urgency, enthusiasm and dedication, as illustrated by young freedom fighters in the novel, the terrorist movement did not go beyond certain urban pockets, partly owing to lack of resources and partly owing to the absence of a charismatic leader of the stature of Gandhi, with the exception of Subhas Chandra Bose, who was in exile. One would also recall the split among the ranks on communal lines as highlited by Malgonkar. Debi Dayal's withdrawal into anonymity in the tea gardens of Assam, after release from the cellular jail of Andamans, illustrates the predicament of several revolutionaries who found themselves rootless and bewildered in the changed situation of the mid-forties[41], charged with communal violence, on the one hand, and repressive war measures on the other, communaalism, as a negation. of all that the nationalists stood for,

appeared an irreversible force, flowing as much from religious
fanaticism and mistrust as from the imperial policies. A statement from a Muslim Leaguer, Hafiz, typifies the communal
perspective :

> "Take Gandhi's own words : 'In the midst of darkness
> light persists, in the midst of death life persists'. Is it non-
> sense? No, it is not. It is the peculiar escapism of Hindu-
> ism; the utter meaninglessness of words. Light in darkness,
> life in death; why not violence in the midst of Gandhi's
> non-violence? . . . In the midst of Gandhi's non-violence,
> violence persists. Violence such as no one has ever seen.
> That is what awaits this country . . ." (p. 93).

This apprehension comes true. What was achieved through
non violence, as Malgonkar stresses, brought with it one of the
most tragic upheavals of history : "Who had won, Gandhi or
the British"? Debi pertinently asked himself, "or had they
both lost through not having allowed for structural flaws
in the human material they were dealing with" (p. 355).
This is a fundamental question, and a legitimate one, raised
by Malgonkar, which should serve as a corrective to the
nationalist myth of non-violence, projected as a universal
phenomenon.

"Yet," as Debi Dayal further reflected "what was the alternative? Would terrorism have won freedom at a cheaper price
and somehow still kept the Hindus and Muslims together?
Perhaps not. But at least it would have been an honest sacrifice, honest and manly not something that had sneaked upon
them in the garb of non-violence" (p. 355). This is as much
Malgonkar's answer as Debi Dayal's to one of the most crucial
questions of India's nationalist history.

Thus, far from being a sketchy[42] or 'an erratic national
calendar'[43] *A Bend in the Ganges* is an indispensable artistic
interpretation of the collaboration and confabulation of historical forces in the final phase of freedom struggle.[44] If in the
contemporary context, Raja Rao's *Kanthapura* is acclaimed as
an outstanding enunciation of faith in Gandhian creed, Malgonkar's *A Bend in the Ganges* is outstanding as its incisive
critique.

Chaman Nahal's *Azadi*[45] begins where *A Bend in the Ganges* virtually ends. *Azadi* is not only a comprehensive reflection upon the savagery and atrocities of the partition; it is also an interpretative probe into the variables that precipitated the tragedy. Azadi synthesizes the portrayal of dilemmas of innocent victims by forces beyond their control (as in Khushwant Singh's *Train to Pakistan*), and the emotional impact felt by the divided communities (as recreated in Attia Hosain's *Sunlight on a Broken Column*). In depicting factual information, *Azadi* is comparable to Balwant Singh Anand's non-fictional narration *Cruel Interlude*.[46]

Although highly commended by some critics,[47] Khuswant Singh (*Train To Pakistan*) primarily writes about rather than create "brutalities committed in his fictional border village, Mano Majra." His characters are, indeed, "hemmed in by their environment and traditions."[48] Chaman Nahal's *Azadi* covers an expansive canvas with discernible political orientations among the displaced masses. Attia Hosain's *Sunlight on a Broken Column*, in an entirely different ethos, had earlier attempted such a politico-psychological portrayal of uprooted individuals typifying the tragedy of the minority communities, especially the Muslims, in India living in nostalgia.[49] Nahal's *Azadi* places this 'alienation' and 'sadness' in perspective, and, thus, transcends sentimentalism and reportage, despondency and utopia.[50]

At one level, *Azadi* registers the apprehensions of insecurity, before and after the partition, suffered by displaced minorities. At another level, it graphically brings out the traumatic incidents that took place in border areas immediately after the announcement of the partition in June 1947, symbolic of the sufferings of the people of Sialkot, now in Pakistan. In both cases, the depiction is authentic and insightful. Beginning with the genesis of the tragedy, as a historian would, Nahal poses the fundamental question: how could it happen?

There is disbelief and bewilderment among the minorities soon to be displaced, in the novel represented by the well-established grain merchant of Sialkot, Lala Kanshi Ram and his neighbours. The partition was not logical in any sense:

"The Congress had a promise to keep with the people. For last thirty years, since that wizard Gandhi came on the scene, it had taken the stand that India was a single nation not two. And Gandhi was not only a politician, he was a saint. He had his inner voice to satisfy too. Would that nagging voice of his let him accept the slaughter of so many? That's what it would mean, if Pakistan would come into existence." (pp. 42-43).

The faith of the masses in Gandhi's charisma, determination and wisdom, however, came under severe stress in the wake of politics of two-nation theory and its consequences. Euphoria of Gandhian ideals was swept away in the anarchy and insecurity let loose by indiscriminate violence. A young Sikh, Niranjan Singh, for instance, wanted to "hack Nehru to pieces" (p. 60) for the latter's inability to control the worsening political situation. Not only individual leaders, but the Congress on the whole, was to blame for not anticipating the critical situation. The Congress policy of appeasement comes under specific criticism in the novel: "Didn't Gandhiji and Rajaji themselves as much as offer Pakistan to Jinnah in 1944? They were the ones who put the idea in his head . . . . until then Jinnah talked of Pakistan, but he did not quite know what he meant by it" (p. 34). Although, it is possible to point out exaggerations in such statements, the appeasement policy of the Congress after 1916 (Lucknow Pact) did have certain negative repercussions, especially in the context of communal politics.

True, the creation of Pakistan, as shown by subsequent events, did not solve the problem of the minorities; "it was going to create new minorities" (p. 80). It was impossible to cut a country in two, where at every level the communities were so deeply intermixed. But the impossible was about to happen through vitiated politics. The "conspiracy of politicians behind the whole move" was obvious, as Arun, the young son of Lala Kanshi Ram, remarks: "Jinnah and Liaquat Ali Khan were coming into an estate, as was Nehru, why else would they rush into Azadi at this pace—an Azadi which would ruin the land and destroy its unity?" (p. 90). The minorities had reason to be unhappy with political leaders, for they had been pushed into the partition; they did not ask for it, din't sanction it in any form whatsoever. And no arrangements had been made to meet the consequences (p. 341).

Lack of adequate rehabilitation facilities, or planned schemes for coping with the enormous problems of displaced persons, highlighted the complete absence of political imagination of those at the helm of affairs. The people at large truly felt cheated: "If unwilling, the government is a party to murder. If incapable, we Indians had no right to ask for freedom" (p. 124). Nahal is, therefore, not uncharitable in his criticism of the erstwhile governments that "they should have devised means of mass migration to begin with, before rushing to partition" (p. 204). The chaos was complete. Political expediency had turned human beings into "refugees," all of a sudden. Neither of the governments knew what rights and privileges, it had in the area of the other.[51] For the refugees, suffering became synonymous with freedom: "Freedom was on its way and nothing could have stopped it. If only they had not given in so easily to partition" (p. 366). It is, nevertheless, a big "if" of India's political history, which Nahal repeatedly emphasizes.

However, in the concluding section of the novel, when the news of Gandhi's assassination is broadcast, there is a feeling of great loss among the people, including the refugees (p. 362). The author concedes that the people, even those who had suffered the consequences of partition, gradually began to realize the blessings which only freedom could bring about and ensure as against the persecution and exploitation suffered during the imperial domination. Thus, although beginning on a note of ambivalence and uncertainties of national integrity in the face of religious fanaticism, moral degeneration and political fragmentation, *Azadi* closes with the affirmation that a nation, resolved to persist with her quest for identity, outlives even annihilating tragedies.

It is interesting to note how the quest for national identity has also given rise to historical fiction dealing both with distant past and with fantasy. For instance, Kamala Markandaya (*The Golden Honeycomb*)[52] and Manohar Malgonkar (*The Devil's Wind*)[53] fictionalize the glorified aspects of the 19th century political history in order probably to straighten record or fill in existing historical gaps.

Whereas Malgonkar attempts an interpretation of the

Rebellion of 1857, Markandaya endeavours to fill in the gap
that exists regarding the historical period following the Rebellion.
It is well known that with the assumption of rule by the
Crown, the relationship of the Indian princely states and the
imperial government underwent significant changes. Legal
measures like the *Sanads* of 1860, the Act of 1876 and the
Ordinance of 1884, changing norms of Succession, reduced the
princely states to the status of vassals. Doctrine of paramountcy
had already paved the way. Introduction of a new institution,
viz., Agent or Resident, deputed in each princely state as
Viceroy's representative worsened matters. It was not until the
end of World War I that progressive forces of nationalism
succeeded in penetrating some of the "golden honeycombs"
protected and pampered by the British imperialists and the
native feudal hierarchy.

Taking up Devapur, a Southern State, as a microcosm of
the tortuous process of transition from supine loyalty to the
alien ruler to self-assertion and protest, Markandaya like
Malgonkar, exposes the crudities of the British rule in India.
The novel spans over a long period of history, from around
1870 to 1918, in the process delineating a variety of responses
to the British hegemony by three generations, ranging from
bewildered acceptance of the situation by the Commoner-King,
Bawajiraj II who succeeded the "Scheming" Bawajiraj I, to
the pliant tenure of Bawajiraj III, followed by rebellious rejection of both, the British authoritarianism and feudal autocracy
by Rabi (son of Bawajiraj III, born of his concubine). The
protracted process of evolution of 'fray' and 'ferment' portrayed
by Kamala Markandaya seems to be inevitable owing to the
contradictions inherent in the feudal-imperial alliance, thriving
on what the novelist describes as the "tie of self-interest, in the
Imperial scheme". (p. 33).

Like Malgonkar, Markandaya attributes the British conquest
of India, not to their alleged superiority of fighting skills but to
their training, discipline and clarity of objective. The dowager
Maharani unfolds the historical irony before her grandson and
comments sadly: "If we had stood together they would never
have conquered us, not with all the bribery and plotting at
which they were experts" (p. 46). In his own time, Rabi learns
the truth and realizes that the British ruling class like 'Clay

obstinately refusing to transform its qualities remained clay . . .'
(p. 184.).

As world history took a decisive turn, political reality in
India assumed sinister proportions with the announcement of
India's involvement in the World War. The erstwhile native
rulers bent over backward to prove their allegiance and loyalty
to the Crown. In one sweeping stroke of servitude the
Maharajas' offerings at the imperial altar included total commitment in terms of their respective states, people and resources,
well illustrated by the novelist. Following the war and disillusioned with the imperial promises, Gandhi gave a stirring call
of integrated national protest. The call had a delayed impact
on the people in the princely states. However, as the novel
projects, it could no longer be stopped.

Kamala Markandaya elucidates the beginnings of the process
of social awareness and political revolt in the princely states,
through the younger generation in Devapur, the progeny of
the native ruling class itself, with poetic justice as it were. The
feudal imperial clique is ultimately forced to yield to popular
demand, through withdrawal of some of the obnoxious taxes,
including the hated salt tax. The novel ends on an optimistic
note celebrating "the splendid beginning" not only of social
consciousness but also of a political struggle for civil rights.

Salman Rushdie (*Midnight's Children*),[54] on the other hand,
fantasizes the three decades preceding independence (in the first
section) in his seminal work. Malgonkar and Rushdie are an
interesting contrast in terms not only of selection of material
but also regarding approaches to history. Whereas Malgonkar's
fictionalization of history is a resolved quest for an ordered,
patterned and logical past.[55] Rushdie's analysis of history moves
through various 'fragmented' aspects into both a comprehensive
fantasy and reality.

Malgonkar's interpretation romanticizing the revolt of 1857,
effectively resembles that of V.D. Savarkar, the renowned militant nationalist: "If the whole of Hindustan had risen simultaneously, history would not have to wait longer than 1857 to
record the destruction of the English empire and the victorious
Independence of India."[56] Such fantasizing, culminating in
Rushdie's work, where each individual instance is "mysteriously
handcuffed to history", may apparently seem to have no 'living

significance', as Lukacs would say, in either documentation of history or in understanding the present. It is, however, not irrelevant, for, as Nehru said "the spirit behind those events did not end with them".[57] "The spirit behind those events", in fact, proved to be the major pace-setter initially in the creation of a politico-cultural awareness of the nation and responsiveness towards the new idiom of national community, symbols, traditions, and, later, participation in the nationalist struggle.

The trials, ordeals, sacrifices and the struggles of over two centuries came to an end, whereas at the stroke of the midnight hour, India was awakened to life and freedom (the hour superbly dramatized by Rushdie), and new kinds of "tryst with destiny" began. Anticipating Rushdie, as it were, Bhattacharya prophesied: "Freedom was the touchstone . . . To possess this touchstone was not enough, for it could wake to life and work its miracle only when acts of faith were done".[58] Quest for national identity, is identified with responsibility and faith, by Bhattacharya. In fact, the national edifice would, to a large extent, depend on how the legacy of the past is transmitted to posterity and to what use it is put.

III

The Emerging Perspective

The Indo-Anglian political novel, from the nineteenth century reformist spirit to protest and radicalism in the twentieth century, has evolved through an ineluctable process of maturing. In the process, it has had to contend with the ambivalence of colonial politics and rise of nationalism, consolidated by subsequent emergence of the Gandhian phenomenon. It is, however, possible to discern a point of distinction between the pre and post-independence novelists. Whereas the pre-independence novelists were intensively enmeshed in the process of national protest as observer-participants in an 'involved' manner,[59] the post-independence writers show an awareness of historical perspective in terms of inevitables of challenges, problems and transition from dependence to self-government. For instance, Raja Rao projected India's national identity in the Hegelian sense of supra-individual, spiritual organism, with

Gandhi's charisma as its central sustaining force (later followed in varying degrees by Nagarajan, Chetale and B. Rajan). Mulk Raj Anand, on the other hand, rejected such metaphysical overtones and portrayed the nationalist urge in terms of the materialist struggle of the oppressed against the oppressors (elaborated subsequently by Abbas and Bhattacharya). The politico-aesthetic interpretation of India's political history, that emerged later, illustrates the enduring relevance of these ideo-artistic conceptions.

The Indo-Anglian novels, projecting nationalist protest, could be identified as effective interpretations of resurgence in independent India, particularly exposing paradoxes of the private and the public norms of conduct. The novelists show an uneasiness at the process of disintegration of the old, familiar and traditional world, challenged by new egalitarian ideals flowing from the west. There is also indignation at the brutalities of colonial repression and denial of freedom to Indians. The novelists, therefore, on the one hand, attempt in varying degree, a re-orientation of the tradition in their respective delineations and, on the other, look to the west for positive inspiration. This kind of ambiguity of perception has resulted in a sort of cultural dualism (if not schizophrenia) in all the Indo-Anglian novelists, with the exception of Raja Rao, who, even at the cost of being accused of orthodox, retrogressive and metaphysical fixations seems to be convinced about his priorities in terms of values. The quest of individual identity, in fact, gets suffused with that of the nation's, on a much larger scale. Nationalism is, therefore, effectively used by Indo-Anglian novelists as a pervasive prism through which idealism, ambiguities, cultural dilemmas and practical uncertainties could be identified in relatively concrete life situations.

Considerable recourse to this technique by Indo-Anglian novelists is useful in illustrating the extent to which contemporary political culture of India is rooted in the collective history of nationalism and the life histories of individuals who decisively shaped it. The novels present particularly interesting dimensions in placing public events through individual experiences and projecting nationalist politics as part of the totality of the social ferment and not as isolated phenomena confined to political leaders and political strategies. Conscious and

aware political fiction at this level usefully supplements documented history, sometimes by straightening the factual record,
at others by interpreting specific events and raising relevant
issues in the light of new sources of understanding. The works
of Anand, Raja Rao, Bhattacharya, Malgonkar, Rajan, Nahal
and Rushdie show how insightful such attempts can prove to
be, once empathy and critical concern are syncretized.

Malgonkar's *The Devil's Wind* is specifically successful in
clarifying several aspects of the revolt of 1857. Raja Rao's
Kanthapura is a characteristic interpretation of Gandhism
during the thirties. Anand's protest novels are pioneering
endeavours at portrayal of political consciousness. Bhattacharya,
Malgonkar, Rajan and Nahal, particularly raise several pertinent questions in relation to Gandhian politics in the forties.
Highlighting the incidence of unprecedented violence and attributing it to the erosion of Gandhian charisma in the wake of
independence and partition; Malgonkar and Nahal seek to
question the unqualified faith in the 'saintly politics' of Gandhi.
They suggest that Gandhian non-violence owed itself as much
to Gandhi's charisma and the popular support as to the liberalism of the antagonist, the British rulers. One should, however,
not forget the shattering blow that the British imperial might
had in the wake of world war II which perhaps left them with
no alternative but to quit. This digression apart, the failure of
Gandhian tactics in the midst of communal frenzy, inevitably
brought out the other alternative, that is, recourse to violence,
however, imperceptibly. Did the Indian people fail to grasp the
spirit of non-violence in accepting it as a convenient weapon to
counter the antagonist and abandoning it as soon as the
antagonist's exit was ensured? Or, was it a saintly miscalcula-
tion of Gandhi to have brought religion into politics?

To be sure, Gandhi used religion as an instrument of reaching out to the masses. The same instrument, however, was
transformed into an aberration by advocates of the other
alternative. How did Gandhi fail to perceive the signs so
strikingly conspicuous toward the end of 1930's? Or, had it
become too late by that time? The myth of 'saintly' political
idiom was exploded by Malgonkar, and Anand, for instance,
whose contributions are replete with firm argumentation.
Suggestive interpretations of B. Rajan, Attia Hosain and Chaman

Nahal on how communal violence could have been minimized (if not totally avoided), are equally relevant. The novelists, on the whole, accept the tragedy of partition as an inevitability, inherent in the events of the preceding decades and, therefore, ruefully note celebrations of India's Independence.[60] For, as Michael Brecher said, "the quest for freedom was finally crowned with success but the pride of achievement was marred by much pain and suffering".[61]

India entered freedom charged with tension. Indo-Anglian political literature, like regional literature, evolved along with this tension. The depiction, however, was not confined merely to pessimism, protest or rejection. Concern with central political values was markedly present. In Indo-Anglian novel, the quest for freedom and justice, for instance, was coincidental with their genesis. All subsequent attempts also idealized these core goal-values as the bedrock of India's evolution to a democratic system. Imperial suppression of these ideals for long made them categorical perceptions of conscious intellectuals and activists alike. Indo-Anglian novelists, as seen earlier, have presented these ideals in a variety of forms, ranging from intellectual, commonplace and activist responses to ethical and metaphysical interpretations.

The hiatus between the social and the political worlds, which was sought to be bridged by the unifying force of nationalism, re-emerged as a challenging chasm as soon as the immediate goal of independence was achieved. The definition of political community was now seriously hampered by another kind of ambivalence, generated by conscious import and adaptation of the western, modern political structure, not fully syncretizing with traditional social structure. Conscious of their self-esteem, the Indo-Anglian novelists, particularly the progressive and the forward-looking, such as Anand, Bhattacharya, Nahal and Sahgal, attempted, in varying degrees, some sort of selection, redefinition and rejection of traditional norms in order to identify innovative socio-political consciousness. Raja Rao, on the contrary, attempted a selection, re-definition and rejection of modern western socio-political categories in favour of Gandhism and revivalism. The contrast of the two aesthetic schools exposed the prevalent hiatus and explained the related ambiguity. The post-independence political vision, however, continued to be influenced by the concept of spiritualization of politics in quest of an egalitarian utopia. It thus remained, at least in part, Gandhian.

In totality, the Indo-Anglian novel has brought forth valuable politico-aesthetic sensitivity to historical evaluation. It is also to be noted that the works cover a vast canvas of India's political history, not only in factual terms but also in regard to political orientations, ranging from ideological apathy to conscious concern. Equally significant is the fact that several major concepts and instrumentalities in evidence during the nationalist movement, such as pacifism, politics of renunciation and compassion, and, 'deification' of nation, have not been subjected to comprehensive exploration as social and psychological bases of Indian nationalism. Consequently, there is no 'magnum opus' on nationalism and national movement in Indo-Anglian contributions comparable, for instance, with Yashpal's *Jhoota Sach* (in Hindi). And, yet, Indo-Anglian political novel presents pervasive insight into modern political history of India, identifying meaningful indices of the legacy and quest of contemporary socio-political alternatives.

References

1. R.G. Collingwood, *The Idea of History* (Oxford University Press, 1961), p. 262.
2. Ashis Nandy, "The Culture of Indian Politics: A Stock Taking", *Journal of Asian Studies*, 30, 1 (November 1970), 57-79.
3. For details see R.C. Majumdar, *British Paramountcy and Indian Renaissance*, part III (Bombay, Bhartiya Vidya Bhavan, 1961).
4. The trend could be seen in the works of Madhusudan Dutt, Bankim Chandra Chatterjee, Sarat Chandra Chatterjee and Premchand.
5. The simultaneous persistence of militant nationalism and also of communalism (along with Gandhian non-violent nationalism) till the very end of the independence movement, indicates that Gandhian methods were not universally accepted. They were sometimes, misunderstood, and, at others, identified as moralistic or even expedient. See Selig S. Harrison, "Hindu Society and the State: The Indian Union" in K.H.[Silvert (ed), *Expectant Peoples— Nationalism and Development* (New York; Vintage Books, 1967), pp. 273-90.
6. Some analysts ascribe the failure to keep united the divided commu-

nities in India to the Hindu Character of the Congress and also of Gandhi.

See for instance, (i) Norman Brown, *The United States and India and Pakistan*, (Cambridge; Harvard University Press, 1953), p. 199.

  (ii) R. Coupland, *The Indian Problem*, Vol. II (London; Oxford University Press, 1944), p. 193.

  (iii) Nirad C. Chaudhary, *The Autobiography of an Unknown Indian* (New York, Macmillan, 1951), p. 432.

  7. Tilak, before Gandhi, and like Vivekanand, reiterated in the *Gita Rahasya*, that the *Bhagvad Gita* taught the synthesis of action and that violence for a righteous cause was morally justified and sanctioned by the divine book. Gandhi, however, interpreted the *Gita* as the teaching of action in terms of courage, fearlessness and sacrifice (*Yajna*) and thus ruled out violence.

  8. Boyd C. Shafer, *Nationalism-Myth And Reality* (New York, Harcourt, Brace and World, 1955), p. 142.

Also see Rupert Emerson, *From Empire To Nation—The Rise To Self-Assertion of Asian and African Peoples* (Boston; Beacon, 1960), p. 85.

  9. These concepts were identifiable in politics much before the emergence of Gandhi. It was, however, Gandhi who imbued them with new perspectives within practical politics. See W.T. de Bary, et. al. (eds), *Sources of Indian Tradition* (New York; Columbia University Press, 1958), pp. 1-36.

  10. Mulk Raj Anand, *Is There An Indian Culture?* (Bombay; Asia, 1963), pp. 79-82.

  11. See L.I. and S.H. Rudolphs, *Modernity of Tradition* (Chicago, Chicago University Press, 1967), pp. 187-190 and 254-269.

  12. See Jawaharlal Nehru, *The Discovery of India* (New Delhi, Oxford University Press, 1981), pp. 380-394.

  13. K.R.S. Iyengar, *Indian Writing in English* (Bombay, Asia, 1962), p. 30.

  14. Amlendu Bose and Pallabsen Gupta are credited to have brought to light these pioneering novels. On the basis of these novels, G.P. Sarma has traced the birth of Indian, not only of Indo-Anglian, fiction to 1835, against the common assumption that Indo-Anglian novel began with either Bankim Chatterjee's *Raj Mohun*'s *Wife* (1864) or with Lal Behari Day's *Govinda Samnta* (1874).

See G.P. Sarma, *Nationalism in Indo-Anglian Fiction* (New Delhi; Sterling, 1978), pp. xvi-xis.

  15. Meenakshi Mukherjee, *The Twice Born Fiction* (New Delhi, Arnold Heinemann, 1971), p. 19.

  16. William Walsh, *R.K. Narayan—A Critical Appreciation* (London; Heinemann, 1982), p. 4.

  17. As Nehru said: Gandhi came "like a powerful current of fresh air that made us stretch ourselves and take deep breaths, like a beam of

light that pierced the darkness and removed the scales from our eyes; like a whirlwind that upset many things, but most of all the working of people's minds". *n.* 12, p. 358.

Also see, Romain Rolland, *Mahatma Gandhi* (trans. C.D. Groth) (New York; The Century Co., 1924), pp. 3-5.

18. For a psycho-political analysis of these concepts see, Erik H. Erikson, *Gandhi's Truth: On the Origins of Militant Nationalism* (London; Faber and Faber, 1970), pp. 417-433.
    Also see Joan V. Bondurant, *Conquest of Violence: The Gandhian Philosophy of Conflict* (Bombay, Oxford University Press, 1959), pp. 16-32 and 190-229.

19. S.R. Bald, highlighting the predicament of the pre-independence novelists, writes that they "occupied an uncomfortable and undefined space" and "fitted a peculiar double category, the privileged under-privileged: privileged because of their education and caste, under-privileged because of India's subjection to Britain". *Novelists and Political Consciousness* (Delhi, Chanakya, 1982), p. 4.

20. Mulk Raj Anand, *Apology For Heroism* (1946), (New Delhi, Arnold Heinemann, 1975), p. 120.

21. Venkataramani, himself living through the history-making epoch of Gandhian nationalism, anticipates the attitude of idolatory towards Gandhi in subsequent years and pleads for imbibing the 'spirit' of Gandhian creed: "Men like Gandhiji instead of being a world phenomenon to be worshipped like the Sun, must grow on every hedge like black berries. At least every cottage must have one Gandhiji, working for its renovation till it is restored to healthy life and needs no Gandhiji for a trumpet call to pure, selfless public work". *Kandan, The Patriot* (Madras, Svetaranya Ashram, 1932), p. 249.

22. *Kanthapura* (1938), (Delhi; Orient Paperbacks, 1971), p. 176.

23. *n.* 15, p. 38.

24. C.D. Narasimhaiah, *Raja Rao* (New Delhi; Arnold Heinemann, n.d.), p. 42.

25. See, C.D. Narasimhaiah, "National Identity in Literature and Language: Its Range and Depth in the Novels of Raja Rao", in K.L. Goodwin (ed) *National Identity* (London; Heinemann, 1970), pp. 153-154.
    Also see, V.Y. Kantak, "The Language of Indian Fiction in English" in M.K. Naik (et. al.), *Critical Essays on Indian Writing in English* (Dharwar; Karnatak University, 1968), p. 157.

26. K.R.S. Iyengar comments that the social structure portrayed in *Kanthapura* neatly divided into the Brahmins', potters', weavers' and Sudras' quarters—is absurdly true of the typical Indian village. *n.* 13, p. 393.

27. V.Y. Kantak, "The Achievement of R.K. Narayan", in C.D.

Narasimhahiah (ed.) *Indian Literature of the Past Fifty Years* (Mysore, University of Mysore, 1970), p. 139.

28. R. Taranath, "The average as the positive—A note on R.K. Narayan", in M.K. Naik (et. al.), *n.* 25, p. 319.
29. *Waiting for the Mahatma* (1955), (Mysore, Indian Thought Publication, 1967), p. 113.
30. H.M. Williams, *Studies in Modern Indian Fiction in English*, (Calcutta, Writers Workshop, 1973), p. 53.
31. A.N. Kaul, "R.K. Narayan and The East West Theme", in A. Poddar (ed.), *Indian Literature* (Simla, Indian Institute of Advanced Study, 1972), p. 223.
32. C.D. Narasimhahiah, *The Writer's Gandhi* (Patiala, Punjabi University of Patiala, 1967), p.71.
33. *n.* 16, p. 94.
34. Balchandra Rajan, *The Dark Dancer* (London, Heinemann, 1959).
35. Prema Nand Kumar, "The Achievement of the Indo-Anglian Novelist", *The Literary Criterion* (Winter 1961), 160. Also see, V.Y. Kantak, *n.* 25, p. 156.
36. Frederick Morton, "New Truths, Old Values", *New York Times Book Review* (29 June, 1958) 6; Also see, Meenakshi Mukherjee, *n.* 15. 156-157.
37. *So Many Hungers* (1947) (Delhi, Orient Paperbacks, 1978), p. 20.
38. There is pride in Kunal's statement: "The soldiers from India have fought and defeated White troops in pitched battles even against heavy odds. The White Man's bubble has exploded in the African air . . . the myth that has been the spine of empires lies in pieces on the desert sands", *n.* 37, p. 104.
39. K.R.S. Iyengar, *n.* 13, p. 414.
40. *A Bend in the Ganges* (London, Hamish Hamilton, 1964), p. 234.
41. Kai Nicholson gives a naive interpretation of the episode: "the underlying theme in the novel has been a praise for the British Empire in India and by making Debi realize the flaws in the Congress Party, he (Malgonkar) has turned Debi finally against the idea of independence".
A Presentation of Social Problems in Indo-Anglian and Anglo-Indian Novel (Bombay, Jaico, 1972), p. 158.
42. Robin White, *Review of a Bend in the Ganges*, New York Times, (14 February, 1965).
43. Meenakshi Mukherjee, *n.* 15, p. 60.
44. E.M. Forster, G.S. Amur and Khushwant Singh, among others are, therefore, justified in their appreciation of the novel. See G.S. Amur, *Manohar Malgonkar* (New Delhi, Arnold Heinemann, 1973), pp. 113-131.
45. *Azadi* (Delhi, Orient Paperbacks, 1975).
46. *Cruel Interlude* (Bombay, Asia Publishing House, 1961), also reports the transit of a convoy, the Sargodha *Kafla*, from Pakistan to India, as in *Azadi*.

47. See V.A. Shahane, *Khushwant Singh* (New York; Twayne, 1972). He characterizes it as a "classic of its own kind, a realistic epic of modern India" (p. 8); and J.F. Adkins, "History As Art Form: Khushwant Singh's *Train to Pakistan*". *The Journal of Indian writing in English*, 2, 2 (July, 1974), 1-12.

48. Chirantan Kulshrestha, "Khushwant Singh's Fiction," *Indian Writing Today*, 2, 4 (Jan-March, 1970), 20 and 25.

49. Meenakshi Mukherjee, *n*. 15. p. 52.
    Also see, David Mccutchion, *Indian writing in English-Critical Essays* (Calcutta; Writers Workshop, 1969), p. 40.

50. See K.C. Bellapa, "The Elusive Classic: Khushwant Singh's *Train to Pakistan* and Chaman Nahal's *Azadi*", *Literary Criterion*, 15, 2 (1980), 62-63.

51. See V.P. Menon, *Transfer of Power in India* (Calcutta; Orient Longmans, 1957), pp. 422-423.

52. *The Golden Honeycomb* (London, Chatto and Windus, 1977) comprehensively portrays the evolution of political consciousness through three generations in princely India covering the period, 1870 to 1918, prior to the beginning of the Gandhian revolution.

53. *The Devil's Wind* (New Delhi; Orient Paperbacks, 1972). Prior to this novel, there was only one novel on the Revolt of 1857, written by S.C. Dutt in 1885, *Shunkur: A Tale of the Indian Mutiny of 1857*. G.S. Amur disputes Malgonkar's claim of being the pioneer of the 'Indian point of view' on the revolt. See G.S. Amur, *Manohar Malgonkar* (New Delhi, Arnold Heinemann, 1973), pp. 123-4 & 130. Apart from professional historians, however, Manohar Malgonkar deserves place as a pioneer of the Indian point of view on 1857 in the literary world of Indo-Anglian fiction.

54. *Midnight's Children* (London, Picador, 1981).

55. Malgonkar is reported to have "spent two years on research, reading over 150 books by both Britishers and Indians on this event of 1857." See James Y. Dayanand, "The Novelist as Historian: Manohar Malgonkar's *The Devil's Wind* and the 1857 Rebellion." *Journal of South Asian Literature*, X, 1 (Fall, 1974), 59.

56. V.D. Savarkar, *The Indian War of Independence, 1857* (1909) (Bombay, Phoenix, 1947), p. 116.

57. *n*. 12, p. 325.

58. Bhabani Bhattacharya, *A Goddess Named Gold* (Delhi, Hind Pocket Books, 1960), p. 303.

59. S.R. Bald aptly remarks: ". . . politically conscious Indians were raising highly charged political questions . . . writing about life, the novelists of 1919-47, in effect wrote about politics," *n*. 19, p. 3.

60. The novelists do not fail to celebrate independence due to a consciousness of "guilt" as Gomathi Narayanan argues. See her

"British Fathers and Indian Sons: Guilt and Pride for the Indian Freedom Movement in the Post-Independence Indian Novel in English. The Art of Scapegoating". *Journal of South Asian Literature*, xvii, 1 (Winter-Spring, 1982), 207-24.

61. Michael Brecher, *Nehru—A Political Biography* (London, Oxford University Press, 1959), p. 334.

4

The Political Structure in India: Aspirations, Challenges and Dilemmas

> Now that we have freedom, we need acts of faith. Then only will there be a transmutation.

> —*Bhabani Bhattacharya*

Contrary to aesthetic conceptions, which perceive contemporary social or political events as unsuitable subjects for a work of art[1], political fiction addresses itself to the labyrinth of contemporary political events, patterns and paradoxes. Political fiction, in this sense, need not be propaganda or journalism. The success and utility of political fiction would depend, to a large extent, on the depth with which it perceives the underlying challenges and paradoxes of the prevailing power-relationships in a given political system. The response of the political analyst and the creative writer to this varied, complex and fascinating dynamics could be approximated with G. Sartori's statement, comparing an economist and a political scientist: "The economist intervenes. His knowledge is applied knowledge. The political scientist awaits. He explains what happens, but does not make it happen"[2]. It is possible to qualify this statement with reference to recent developments in political science, specially policy science and action-oriented researches, which cut across the distinction made by Sartori. However, if this comparison is extended to include the creative writer as well, he would be closer to the economist on the assumption that he possesses the capacity for 'making things happen' through his creative imagination and critical comprehension, the magnitude of the challenge, notwithstanding.

The present chapter enquires into various aspects of challenges, aspirations and dilemmas of India's political structure and processes as perceived in major Indo-Anglian political novels.

I

Political Structure: Image and Reality

India's independence marked not merely the end of colonial domination but also the beginning of a new journey. The transition to Freedom was, indeed, transition to the challenges of state and nation-building. It was a historic watershed, nevertheless, "a moment", as Nehru said, "which, comes but rarely in history, when we step out from the old to the new, when an age ends and when the soul of a nation long suppressed finds utterance".[3] The "utterance" was duly incorporated into a legal framework, the constitution, subsequently translated into practice through concrete structures and processes as identities of independent India.

Independence in India's case marked both continuity with and a departure from the past. On the one hand, it entailed transformation of the whole pattern of political life—"a metamorphosis of subjects into citizens",[4] although not "total, complete and absolute substitution", as Fanon would associate with decolonization.[5] Change in power structures also brought about urgency and concern with political structures, expected to be responsive to the aspirations of the nascent nation and perceived in awareness of the challenges inherent in the situation. Concern with authority and legitimacy also brought about renewed emphasis on the nature and processes of government and their potential to ensure stability.[6] The concern for stability marked the process of continuity with the past. The long and entrenched experience of the national movement consolidated awareness and sense of involvement. It was an enriching legacy. Also, the Indian National Congress which had provided leadership to the nationalist movement turned itself after

India's independence into a political party and also formed the government. This was much against the wishes of Gandhi. There was also continuity in administrative machinery, personnel, institutions and even the governing norms. One could even argue that on the eve of independence change in some way was visualized more in terms of continuity than break with the past.

Values of justice, liberty and equality, as substance of liberal democracy, were statutorily incorporated in India's constitution. India *consciously* imported the political structure of parliamentary democracy, as a theoretical model which was later subjected to the pulls and pressures of indigenous needs, aspirations and challenges. In the process, several paradoxes and contradictions have crept in, seriously affecting the operation of the political system. This however, was inevitable in order to encapsulize, in a short span of time, the objective of three-fold transformation, political integration, social regeneration and economic reconstruction. Democracy, as western analysts often assumed, was not merely a matter of pre-existing conditions but also of 'political will' to create and maintain conditions, conducive to the attainment of ideologically and constitutionally conceived goals.[7]

The newly created political structure sought to bring about basic transformation in society and economy through polity. Aspiring to attain a just, free and egalitarian society as epitomized in the Preamble and the Directive Principles, the political structure began by attacking, and partly succeeded in abolishing, feudal privileges based on oppressive 'superior-subordinate' hierarchy. The institutional structure included, among other arrangements, periodic elections based on adult franchise. The dynamics of competitive politics worked through party system and participation was sought and realized through representation system. Altogether an effort was made to operationalize the spirit and ideals of constitutional democracy by breaking down isolation of the rural community and stirring the dormant urban population. The process of political awareness, involvement and articulation had, thus, been set in motion, as a basis of political 'literacy'.

Creation of structures, however, symbolized an approach meant to be conducive to the viability of the political system.

The constitutional ideals of the new polity were put to test by numerous challenges from the very beginning. There were several problems, for instance, of incorporation of 562 princely states (covering one-third of the land area) into the Indian union, and the turmoil and communal travail of riots, both preceding and following the partition; apart from divergent linguistic and regional claims and divisions.[8] In order to attain enduring political structures, an imperative need in the given circumstances, the constitutional ideal of democratic decentralization was supplemented by strong central authority, federal autonomy by centralized planning and other requirements of national integration. The norms of participation could not be qualified nor inhibited by the pluralist context, though there persisted incessant majority-minority dichotomy. This *modus operandi* explains, to some extent, the flexibility, adaptability and diversity of political beliefs, attitudes and norms, perceived at both the elite and the mass levels in Indian politics, notwithstanding, the existence of certain unifying norms. Probably, the pluralistic code of ethics, highly valued in Indian culture, justifies, rather than discourages tolerance of antagonisms and neutralizes sharp choice, radicalism or even rebellion, without mediating structures.[9] In a way, one of the results of this dynamics has been politics of compromise and accommodation which has emerged as a persistent feature ever since the genesis of the nationalist movement.

The Indian political structure has been largely shaped by the unique phenomenon of the convergence of the Congress party, the government and personal power and the charismatic leadership of Nehru in the initial decades after independence. The trend apparently continued for long after Nehru. The historical consensus inherited from the nationalist movement was converted into the 'left of the centre' democratic ideology. In operational terms, the Indian political structure has been considerably influenced by the increasing role and the complexity (including its perversions) of electoral politics and the associated paraphernalia of competitive and party politics, in addition to the growing role and intervention of politics and government in socio-economic and cultural affairs.

In its evolution towards a viable polity, the Indian system has undergone several crises. It has, however, managed to

survive owing probably to the inbuilt devices through which
it has been possible to throw up leadership at regular intervals
in a democratic manner, rather than through violent methods
such as 'coups'. Informal personal arrangements, facilitated by
one-party dominance for most of the early decades of the new
polity, rather than conventions, have played their own part in
countering the lurking crises.[10] In attitudinal terms, this
phenomenon may be explained with reference to the cultural
predisposition in Indian society to personalize all phenomenon,
including struggle, to exalt the leader by attributing to him/her
unilimited potential for changing the course of events, with
complete disregard for impersonal forces that equally
govern the trend of events. Such perception of leadership as
charisma, however, is inadequtate for comprehending the
complexity of the political process. The ideal situation of
employing power as an instrument to achieve the constitutional
or ideological goals is attainable only when there is agreement
on the basic 'rules of the game' and related defined goals. In
such consensual situations the pursuit of power and authority
becomes essentially a task of integration or accommodation of
various groups and individuals in pursuit of common public
objectives. In practice, however, the political process is far
more complex than the simple ideas of 'accommodation' and
'reconciliation'. There is no dearth of evidence to show how
larger public interest is subordinated to personal gains, both
political and economic.

When the demands of narrow interests collide with larger
public needs, the inevitable dilemma of balancing order and
change, integration and adaptation, becomes more acute.
Whereas maintaining harmony, unity or integration is absolutely essential, the goals of liberty, justice and development cannot be taken as static or perceived for all times. The goals
have to be change-oriented. Here one is struck by a notable
absence of a carefully considered conception and design of
change in India. Inadequacy of implementing the professed
measures of change, notwithstanding the 'radical' intentions of
some of the socio-economic objectives of the Indian National
Congress[11] and policies of the government, becomes all too
apparent.[12]

The reasons for the persistence of the dilemma in one form

or the other and the inadequacy of efforts to resolve it in favour of orderly, purposive and progressive change, may be perceived in the composition of the political structure itself. For instance, Rajni Kothari in his ingenious diagnosis of the crisis areas in Indian political system highlights the failure of Indian leadership on the front of distributive justice. In a simultaneous attempt at national integration, democratic consensus-making and economic development, the Indian leadership, according to Kothari, adopted the approach of "aggregative performance", paying little attention to ensure distributive performance. It had probably been the assumption that aggregative performance would automatically result in distributive performance. That there were inbuilt constraints, Kothari stresses, on such a progression from aggregative to distributive performance, was not adequately perceived.[13] This resulted in inevitable failures on economic and distributive fronts, putting to test the sincerity of the national leadership regarding professed socialistic principles.

In order to accomplish the goals of democracy as well as those of socialism, some sort of fundamental, institutional as well as attitudinal innovations should have been visualized.[14] Experiments of institutional innovation, such as Community Development programme, have not succeeded in achieving the cherished targets. Similarly, attitudinal innovation through political education and 'cadre formation' have not been attained.[15] Cadre formation may prove to be an important technique to control and check the tendency of 'ad hoc' programmes followed by most parties. It may also help in diluting inherent incongruities of the ideology of democratic socialism by ensuring programmatic politics. It is essential to redefine and modify theoretical framework and concepts of both democracy and socialism in a pragmatic manner. Concrete programmatic politics aimed at progressive consciousness should now be the most pressing priority in India in order to rectify the past record of what Kuldeep Nayar calls "good intentions and bad performance".[16]

As Nehru said, even the best of constitutions and institutions will fail if the spirit to operate them properly is absent. True restoration of public morality and spirit, reminiscent of the freedom movement, of service before power and principles

before self, needs to be inculcated through education,[17] volun-
tary associations and cadre-based parties. As the final test of
any polity, more so of a polity simultaneously committed to the
ideals of democracy and socialism, what stands out is performance rather than professions, legitimacy rather than appearances. The crisis-points in the Indian political structure are
indeed the crises of change. Besides institutionalization of
protest through social agencies in attitudinal terms, the
Hegelian 'false happy consciousness' (against which Herbert
Marcuse cautions the modern world), needs to be replaced by a
reorientation toward the socio-political phenomenon, based on
a change-oriented progressive consciousness. In a society
not yet liberated from several constraints, purely idealistic
exhortation would exacerbate the crises. Thus there is need of
emphasis on political will and political initiative through programmatic politics, working through cadres. The unavoidable
centrality of politics in the context of India entrusts to the
political structure an extra-political role as well. The perennial dilemma for analysis of Indian politics seems to be how
best to balance mechanically oriented administrative outlook
against scientific, on the one hand, and innovative and creative
perspective against pragmatic posers, on the other.

II

Major Indo-Anglian Novels: Themes and Issues

The internal dynamics of the political structure in India
presents to a creative writer almost an inexhaustible material
for scrutiny and analysis. There is a remarkable mix of situations, incongruent and facile, of human weaknesses and determination, of affluence and poverty, splendour and squalor,
commitment and frivolous pretence, ideals and hypocrisy.

The Indo-Anglian novel in response to this challenge, however, has taken up a complacent view. The socio-political optimism and aesthetic rebellion of pre-independence era seem to
be giving way to some sort of anxiety and despair. Although
unapologetic, the novels are not particularly ambitious so as to
project an architectonic perception of Indian politics. As delineations of specific aspects and dilemmas of political life,

however, they are valuable. By way of preface it could be said that the Indo-Anglian novel begins to grasp the new political reality only marginally in the 1950s, matures through protest against the ills of political populism, corruption and moral degeneration in the 1960s and the 1970s and seems to be coming to a fuller understanding of the political reality in a broader perspective in the 1980s. Mulk Raj Anand, Manohar Malgonkar, Nayantara Sahgal, A.G. Sheorey and Salman Rushdie have specifically contributed to comprehending varied aspects of the socio-political conflicts and anachronisms that have arisen in post-independence Indian politics with a view to re-assessing the impact of democratic political structures in a former colony.

One could begin with the challenge of territorial consolidation as perceived by Anand and Malgonkar. Mulk Raj Anand's *Private Life of an Indian Prince* is a therapeutic concern in artistic terms, of a physician, seriously engaged in pathological analysis of a chronic patient. Indeed, the Indian political structure was in a serious pathological state at the time of independence, balkanized into several hundred princely states. The situation could not have been worse. The transfer of power not to a united Indian government, but to two governments (India and Pakistan), further complicated by some of the princely states nursing aspirations for independence, created a situation of near anarchy, as symbolised by Anand's prince, Victor Edward George Ashok Kumar. This was the most tragic legacy of the imperialistic policy of *divide-et-impera*. Saros Cowasjee rightly states that on the surface of it, Maharaja Ashok Kumar's bid (as also of Maharaja Hiroji in *The Princes*), for independence might seem the act of a lunatic, but not so if one bears in mind what the British had led the Indian princes to believe for nearly a century.[18] In 1858, with the establishment of the rule of the British crown, Queen Victoria, in her royal declaration, pledged to 'respect' the rights, dignity and honour of the native princes. These promises were, time and again, repeated in the subsequent century. Since the Butler Committee report in 1928, the British virtually assured the chamber of princes that in the event of any political change in British India, paramountcy would lapse.[19] The 'lapse of British paramountcy' was interpreted by the princes as synonymous with independent status for their respective states. The resistance bordering on recalcitrance exhibited by several rulers (Hyderabad, Junagarh and Kashmir) at the time of independence can be understood in the light of this explanation. In actual practice, however, the states had never possessed any sovereignty or independence.[20] On the other hand, the native states had served as pockets of reaction and suppression of popular movements. With the advent of independence, it was only logical that the anachronistic feudal order should give in to the 'paramountcy of the popular will,' as Sardar Patel said. Anand and Malgonkar, though differing in ideological viewpoints, show how arduous the task of the newly created States Department was in drilling basic commonsense into the hardheaded native princes, despite the provision for privy purse settlement (amounting to Rs. 580 lakhs per annum) and numerous other privileges.

Whereas Anand's *Private Life of an Indian Prince* is a psychopathological probe into the feudal political culture of India in decadence, Malgonkar's *The Princes* is a historic-sociological analysis of the process of decay being resisted. The portrayal of the prince as an eccentric, neurotic and (Dostoevkian) 'idiot' shows Anand's contempt for feudal anachronisms.

Private Life of an Indian Prince, at one level, is the story of a prince removed from normal life experience, caught between the erotic influence of his nymphomaniac mistress, Ganga Dasi and the stubborn resistance against denial of rights by his estranged wife, Indira. The familiar palace intrigues, Ganga's plotting against Indira and her son and Indira's retaliation in her appeal to the central government not to recognize Ganga as the official Rani, all typify the decline of the princely order. The life of the prince does not remain 'private' any more. That precisely seems to be Anand's purpose; to expose the contradictions of the 'private' and the 'public' stances when the two interact, as they inevitably do. Confused and tentative in his perception of the political reality and adamant in his approach, Maharaja Ashok Kumar ultimately agrees to sign the Instrument of Accession in Delhi, thus acquiescing in the new political order. On the other hand, having failed to achieve official recognition as the rightful and wedded consort of the prince and also aware of the impending doom of princely order,

Ganga deserts the prince. The Maharaja finds it hard to bear Ganga's departure in addition to the loss of his kingdom, and ultimately lands in a mental asylum. The novel ends with Dr. Shankar's (the conscience-keeper of the prince) realization of the 'absurdity' of the whole situation as Albert Camus would have said: "In a way the whole of India was a kind of lunatic asylum, part of the bigger lunatic asylum of the world, in which only those who struggled against the *status quo* and gave battle to authority seemed to find some sense of balance through the elaboration of a new sense of values" (p. 336). And he resolves to return to Shampur, amongst the people, to the sources of strength, to struggle, probably to realize "freedom".

Thus, Anand succeeds in exposing the myth that the princely order, 'the sons of the Sun and the Moon', were not as handsome as they were made out to be; their image, bolstered by the British, was bound to wane in the face of the new forces of popular revolt against their maladministration, autocracy and whims. The disintegration of Anand's prince was inevitably a part of the larger historical process.

Manohar Malgonkar's *The Princes*, on the other hand, rich in documentation of details of the palace life, intricacies of the *modus operandi* of the princely rule and the mysterious happenings in the states, shows the novelist's predisposition for facts and intimate knowledge of his subject.[21] Thus, a reviewer should characterize Malgonkar either as a 'very royal prince' or a 'ghost of one'.[22] Malgonkar's portrayal of the tumultous transition from feudalism to democracy (from the point of view of the heir-apparent who later becomes the king, having stakes in the system—rather than from an observer's point of view without substantial personal stakes, as in Anand's novel), distinguishes his conservative political premises from Anand's radical ideological flamboyancy. Whereas Anand is convinced of the dialectics of historical inevitability, wherein the old order is doomed to die. Malgonkar is conscious of the forces of resistance and suggests that old order dies hard in practice despite political revolutions.

The arrogance, helplessness, anger and gloom of Maharaja Hiroji as characterized by Malgonkar, in fact, typified all the erstwhile normal princes (unlike Anand's neurotic prince), as confirmed by V.P. Menon's historical account. No ruler had

believed even a month before independence that he would have
soon to part with his sovereignty, however farcical over the
state and rights of rulership. Exclusive privileges enjoyed over
generations and somehow regarded as sacrosanct had disappear-
ed, as it were, in the twinkling of an eye. "Though all of them
put a bold front, the mental anguish they were going through
was writ large on their faces".[23] The delusions of grandeur,
and false security, cloaked in their dreams of establishing a
third force as a counterweight to the Congress and the Muslim
League, and later of setting up a union of Princely States, 'the
India of the princes, powerful, solid, deeply rooted in tradition',[24] were over with the proposed Instruments of Accession
and merger. Covenants of merger were signed with the rulers
of semi-jurisdictional and non-jurisdictional estates.

In fact, there was no alternative left for the princes. Owing
to maladministration, which they had carried on under the
protective shield of British paramountcy and having no direct
contact with their subjects for one and a half centuries, they
had forfeited the sympathy of the people.[25] In 1938, the All
India Congress at Haripura had passed a resolution to support
democratic movements in princely states. The princes, however
refused to heed the warning and persisted with their illusion of
sustaining absolute power. Maharaja Hiroji, for instance, did
not like the "nonsense about people's movements" (239). The
megalomania of the Maharaja was undisguised: "There will
always be Begwad and there will always be a Bedar ruling it—
so long as the Sun and Moon go around" (p. 322). When the
Maharaja became cognizant of the irreversible course of events
he preferred death to signing the Instrument of merger by going
unarmed before a tiger.

Yuvraj Abhayraj, taking over the regime for the final and
last fortynine days, also does not give evidence of qualitative
difference in his approach particularly with regard to the
popular 'Praja Mandal' movement. Malgonkar's politico-
aesthetic judgment, however, aptly summarizes the situation:
"Abhayraj's highest moment of awareness of his identity as a
prince has a strange coincidence with the disappearance of his
princely inheritance itself".[26] He was "bewildered and unsure,
thoroughly alarmed at how things were going, really concerned
for the first time for what we were about to lose" (p. 283).

That is the reason why V.S. Naipaul identifies *The Princes* as 'the medieval tragedy of a medieval Indian petty prince".[27] For, in spite of living in the middle of the twentieth century which witnessed revolutionary upsurge, the attitudinal stubbornness and the resistance to change shown by the princes is truly medieval. Malgonkar portrays the critical dimensions of conflict between feudalism and democracy. Nothing brings that out better than the contemptuous attitude of Abhayraj toward Kanak Chand, an untouchable, and a leader of the 'Praja Mandal' movement in the Begwad State. At best, as G.S. Amur reflects, Malgonkar knows some facts about the new types of the politician but these "are not *his* facts. They are not, of course, the only facts worth knowing about them".[28]

For Malgonkar, the princely world "was a rather nice world. . . it was like some bit of colour in a very drab India".[29] This nostalgia for feudal 'colour' on the part of Malgonkar, should rightly make students of 'Change' in the wake of democracy feel rather uneasy. However, so far as the historical aspect is concerned, Malgonkar's portrayal is accurate and does not submit itself to criticisms such as novelist, P.S. Bawa's: "We (the princes) are the victims of a misdirected or jaundiced image which the authors have projected for their fond readers".[30] Malgonkar, one might sum up, is excellent at history but fails to go beyond, as Anand does.

The successful accomplishment of the integration of princely states marked an important landmark in the process of national evolution. In their counter-hegemonic role, however, the princes substantially affected the working of the new political structure, through what may be identified as the 'politics of privy purses' until the 24th Constitution Amendment was passed in August 1971, derecognizing princes and abolishing privy purses. In post-1971 phase, the erstwhile princes seem to be showing marginal political involvement. They, however, continue to wield power through their resources and alignment with capitalist forces.

Territorial consolidation, as subsequent events proved, was only the first step in the hazardous process of national integration.[31]. The challenge, partly countered through linguistic reorganization in 1956, continues to persist in varied forms of regionalism.[32] The Indo-Anglian novelist, however, has not responded to this challenge.

Among the Indo-Anglian novels, Nayantara Sahgal's *Storm in Chandigarh* is the only attempt addressed to some aspects of the problem of cultural pluralism and national integration in India, with reference to the linguistic bifurcation of the erstwhile Punjab into Punjabi-speaking Punjab and Hindi-speaking Haryana in 1967. She seeks to interpret the issue as a pathological aspect of the body-politic of India, without hiding a liberal democrat's impatience with unexpected changes in the seemingly harmonious state apparatus. For example, the novel begins with political distress: "The map of India, once a uniform piece of territory to administer, was now a welter of separate sensitive identities, resurrected after independence."[33] This distress further rests on the assumption that "psychology seemed to play as important a part in understanding them as did history, geography and economics".[34] The contextual problem depicted in the story factually relates to the disputes over boundaries, water, power distribution and the capital (Chandigarh) between Punjab and Haryana. However, in the portrayal of chaos, violence, dwindling loyalties and crisis of social and political values, the novel moves beyond the dated crisis.

Illustrative of the unseemly trend, a typical report read: "Outburst of brutal, calculated violence had become a feature of the cities. There were too many in the congestion and chaos who had nothing to lose by violence, too many others who sat inert and indifferent, their sap sucked dry, watching the mount and ebb like some great tidal wave waiting for it to engulf them . . . Violence had become routine and expected. It was given different names, indiscipline, unrest, disorder" (p. 6). One might dislike the depiction of violence it is, however, unfortunately as true (or even worse) of Punjab today as it was when the novel was written.

Going deeper into the crisis, Nayantara Sahgal identifies the erosion of Gandhian ideals and Nehru's vision *vis-a-vis* the present generation of politicians by contrasting the political styles of Gyan Singh (the Chief Minister of Punjab) and Harpal Singh (the new Chief Minister of Haryana). Polarized politics of the two leaders is sought to be mediated and moderated by the central government through deputing a brilliant young civil

servant, Vishal Dubey, to Chandigarh. Individual efforts, however, prove inadequate for controlling and resolving collective
ills, such as, wanton killing and extraction of money by police
officers (p. 55), proclamation of high ideals and corrupt practices by ministers (p. 141), the government service running 'at
snail's pace' (p. 165), and inconvenience caused by employees'
strikes in essential services (p. 204).

Concretely speaking, therefore, nothing substantial gets
accomplished through Vishal Dubey's efforts except the acceptance of the Punjab chief minister's challenge of resorting to
general strike by the Haryana chief minister. During the course
of events, the Haryana chief minister gets injured and the
Union home minister (portrayed as a relic of the Gandhian
past), also expires. Vishal Dubey goes back to Delhi amidst
temporary lull. The problem, however, continues to smoulder.
The novel thus initiates a psycho-cultural perspective to the
phenomenon of political crisis generated by linguistic regionalism during the 1960s in India. For several literary critics, the
novel is valuable not so much as a political novel, but as an
exploration of inter-personal relations and values.[35] Nevertheless, Nayantara Sahgal's portrayal of political issues as current
public and collective concerns assumes an interaction between
individual ethics and public norms. The interaction is visible
in leadership roles, especially in times of crisis, adequately
illustrated in *Storm in Chandigarh.*

Crisis of politico-cultural integration, combined with crisis
of individual identity, has manifested itself in a deeper crisis of
legitimacy of the power structure operative in Indian polity.
Unlike those of the thirties and the forties, contemporary
novelists are not linked together against a common enemy; they
do, however, in differing degrees, delineate the dilemmas of
democratic life in a nation, that has not as yet imbibed democracy as a 'faith'. A.G. Sheorey's *Dusk Before Dawn* and
Nayantara Sahgal's *This Time of Morning* explore the operational contradictions of democratic political structure, simultaneously confronting the task of state and nation-building. In
striving for quick results, the novelists highlight that democratic
norms sanction centralization of authority, which ultimately
gets degenerated into none-too-ennobling pursuit of power.
Politics, the nationalist 'vocation' in pre-independence India, is

perceived to be surviving as a necessary evil in post-independence context. Sheorey and Sahgal evaluate the process of degeneration with the yardstick of Gandhian norms of public conduct.

Both the novelists advocate freedom of press and of public institutions as custodians of India's nascent democracy. The ideological preference for liberal democracy is so strong, in both that socialistic postures and goals, professed so often by India's leadership, are given scant attention. By implication, however, the humanitarian core in the Gandhian framework comes to be identified in the equation of 'freedom' with 'progress', perhaps in quest of identity. Nayantara Sahgal's *This Time of Morning* has been described as "one of the best political novels"[36] addressed to the national political scene in India. A.G. Sheorey's *Dusk Before Dawn* deserves to be assessed in a similar vein, as an indispensable analysis of aspects of state-politics in India (in many ways comparable to the famous Bengali novel, *Mukhya Mantri* by Chanakya Sen, that is, Bhabani Sen Gupta).

Dusk Before Dawn is the story of persecution and political vendetta launched by a State government against an editor (Dhananjay) of a newspaper (*Yug Samachar*). The editor criticizes the irresponsible and deplorable conduct of an erring minister (PWD), the growing climate of corruption, followed by indictment of the head of the anti-corruption squad. The novel expresses how, eager to hold public offices but hostile to public criticism, diehard elements in the government and the police department decide to punish the newspaper and its editor for outspoken and critical journalism. Through the story of this case the novelist raises the fundamental question: "Whether a newspaper enjoys complete freedom to which the press is entitled under a free, democratic society, whether politicians or men in power will tolerate a free press and allow it to grow and function according to its own light, without any hindrance."[37] The expectation was in keeping with the value that democratic governments uphold discussion and debate, disagreement and consensus. With independence, a new constructive phase of journalism was also conceived to carry out "notable task of public education, so that the masses were taught to exercise their power guaranteed through adult franchise in a proper, responsible manner", (p. 33) with complete dedication to help the national government build a new social order. In practice, however, the novelist notes with concern that these ideals were being eroded even before they were consolidated in some form. Politics came to assume postures of acutely self-centred priorities, intolerance, short-sightedness and ruthless liquidation of opponents. Power proved to be "a corrupting intoxicant", as apprehended by Gandhi and other freedom fighters. Parading Gandhi's name and making platitudinous exhortations, ministers in free India "seemed to be on perpetual holiday", betraying "utter lack of application and hard work" (p. 49) "swept off their feet by the first flush of power" (p. 84), whereas Gandhi himself is known to have "advised central ministers to shun pomp and show" and "live simply in austerity in keeping with the poverty of the nation." (p. 52).

The novel seeks to show how politics had made such a vast change within the first decade of independence that a veteran freedom fighter (now a chief minister) got another freedom fighter (the editor of *Yug Samachar*) hauled up on a framed-up criminal charge and sent him to penal servitude. Having, however, failed on the legal front, the government turned to coercing the newspaper by withdrawing advertisements and other normal facilities to which journalists are entitled. The unthinking vindictiveness resulted in nine cases cooked up against the editor (civil, criminal and under the Companies Act). Consequently, the editor was compelled to attend law courts twenty days in a month and spend Rs. 2,000 per month on litigation, even when some of the lawyers came forward to work 'gratis'. The tide of public opinion subsequently turned in favour of *Yug Samachar*. People came forward to contribute voluntarily to its defence fund. Every rupee thus contributed was like a vote of no-confidence against the state government. The central government under Nehru did not wish to intervene, probably, because, constitutionally speaking, press was in concurrent list and the states were sensitive about their rights.

Finally, on appeal from the editor, the Supreme Court ordered appointment of special judges under the direct supervision of the High Court to try the cases. Within a year, the judicial verdict was pronounced, indicting the government of

cheating and forgery. With this the Chief Minister's reputation
went under a cloud. He was denied the Congress ticket for the
second general election and subsequently commited suicide. The
novel ends with Dhananjay visiting the grave of the late chief
minister praying that his soul may rest in peace, with an affirmation of Gandhian values, independence and sanctity of the
judiciary and an artistic commitment to the cause of democratic
rights of citizens.

Moving from the scenario of state-politics to the larger,
national political spectrum, Nayantara Sahgal's *This Time of
Morning* portrays the 'dusky' as well as 'bright' aspects of
India's experiments in democratic nation-building in the initial
decades. The novel, however, seems to assume that transformation was a tedious and complex process. Like B. Rajan,
Nayantara Sahgal also accepts the Indian Civil Service, the
defence forces and the English language as positive aspects of the
British legacy in post-independence India. It is another matter
that the ICS continued to be manned by officers for whom
Whitehall continued to represent the most reliable approach to
world affairs. (p. 25). The Indian Foreign Service, soon caught
the infection of 'lording' and 'politicking': "Things drift.
Decisions pend . . . the riddle of who is appointed where and
why becomes more and more unfathomable". (p. 124).[38] The
inconsistencies persistently multiply. Unlike any other Indo-
Anglian novel, *This Time of Morning*, thus, draws our attention
to the anachronisms of administering an independent polity
through a colonial framework. The novelist suggests that what
we most urgently need is not so much as administrative or
monetary outlook as political imagination on how to harness
the energy lying idle. (p. 119).

Nayantara Sahgal concedes that politics has to play a central
role in nation-building in India. However, 'politics' for her has
connotations of pre-independence ideals. For instance, in the
novel, she highlights aspects of Gandhi's charismatic politics
(pp. 172-76) and the role of Indian National Congress in the
long freedom struggle (pp. 171-84). The foremost challenge
before post-independence 'politics', as Sahgal perceives, is
institutionalization of these values in the formal political
structures. As a veteran freedom fighter explains in the novel:

"The framework we have today is from the British but humanity we learned from the Mahatma". (p. 183). Attempts to reconcile the two, however, have resulted in acute tension in the Indian political process. The novel seeks to explore several dimensions of this 'tension' through polarization of two characters, Kailas Vrind (a Gandhian idealist) and Kalyan Sinha (a non-Gandhian, pragmatic activist), culminating paradoxically in the foundation of a Peace Institute which only aggravates the murky political scene.

Kailas Vrind represents the generation that grew with the magic and the dedication of Gandhi and lived for such ideals in post-independence India. Interestingly, Kailas Vrind attributes the growing asymmetry in Indian political culture largely to the transition of the Congress from a movement to a political party. The process has been frustrating in both normative and pragmatic senses. Kailas Vrind is aware that, though the party had always been amorphous, it was, however, disciplined. In the changing conditions, it could not mean all things to all the aspirants. Congress was drifting from Gandhian values. The forces of change were too powerful to be checked. For Kailas Vrind, politics was identical with Congress and freedom during the pre-independence period. They remained identical in another sense in post-independence India, namely, through convergence of the government and the party in important respects.

The amorphous character of the Congress resulting in an ideological ambivalence gets reflected in the larger political milieu of the nation. Befitting a new-born democracy, changes are perceptible at every level of society, economy and polity sometimes conveying a sense of perpetual crisis. Kailas wishes ideals and actions to be harmonized as during the freedom struggle. He considers it futile to keep on blaming the British. It is time to realize that their business had been to sustain the empire, not nation-building. The empire was, therefore, defied by the "tidal wave of patriotism against the framework of justice being used to supress the reality of justice" (p. 41).

In the changed ethos, Kailas thinks it is possible to revaluate Gandhism as a philosophy of life and as the guiding principle for a sovereign state. The creeping crisis of values does not signify the end of all that Gandhi and the Congress stood for, but a realization of the new challenges of transition.

Congress, he believes, continues to have a vital role to play in Indian politics. Politics in post-independence India is not inevitably a dirty game, for any game is a dirty game when dirty people play it. If there are unscrupulous doctors and lawyers and businessmen, and also dishonourable politicians, there are honourable ones too. (p. 185). In Kailas's view, therefore, a rejuvenation of Gandhian values is urgently needed to see India through the crisis of values and attitudes.

The Gandhian idealism of Kailas Vrind is counter-balanced in the novel by the pragmatic realism of Kalyan Sinha as the proverbial strongman, exhibiting the ability to shed all non-essentials and go directly to the heart of the matter and get things done. (p. 17). Disenchanted by both Gandhian and the terrorist methods, Kalyan had established an India Centre in the U.S. in 1935 with the object of stirring public opinion in support of India's freedom. Even after independence, educating foreign public about India is as laborius a task as it had ever been. Katherine Mayo's *Mother India* had not lost its hold and men like Kalyan are needed to dispel that image. Despising conventional morality and idealism, Kalyan advocates the methods of "catching up fast" through collective action. After all, whose ego is so sacred that it must flourish at the expense of the community? (p. 63). Faith and compassion are hollow words for Kalyan: "As long as there were starving, ignorant men, there could be no relationship between a government and the governed, except in terms of rapid accomplishment" (p. 13). Kalyan Sinha's rejection of Kailas Vrind is, therefore, much more than personal. It symbolizes the divergence of two perceptions of life, politics and values.

Nayantara Sahgal, however, conceives of the possibilities of reconciliation of Gandhian ideals and new pragmatism (as perceived in the personality of Prime Minister Nehru), among the aware segments of the younger generation represented in the novel by Rakesh (a young IFS officer, who is also the central consciousness of the novel) and Rashmi (the 'separated' daughter of Kailas Vrind). The novelist's adoration for Nehru (through various characters and on a variety of issues such as the language controversy, the Peace Institute and Foreign Policy), is undisguised. For instance, the Prime Minister is commended for having "taken upon himself a challenge unique in history: that of raising a people to modern times with their own consent".[39]

This Times of Morning is a graphic account of the process of political change as also of the initial travails of nation-building in an emerging democracy. The novel not only exposes the paradoxes of operational politics in India, but also raises several pertinent and basic questions related with the nature of the polity, such as the issue of committed or neutral bureaucracy, the problem of public ethics and its erosion, and, the emerging styles of leadership. As a conscious political novelist, Nayantara Sahgal fully supports Nehruvian style of political leadership and, as if anticipating the emergency of 1975, concludes: "No one will deny that efficiency is what this country needs, but we are afraid and shall continue to be afraid, of efficiency when it is accompanied, as it so often is, by ruthlessness". (p. 218).

Nayantara Sahgal's concern with erosion of Gandhian ethics and Nehruvian values and the suspicion of the emerging leadership continues in her subsequent novels as well. *The Day in Shadow*, as the title itself suggests, highlights, though does not adequately probe, the dismal aberrations of the Indian system, social hypocrisy, cultural shallowness and political corruption.[40] The two principal characters in the novel, Som Raman and Sumer Singh, the former obsessed by material ambitions and the latter by lust for power, are drawn to typify the decaying socio-political morality in India. Simrit, the divorced wife of Som and protagonist in the novel, brings out a suggestive comparison of Som and Sumer Singh: " . . . though they might be on opposite sides of the fences politically, big business and radical politician; there is no human difference between them". (p. 222).

The supposed climax of political crisis occurs with the official acceptance in parliament of (Sumer Singh's proposal) the Russian offer to explore oil in the region of Jammu and Kashmir (a sensitive and strategic region) in contravention of the senior cabinet minister's (Sardar Sahib) advice to accept a neutral country's offer.[41] Through Sumer Singh—who initiates the proposal, not so much motivated by sincere commitment to socialism or even to nationalism, as by his calculations to bag the chance of promotion to foreign ministry from ministry of petroleum—the novelist's treatment of left-orientation in Indias domestic and foreign policy stands misrepresented. The novel exhibits undue apprehension of violation of the principles of non-alignment through Indo-Soviet collaboration. As vindicated during subsequent decades, Indo-Soviet friendship and collaboration, far from hampering the pursuit of goals of non-alignment, has been largely conducive to organization of non-alignment as a strategy of change in international arena to combat the prevalent structures of dominance.[42] Totally oblivious of the changing international situation, the novel isolates a specific dimension of foreign policy and misrepresents a vital issue by over-simplification and sentimentalism.[43] True, India did pass through critical years of indecision and uncertainty after Nehru's demise; the socialist professions and inclinations in India's domestic or foreign policy, however, did not aggra vate the crisis, as the novel assumes.

In *A Situation in New Delhi*,[44] Nayantara Sahgal moves beyond the Indian liberal's brooding mood over the vanishing Gandhian values from public life and comprehends the complexities of the political process in view of the upcoming political repression, preceding the emergency. In exploring the sources of the creeping politico-cultural conformism and loyalism, the novelist examines the pertinent attitudinal variables of guilt and responsibility, ideology and action, commitment and neutrality, in private and public life. By choosing articulate personalities, academicians, educated politicians and aware businessmen, as the principal characters in the novel and making them 'act' with or besides their accepted political positions, Sahgal transcends the liberal dilemma (of ideology *versus* action) in an almost Sartrian manner. That, probably, makes it her best political novel.

A Situation in New Delhi is a triangular diagnosis and analysis of the systemic crisis which India faced in the late sixties and the early seventies. The novel begins in a nostalgic tone with the news of sudden death of the Prime Minister, Shivraj (meant to be identified with Nehru) symbolizing the end of an era, a way of life, a set of norms and a style of politics. The loss is too big to be taken philosophically on either personal or national level, as in the novel typified by Devi (Shivraj's sister and later education minister), Michael Calvert (a British

admirer of Shivraj, family friend and later biographer), and
Usman Ali (Shivraj's friend and later Vice-chancellor of Delhi
University). Shivraj is portrayed as the beacon light of the
generation that upheld freedom as a sacred word amounting
almost to an oath. Michael Calvert admired Shivraj as an
"Asian who believed there was a middle road between capitalism and communism" (p. 5), conveying "whole visions and
possibilities and get people to work for them" (p. 8). Devi
identified her brother with "the sense of values" he had
"planted like roses with his two hands". It was their fragrance,
something as ephemeral as that, that had bound the country
together in a unity, not any hide-bound principle or rule from a
book" (p. 42). Usman praised Shivraj for his leadership
qualities—his "gift of putting things in perspective".

How did Nehruism end with Nehru? Probably like
Gandhism, Usman thought it was not Shivraj's enemies who
were undoing what he had done. It were "his friends, his
following, those who had written paeans of praise to him"
(p. 28) Devi argued that "Shivraj's successors, playing at
revolution, have set the clock back dangerously". (p. 16)
Michael found it hard to accept the general 'drift' of policy in
the direction of more censorship, intolerance and uniformity.
He felt, "When this kind of thing begins to happen, interpretative writing disappears". (p. 108) Nayantara Sahgal's,
writing, however, tends to become nostalgic, rather than interpretative with reference to Nehru: "But we are nostalgic for
kings, or charismatic leaders, or some shining example that
stands out from the millions, republic though we might be.
Five thousand years of memories and attachments don't vanish
at the sound of three syllables." (p. 22)

There is, on the other hand, the younger, post-freedom
generation in India, born free, wishing for change, yet every-
where in chains, as Rousseau would say. The novel portrays
this generation's perceptions through several specific instances:
the seeming contentment in affluence of Pinky; brutal rape of a
young girl, Madhu, on the University campus; and, the creed
of violence practised by Rishad, the nineteen-year-old son of
the education minister, Devi. Whereas descriptions of lavish,
extravagent parties at the Puris (Pinky's parents) reflect the
world of inert affluence, portrayal of Madhu's plight exposes

the utter defencelessness of women in India. Rishad's addiction to violence raises the question of legitimacy of non-violent incremental change in the changed context. Rishad's contention is that others also in their time have fought against wrong; however, "if that had been the right kind of struggle (freedom movement) . . . why were there still so many wrongs"? (p. 125) For Rishad, socio-economic freedom is as important as political freedom :

> "The huge population, described as casteless (the untouchables) 'under-privileged', the weaker section of society, hadn't yet known they were human beings. The law, of course, said they were, and all their rights were on the statute book. But they couldn't read and those in authority had not taken the trouble to see that the laws were observed, and if they did, justice was slow and layers of sluggish procedure clogged each step of it. The outskirts of Delhi or the fringe of society or the edge of history, it was all the same thing" (pp. 97-98)

Was it time for upheaval again? The novelist raises the uneasy question. The signs were rather ominous, confirmed by the growing discontent among the educated, turmoil and disorder in the universities, and spread of the cult of violence in the countryside. Politics of alienation and despair was overtaking purposive protest. The murkiness of the socio-political situation seemed to have infected large segments of the population, especially the youth. It was a reprehensible situation for Gandhi's India, as Sahgal perceived.

The sense of impending doom continues to mount till the end, when public and private issues completely merge into each other: Madhu, the victim of rape on the campus, commits self-immolation; Usman Ali resigns from Vice-Chancellorship and actively joins the fray; Michael Calvert gets back his unfinished biography of the late prime minister, taken away by the authorities for scrutiny; Rishad gets killed in a bomb-explosion in a cinema-hall; and Devi resigns from education ministership. The novel, thus, conveys the gravity of the national crisis, urging intellectuals to act before it is too late. The mounting nihilism is counter-balanced by the reassuring, closing remark in the novel by Michael Calvert: "Perhaps we've been in too much of a hurry to say he (Shivraj/Nehru) is dead" (p. 165)

Transcending despair, the novelist proposes three possible alternative courses to combat contemporary crisis. In the first place, Usman Ali visualizes the past: ". . . another form of government, one that didn't build up and up into a formidable state apparatus. His would build down with maximum power to the small community. How else, in India, would exhausted resources; human and natural, ever recover their strength?" (pp. 83-84). Secondly, the young revolutionaries, represented by Naren and Rishad in the novel, imagined to build a new world by razing to the ground the old one. The way to do it was through systematic creation of panic, chaos and ruin; and out of ruin, open revolt and power: "This cult of violence had to be clean, cold and disciplined . . . . violence of the sane, with a passion for justice. . . Only then could the new social order arise . . . Utopia for the poor and the downtrodden. An Indian utopia" (p. 58). Disagreeing with both, Devi represents the third view, the liberal, reform-oriented vision of political change. "What Rishad and Michael had called 'the Left-Wing phenomenon' understood so clearly a fuzzy emotional egalitarianism backed by force, or threat of force, but had no understanding of the bigger slower human process of a struggle that learns through its own experience". (p. 90). Devi's disdain for violence, including revolutionary violence, is undisguised.

Sahgal presents a double critique of the Naxalite creed to emphasize her point. At one level, she questions the psychology of destruction. For instance, a young college girl, Suvarnpriya Jaipal, by helping Rishad raid her own house, demonstrates that revolution begins with oneself. It is not a lesson given to others as the young Naxalities so often assume. One may disagree with this sort of portrayal, yet it has a definite authenticity. Usman Ali has a relatively considered view: "The state owns the big guns. Any confrontation with it, if it's to succeed must be non-violent. There never was another way. Besides. . . it's the only way most people in this country understand and will give their allegiance to." (p. 116). The novel, thus, projects militant movements as antithetical to the basic value premises of India's political culture.

Although there is a characteristic liberal predilection in Nayantara Sahgal to avoid 'confrontation' as far as possible, she serves an exhortation for both dejected liberals and disillusioned radicals in India by urging them to protest and defy authority.[45] The intensity of mixed perceptions of pathos, concern and non-compliance, available in the novel, calls for "something stronger than the neutral word, 'situation',[46] used in the title of the book. The situation interwoven with experience, ultimately presents an artistic integration of "freedom, justice and aesthetics" having no frontiers.[47]

It is in Salman Rushdie's *Midnight's Children* that the Indo-Anglian novel achieves an architectonic articulation of Indian politics, transcending both conventional aesthetic idiom and political perceptions. As a cultural quest for political relevance and *vice-versa*, the novel is a valuable study in contradictions of the hegemonic process in India. In terms of experimentation in form, *Midnight's Children* is comparable to Raja Rao's *The Serpent And The Rope*, a novel that had revolutionized Indo-Anglian writing two decades back.[48]

Midnight's Children, demonstrating several layers of meaning, could be interpreted in a variety of ways; as a fantasy, imagining the improbable; as a parable indulging in verisimilitude of incidents; as history revealing shades of overt and covert national and sub-continental events, and, also as psycho-cultural interpretation of contemporary political ethos. India's "tryst with destiny," both at individual and national level is, thus, portrayed as part fiction, part fact, part fantasy and part politics. The language of politics is not simple, nor is political reality without complexities. Rushdie presents, with some justification, Indian politics as an elusive reality, speaking in a variety of languages, with differing accents. The variety portrayed is as rich as India herself and perhaps as diffuse. The myths of the land are deliberately and intellectually interpolated into contemporary political world, in a manner that both politics and history begin to acquire a 'flavour' of illusion, magic, nightmare and hallucination.[49] The ultimate output is what he calls "the chutnification of history",[50] a flavoured potpourri of events and their participants.

The individual's relationship with history is inevitable and not a matter of choice. Rushdie laces this 'inevitability' with blessings and curses, satire and anger, overpitched melodrama and undue pessimism, resulting in a "counter-pointed harmony".[51] The novel explores various dimensions of the inevitable linkage and interaction of the individual and history through the organic approach.[52] Rushdie proceeds with an identification of the individual and the state, as Raja Rao does, with regard to individual and society. Raja Rao's quest results in fathoming the vedantic philosophy of cosmic harmony. And, Rushdie reaches a Marxist conclusion without a Marxist methodology that history shapes individuals and that historical transformation is unthinkable without collective consciousness and action.

The metaphor of the individual as State begins in the opening paragraph itself: "I was born in the city of Bombay. . . on August 15th, 1947. . . . On the stroke of midnight. . . mysteriously hand-cuffed to history, my destinies indissolubly chained to those of my country. For the next three decades, there was to be no escape" (p. 9). The novel portrays in some detail the ups and downs, development and decay, in the lives of Saleem Sinai and India, the twin-protagonists of the novel during 1947-1977. Besides a perspectival comprehension of three decades of post-independence India, the novel also incorporates events and issues from pre-independence period (beginning with 1915), that affect the lives of grandparents and parents of Saleem Sinai, consequent upon the inception of the Gandhian movement. For instance, the Heidelberg-returned physician, grandfather of Saleem, Aadam Aziz is hailed for his progressive consciousness and for his resolution in 1915, of never bowing before god or man, once he bumps his nose, while performing *namaz*. Similar resoluteness enters Indian nationalism with the emergence of Gandhi. The evolution of progressive conciousness, subsequently gets hampered by the serious drawback of a "perforated sheet", also symbolizing a fragmented attitude and endeavour both at individual and national levels. And, above all, both individual and national lives are inhibited by the constant presence of a "hole" symbolizing an emptiness, a vaccum, a crisis of identity. Fulfilment is a hazardous process. The course of Indian history takes decisive turn when a soldier (Lord Mountbatton) arrives with a "knife that could cut subcontinents in three" (p. 65) Saleem (and the new generation in India) thus, is born to a 'wild profusion' and confusion of inheritance; "In fact, all over the new India, the dream we all shared, children were being born who were only partially the offspring of their parents—the children of midnight were also the children *of the time*: fathered, you understand, by history" (p. 118)

All of the 10001 children born in the first hour of India's independence at midnight, 15 August 1947, are endowed with special gifts and magical powers. The two babies born in the same Bombay nursing home on the stroke of midnight, are exchanged by a maid-servant, giving the poor baby (Saleem) a life of privilege and condemning the rich-born (Shiva) to poverty—a sort of "her own private revolutionary act" (p. 117). Saleem Sainai's birth gets celebrated through newspapers. Jawaharlal Nehru congratulates him on the happy accident of his moment of birth. At the age of nine, Saleem bumps his head while hiding in his mother's washing chest and discovers his gift for telepathy. Through his telepathic powers, Saleem can see through walls, enter other people's lives and plumb all secrets. He also discovers the miraculous gift of other midnight-children (pp. 196-200). For instance, one of these children, who could travel through time, predicts long before 1977, that India would also be governed by a urine-drinking leader. With a view to utilizing the resources of these gifts, Saleem, through his powers, calls a conference of the midnight's children.[53] The gifted children discuss the notions of purpose and meaning of their existence in conceptual terms such as collectivism, individualism, filial duty, capitalism, altruism, scientific endeavour, women's rights and problems of untouchables aspiring for and fantasizing power.

Corresponding to the actual reality in India, the gifts and resources of the midnight's children, however, are never pooled partly because of Saleem's apprehensions and guilt (concerning Shiva, whom he knows to be the rightful heir of all the privileges), and partly owing to protracted dissensions leading to diverse, often conflicting, manifestation of interests and attitudes within the group.[54] Rushdie diagnoses it as the curse of inheritance, "poison of the grown ups" (p. 256). When the midnight's children do finally meet, during the emergency, the political world has already undergone a metamorphosis, compared to the eve of independence. Meanwhile, Saleem has been to Pakistan, witnessing the military *coup d'etat* in 1958 and participating (as his participation or its claim in language riots and the 1957 elections in India) in the 1965 and the 1971 Indo-Pak wars, also losing and regaining memory.

Saleem's return to India coincides with the supposed political rebirth of Indira Gandhi (p. 385). To his dismay, he finds the country under the "twin spells of power and astrology" (p. 392), with "gangs of Sanjayas all over India", (p. 395)[55] and he himself like million others, finally consigned to the peripheries of history" (p. 395). In his private life, Saleem finds himself a destitute, forced to the slums, having been turned out from the house of his uncle, Mustafa Aziz, a senior officer in Indian Administrative Service. Toppled from the privileged position and forced to the lowest level of humanity, Saleem begins to see the relevance of socialism for a poor country like India, a notion dear to his heart since childhood. In an interesting description, he analyses the country's 'black', corrupt economy, which had grown as large as the official 'white' variety "as an analogue of a Prime Ministerial hair style". (p. 400). Along with economic corruption, Saleem also discovers political and moral corruption, for instance, in "poll-fixing" in Kashmir. It is shameful to see cabinent ministers acting as ministers for bribery, mocking Indian democracy. Saleem is disenchanted with his powers to shape or influence the course of events in his country, painfully realizing his powerlessness, in addition to rootlessness.

There was, however, protest. The nuclear implosion of May 18, 1974, a proud achievement of the nation, also could not contain growing protest. The JP movement of Bihar soon spread to other parts of the country. Meanwhile, the Prime Minister, Indira Gandhi was indicted for malpractice during the election campaign of 1971 by the Allahabad High Court. As forces of change, the midnight's children had little role to play. On 25 June 1975, apprehension about the emergency were confirmed through "suspension of civil rights, censorship of the press, armoured units on special-alert and arrest of subversive elements". True, "something was ending, something was being born" (p. 419). Anticipating his impending doom,

Saleem wondered whether Indira Gandhi was competing with him for a place of centrality in Indian political history: "was my life-long belief in the equation between the State and myself transmuted in 'the Madam's' mind into that in-those-days-famous phrase; *India is Indira and Indira is India?*" (p. 420). Saleem investigated that the emergency had a white part, public, visible, and documented, and a black part, which was secret, macabre and untold—again analogous to the prime minister's hairstyle (p. 421). It smelt of "the sharp aroma of despotism" (p. 424), sterilization and hasty city-beautification programmes, lopsided bureaucratization and total centralization of power.

Some of the excesses of emergency, mentioned in the novel are partly verifiable, yet many of them are exaggerated and figments of imagination of Saleem Sinai and Salman Rushdie. They are sometimes crass enlargements of contrived negatives, gleefully distributed by the Western press. Aspects of the personal life of Mrs. Gandhi (for instance, constantly referring to her as the widow) are crude and in bad taste. In the midst of his misplaced exaggerations, the real thrust to what could have been a powerful critique of Indian politics has been lost. Rushdie's blinkered perspective could lead only to a rather hasty conclusion that the midnight's children are sperectomized, that is, drained out of hope. True, the children of midnight (only a handful of them and not all, as Rushdie reports), representing the vast multitude of India, might have suffered humiliation through forced sterilization and other means of subversion. Birth of another generation of children, nevertheless, should symbolize optimism.

Rushdie does hint at the possibilities of regeneration, for instance, through the birth of a son to his wife; ". . . he, emergency-born, will be, is already more cautious, biding his time, but when he acts, he will be impossible to resist." (p. 425). The novelist also stresses the imperative of responsible citizenship in a democracy: ". . . do we not get the leaders we deserve?" (p. 435). He is, however, not willing to accept the new Janata government (1977-1980) as representing a new dawn. On the other hand, he interprets the Janata victory as an instance of the incapable judgment exhibited by the Indian multitude. Yet he is hopeful of "a second generation of magical children who would grow up far tougher than the first, not looking for their fate in prophecy or the stars, but forging it in the implacable furnaces of their wills." (p. 447). That will be the fulfilment of the democratic socialist childhood dream of Saleem Sinai and Salman Rushdie: a "sort of loose federation of equals, all points of view given free expression". (p. 220). The novel in this respect attempts, however partly, to transcend the democratic myth of citizen competence but remains vague in its alternative vision.

Although, as Rushdie claims, despite being an expatriate, his sensibility is rooted in India;[56] an essential western tendency to present India as either exotic or antiquated is visible at several places in the novel. Contemporary India is more than myth and history, theatre and tragi-comedy.[57] In addition to a hoary tradition, India is also a modern nation-state grappling with challenges and dilemmas of nation-building as a newly emergent sovereign state, trying to sustain and consolidate liberty and justice. The limits of Rushdie's interpretation are, therefore, the limits of the organic approach he employs to explore the dialectics of Indian history. The twin extremes of the metaphor, of the individual as state and then the 'rootlessness-powerlessness' of citizens in modern democracies, are meaningful devices to begin with, but the bleakness of vision that enters the narrative by the time the third part of the book begins makes them only a little better than a fragile psychological conceptualization. Rushdie's bleakness of vision is comparable to V.S. Naipaul's in many ways.[58]

It is also interesting to compare the antipodal assessments of emergency in India by Rushdie and Naipaul, despite some similarity of perspective. Whereas for Rushdie, emergency marked an end to an epoch of Indian history extinguishing freedom for ever; for Naipaul "the very fierceness of the Emergency answered the public mood, assuaged old frustration". The much talked about horrors were nothing more than the opposition's figment of imagination.[59]

Midnight's Children thus, portrays Indian politics as dramatically elusive and India's tryst with destiny as perennial. However, Rushdie as an indologist, belonging and yet not belonging to India, indulges in a disproportional mix of flavours of fantasy and facts and too often elevates the trifle to the climax. As a result, he quite often fails to perceive the central enjoinment of India's cultural creed: 'the art of self-control';

whereby Rushdie both transcends and eludes Indian culture
and politics, an advantage and disadvantage of living on the
frontiers of more than one culture and one nation. It is also
interesting to note how Rushdie has woven certain aspects of
Western aesthetic philosophy (such as Albert Casmus' conception of the 'absurd', Sartre's idea of freedom as 'choice' and
'existential consciousness' and J.S. Mill's thesis of success as
happiness) into his narrative.

In fact, with Salman Rushdie's *Midnight's Children*, the
Indo-Anglian political novel comes a full circle, a culmination
of "a national longing for form" (p. 300), begun by Mulk Raj
Anand, with politics as the staple of protest novel, way back in
the nineteen thirties.[60] Personifying politics as a vibrant continuity, *Midnight's Children* has come as a refreshing interpretation
of the changing politico-cultural ethos of India.

III

The Emerging Perspective

As the preceding analysis shows, the Indo-Anglian novel,
broadly speaking, has not shied away from contemporary political events, problems and paradoxes of interaction of liberty
and authority. In its attempts, however, to interpret and explain
the changing dimensions of hegemonic process, the Indo-Anglian
novel has rarely moved beyond political ideas already in circu-
lation. The resultant complacency seems to 'reassure' rather
than 'disturb' faith in the existing democratic system in India.
Judged from a revolutionary angle, Indo-Anglian political
novel is not adequately ambitious. However, it is valuable as a
critique of specific aspects of operationalization of the political
structure.

The new political structure, in essence, has been identified
and evaluated by the Indo-Anglian novelist with some core
democratic values: freedom, equality and justice (interpreted as
'liberal' by Sahgal and as 'socialist' by Anand). Thus there is
marked resentment at the constant erosion of Gandhian ideals
of public morality and Nehru's vision of political responsibility.
The major novels of Nayantara Sahgal, A.G. Sheorey and
Salman Rushdie, bring out this concern, during various phases

of post-independence politics. Whereas Sheorey is emphatic about the ideals of Gandhian legacy with special reference to freedom of press in a democracy, Nayantara Sahgal's exposition revolves aroud manifestations of Nehruvian perspectives which for her also represent the best aspects of Gandhian politics. In her later novels, Sahgal becomes almost nostalgic about the Nehru-era and is acutely critical of post-Nehru leadership for bypassing both Gandhian and Nehruvian legacy. In fact, she does not highlight the fundamental differences between the two. More than Sahgal Sheorey, seems to be deeply committed to Gandhian principles and practices. Both, however, are suspicious of change of any deviant variety, unlike Anand and Rushdie.

In tracing the sources of current political crisis, Sahgal displays keen awareness and undertakes an indepth analysis of the nuances of operationalization of democratic political structure in India. In *A Situation in New Delhi*, Sahgal diagnoses the erosion of Nehruvian politics of consensus ever since 1969, when the Congress was split. She considers consensus to be the essence of democratic ethos, where discourse is carried out in a civilized manner, without doubting mutual trust and compliance of ground rules. Sahgal is dissatisfied at the unhappy turn of events and the emerging political orientations after Nehru's departure, especially because there has come about a latent, if not manifest, qualitative change in commitments and ideals.

Such predilections of novelists like Nayantara Sahgal (and at times Rushdie) betray an exaggerated identification of a republican state with an individual leader. True, in Indian democracy, the legacy of 'charisma' has been carried over from the days of the freedom struggle to post-independence ethos with all its positive and negative dimensions. Charisma, of Gandhi, Nehru and, later, of Indira Gandhi, has generally been accepted as one of the crucial variables of stability of Indian democracy. Nevertheless, the novelists are on sticky ground as they seem to be justifying inevitability of personality cult, instead of adequately exploring the historical forces that have shaped and transformed the political milieu since independence.

Nayantara Sahgal's *A Situation in New Delhi* and Salman Rushdie's *Midnight's Children* specifically criticize Indira Gandhi for her authoritarian political style, intolerance of dissent and erosion of democratic norms, preceding and during the emergency. Conceding all these lapses, it would, however, be uncharitable to doubt Indira Gandhi's concern for nation-building in India. Sahgal and Rushdie are justified in their indictment of popular leaders indulging in suppression of freedom, fundamental rights, press and ideas. However, following the emergency, the otherwise-illiterate electorate of India, demonstrated a remarkable degree of "political literacy" and capacity for 'political judgement' (which Salman Rushdie doubts) and voted Indira Gandhi and the Congress out of power.[61]

This kind of analysis would suggest that politics in India has been both less and more than the leader-and-prime minister paradigm. There have always been manifold forces at work. The Janata experiment of the post-emergency phase (as Rushdie also anticipated) proved a fragile alternative. And, with her 'comeback' to power in 1980, Indira Gandhi had once again become the centre of political debate in the country as in 1969 and in 1975. Sahgal and Rushdie are, however, partly justified, for given the political structure in India and the pronounced effectiveness of the prime minister's role, it was expected of her and those who ruled in her name, that public morality, non-partisan perspective on national issues and procedural fidelity were upheld. The novelists, however, need not identify political activity with the personalities that practise it, as the game of power played by these personalities is not always the be-all and end-all of political life.

This is not to dismiss the Indo-Anglian novelists' concern for the contemporary state of affairs in India, as unjustified. On the contrary, this 'concern' needs to be projected as a powerful protest. The imperative of creative intervention assumes urgency in times of crisis. Comparable to critical periods in pre-independence history, serious fissures are currently showing up in India's politico-cultural system. Assam and the adjoining north-eastern areas and Punjab are two such souring instances. They are severe tests not only for political leadership but also for the democratic structure.

It seems that the Indian political process has come to such a sorry pass that concerted and purposive protest and even a modicum of adventure are lacking, sometimes, entirely. Perhaps that explains the fact that even the 'fictional' adventurist Saleem Sinai in Salman Rushdie's novel feels isolated and exasperated, pitted against pervasive conformism and apathy in the Indian context. That is a trend, prefacing imminence of alienation adversely affecting and vitiating the political structure. If that is assumed to be symptomatic of the festering systemic malady, there is adequate reason, and also comprehensive challenge, for the creative novelist to identify and evaluate the issues, problems and challenges. To say that India is a complex and baffling amalgam serves little purpose.

It is conceded that being in very close proximity with the events and issues, the requirements of objectivity may not measure up to expectations. However, reasonable success of the Indo-Anglian novel in exposing and demolishing illusions of grandeur and glamour surrounding the edifice of the democratic structure in India, may further result in an aesthetic identification of the beacon for the aspired political future.

References

1. See for instance C. Paul Verghese, "The Problem of the Indian Novelist in English", *The Banasthali Patrika* 12, (Jan. 1969), 87. For a powerful counter-argument see, Bhabani Bhattacharya, "Literature and Social Reality", *The Aryan Path*, (9 Sept. 1955), 392-396.
2. Giovanny Sartori, "Political Development and Political Engineering" in J.D. Montgomery and A.O. Hirschman (eds) *Public Policy*, Vol. 17, (Cambridge, Mass, Harvard University Press, 1968), p. 261.
3. Jawaharlal Nehru—*Independence and After* (Delhi, Publications Division, Govt. of India, 1949), pp. 3-4.
4. Clifford Geertz (ed), *Old Societies and New States: The Quest For Modernity in Asia and Africa* (New Delhi, Amerind, 1971), p. 119.
5. Frantz Fanon, *The Wretched of the Earth* (Trans: C. Farrington) (New York, Grove Press, Inc., 1963), p. 35.
6. See for a broader perspective of Third-world countries, undergoing similar experiences, David E. Apter, *Political Change: Collected Essays*, (London, Frank Cass, 1973), pp. 181-182.
7. For a contrary interpretation see M. Seliger, *Ideology and Politics* (New York, The Free Press, 1976), pp. 275-76.
8. V.P. Menon, *The Transfer of Power in India*, (Calcutta, Orient Longmans, 1957), p. 422.

9. Crawford Young, *The Politics of Cultural Pluralism*, (Wisconsin, University of Wisconsin Press, 1976), p. 274.

10. See Rajni Kothari, "The Congress System in India", *Asian Survey*, VII, 12 (Dec. 1962), 1161-63.

11. Rajani Palmedutt, *India Today*, (Calcutta, Manisha, 1970), pp. 631-640.

12. See Uma Vasudev, *Indira Gandhi—Revolution in Restraint*, (New Delhi, Vikas, 1974).

13. Rajani Kothari, *Democratic Polity a nd Social Change in India*, (New Delhi, Allied, 1976), p. 19.

14. Rajani Kothari has proposed a valuable comprehensive scheme of institutional innovation, *n*. 13, pp. 72-97.

15. The idea was considered by Indira Gandhi and the Congress in 1969 after the split. It was envisaged that at least one trained cadre would be stationed in each of India's three hundred districts, but by 1972 only four cadre-building camps had been organized.
    See K.D. Malviya, "The Congress Must be a Cadre-Based Party", *Socialist India*, 5 (June 3, 1972), 16.

16. See Kuldeep Nayar, *India After Nehru*, (Delhi, Vikas, 1975), p. 100.

17. See Iqbal Narain, *Twilight or Dawn: Political Change in India* (Agra, Shiva Lal Agarwala and Co., 1972), pp. 215-228.

18. Saros Cowasjee, "Introduction", *Private Life of an Indian Prince* (1953), (Delhi, Hind Pocket Books, 1970), p. 9.

19. V.P. Menon, *n*. 8, pp. 46-70.

20. Kamala Markandaya's *The Golden Honeycomb* sensitively recreates this historical theme.

21. Besides politico-historic fiction on princely India, Malgonkar has also written historical documents: *Puars of Dewas Senior* (Delhi, Orient Longmans, 1963), and *The Chatrapatis of Kolhapur* (Bombay, Popular Prakashan, 1970).

22. See *The Times Literary Supplement*, (21 June, 1963), 457.

23. V.P. Menon, *The Story of The Integration of The Indian States* (Bombay, Orient Longmans, 1956), p. 193.

24. *The Princes* (1963) (New Delhi, Orient Paperbacks, 1970), p. 244.

25. See the highly informative, although at places exaggerated, story of the appalling state of administration in the princely states, Dewan Jarmany Dass, *Maharaja*, (New Delhi, Allied, 1969); Also K.L. Gauba, *His Highness* (Lahore, Lion Press, 1930).

26. G.S. Amur, *Manohar Malgonkar* (New Delhi, Arnold-Heinemann, 1973), p. 84.

27. V.S. Naipaul, *An Area of Darkness* (London, Andre Deutsch, 1964), p. 62.

28. G.S. Amur, *n*. 26, p. 96.

29. James Y. Dayananda, "Manohar Malgonkar on his Novel *The Princes*: An Interview", *Journal of Commonwealth Literature*, 9, 3, (April 1975), 26.

30. P.S. Bawa, *Memories of the Raj* (Delhi, Hind Pocket Books, 1981), p. 11.

31. See K.R. Bombwall, *The Foundations of Indian Federalism* (Bombay, Asia, 1967), pp. 257-276, and Kousar J. Azam, *Political Aspects of National Integration* (Meerut; Meenakshi, 1981), pp. 91-110.

32. See Iqbal Narain, "Cultural Pluralism, National Integration and Democracy in India", *Asian Survey* XVI, 10 (Oct., 1976), 903-919 and M.N. Srinivas, "Is the Sun Setting?" *Seminar*, (Feb. 1967), 12-16.

33. *Storm in Chandigarh*, (Delhi, Orient Paperbacks, 1969), p. 13.

34. *n*. 33.

35. See Marcia P. Liu, "Continuity and Development in the Novels of Nayantara Sahgal", *Journal of Indian Writing in English*, 8, 1-2 (1980), 48.
and T.K. Thomas, "The Hindu Ethos—A Novelist's Perspectives," *Religion and Society*, xx, 4 (Dec. 1973), 56-57.

36. K.R.S. Iyengar, *Indian Writing in English* (Bombay, Asia, 1962), p. 473.
Also see, Ruth Van Horn Zuckerman, Review of *This Time of Morning* and *Storm in Chandigarh*, *Mahfil*, VI, 4 (Winter, 1970), 84-87.

37. Anant Gopal Sheorey, *Dusk Before Dawn—A Novel of Post-Freedom India* (Delhi, Vikas, 1978), p. 157.

38. For instance, there is an interesting and apt report in an evening newspaper, *Way Farer* on "Who is going to Burma?", illustrated by a cartoon and a doggerel:
      "If all the world were western,
      And all its people white,
      The ICS would have such fun,
      And every post be right."
This Time of Morning (1965) (New Delhi, Orient Paperbacks, n. d.), p. 120.

39. Kai Nicholson is partly right in evaluating the novel as "a political assessment of India's capabilities put forward with much beating of the official drum", but absolutely incorrect in identifying Kailas Vrind with Jawaharlal Nehru. See Kai Nicholson, *A Presentation of Social Problems in the Indo-Anglian and Anglo-Indian Novel* (Bombay, Jaico, 1972), pp. 130-167.

40. *The Day in Shadow* (Delhi, Vikas, 1971).

41. See Nayantara's own views on the Novel: "Fiction often foreshadows fact. *The Day in Shadow* had had as an accompanying backdrop to Simrit's divorce settlement. the growing Soviet influence on our sub-continent and a definite Indian tilt in that direction". *A Voice For Freedom* (Delhi, Hind Pocket Books, 1977), p. 20.

42. See A.P. Rana, *The Imperatives of Non-Alignment* (New Delhi, Macmillan, 1976).

43. Irene Gilbert is right in her remark that Nayantara Sahgal "writes from the fringes of Indian Politics", "Review of *The Day in Shadow*" *The Journal of South Asian Literature* XII, (Fall, 1974), 187.

44. *A Situatiou in New Delhi* (London, London Magazine editions, 1977).

45. See Nayantara Sahgal, *n.* 41, pp. 10-25.

46. Marcia P. Liu, "Continuity and Development in the Novels of Nayantara Sahgal", *Journal of Indian Writing in English* 8, 1-2 (1980), 52.

47. Nayantara Sahgal, "Testament of an Indo-Anglian Writer", *Indian and Foreign Review*, X, 4 (Dec. 1972), 17-19.

48. See for instance, Darshan Singh Maini's comment: "Although there are no great earth-shaking ideas either in *Midnight's Children* or in *Shame*, what really makes them so compulsively readable is the stupendous nature of the Dickensian imagination at work, and the Joycean gaiety in the use and abuse of language ... In fact, the portmanteau technique finally leads to the bastardizing of the novel form itself". "The Aeging Lions", *Gentleman*, (July, 1984), 87.

49. Rushdie himself characterizes his realism as "magical realism". Quoted by Tavleen Singh, "Magic, Mystery, Madness", *The Sunday Statesman*, (13 Dec. 1981), 2.

50. Salman Rushdie, *Midnight's Children* (1981) (London, Picador edition, 1982), p. 159.

51. Clark Blaise: "A Novel of India's coming of Age: *Midnight's Children*", *The New York Times Book Review* (19 April, 1981), 19.

52. The organic approach, pursued in varying degrees in the writings of western philosophers such as Plato, Marsilio, Hobbes, Hegel and Spencer and in the Vedantic philosophy in India, has been most effectively used in Indo-Anglian fiction, for artistic purposes, by Raja Rao in *The Serpent and the Rope* (1960). (New Delhi, Orient Paperbacks, 1968).

53. Midnight's Children' can be made to represent many things: "as the last throw of everything antiquated and, retrogressive in our myth-ridden nation, whose defeat was entirely desirable in the context of a modernizing, twentieth century economy; or as the true hope of freedom", *Midnight's Children*, p. 200.

54. This point has been discussed in detail by Uma Parameswaran, "Lest He Returning Chide: Saleem Sinai's Inaction in Salman Rushdie's *Midnight's Children*," *The Literary Criterion*, XVIII, 3 (1983), 57-66.

55. Rushdie has since tendered apologies for such references, following a legal settlement in London. *The Times of India*, 30 July, 1984.

56. See: Salman Rushdie's interview with Rani Dubey in *Debonair* (June 1982), 56.
Also see, Robert Towers, *Review of Midnight's Children*, entitled "On the world Mountain", in which he describes the novel as "profoundly 'Hindu' in its sensibility". *New York Review of Books* (24 Sept., 1981), 28.

57. V.S. Pritchett calls it "Pure Arabian Nights Intrigue", *New Yorker*, 57, 23 (27 July, 1981), 84.

58. Iqbal Masud, writing on Naipaul, goes to the extent of saying: "In fact, for people like Ved Mehta, V.S. Naipaul and Salman Rushdie, the third world is a kind of *tamasha* . . . a thing they can make use of". There is truth in this statement, although its comparative applicability would place Rushdie in a much less biased position than Naipaul for the simple fact that Rushdie was born in India, grew up in Bombay, 'entirely Indian', and left the country at the age of 14, whereas Naipaul grew up totally as a west-Indian. Iqbal Masud, "Naipaul's views on The Third World are biased". *Gentleman* (February, 1984), 50.

59. V.S. Naipaul, *India: A Wounded Civilization* (Harmondsworth, Penguin Books, 1979), pp. 136-150.
For a scholarly and objective analysis, see Mary C. Carras, *Indira Gandhi: in the Crucible of Leadership* (Bombay, Jaico, 1980), pp. 204-214.

60. To this extent, Clark Blaise's comment is justified: *"Midnight's Children* sounds like a continent finding its voice", *n.* 51, 18.
Also see, Valentine Cunningham's characterization of *Midnight's Children* as an ambitious novel, "nosing out the Indian reality" and "the real world of the sub-continent". *Times Literary Supplement* (15 May, 1981), 535.

61. For a contrary interpretation, see V.R. Mehta's statement: "The election was not so much an affirmation of the liberal democratic framework, as a negation of arbitrary rule . . . flouting all known canons of justice as commonly understood". *Ideology, Modernization and Politics in India* (New Delhi, Manohar, 1983), p. 48.

5

The Socio-Economic Infrastructure in India: Limits of Political Democracy

The national and social issues are closely intertwined, and the understanding of this interconnection is the key to the understanding of the Indian situation.

—Rajani Palme Dutt

Political fiction is genuinely expressive when it transcends 'representation' of contemporary events and conveys innovative meaning to the intellectual reserves of the genus of *homo sapiens*. Inspired by a sense of 'involvement in life', political fiction has a broad span of politico-aesthetic possibilities, ranging from the historically specific types of consciousness to an integrated sensibility of the era. In his awareness of responsibility to society and art, the political novelist seeks to realize the limits of individual self-awareness and assimilate concrete human interactions into an integrated aesthetic conception. The urge of the progressive artist to reveal the vital content of the problems of everyday life filled with tensions and unmask the essential aspects of the socio-economic reality unacceptable to him, results, on the one hand, in questioning the prevailing absolute notions of social and cultural evolution and, in formulating aesthetic convictions in which bold realism is inseparable from critical imagination, on the other. The quest of political fiction in exploring dimensions of changing hegemonic process in society thus remains essentially anthro-pocentric.

The present chapter examines the politico-literary percep-tions available in Indo-Anglian novel, regarding tension areas in the socio-economic infrastructure vis-a-vis political order in India.

I

Socio-economic Infrastructure: Challenge of Transformation

The movement for India's freedom was not meant to be confined to the political dimension. Pioneer activists such as Ranade, Naoroji, Gokhale, Tilak, Aurobindo, Gandhi and Nehru, among others, were acutely conscious of the corres-ponding imperatives of political aspirations, namely socio-economic justice and opportunity. The challenges flowing from a social system, vitiated by hierarchical and authoritarian predilections, could not be permitted to co-exist with aspira-tions for political freedom. Political exertions, it was con-ceded, could not attain the desired efficacy in a climate that sought to sustain socio-economic ambivalence. It is not surpri-sing, therefore, that the movement for socio-religious reform preceded organized efforts to ensure political autonomy. The priorities of India's national movement clearly indicated that a comprehensive view of problems and issues was taken. The task was neither facile nor without hazards, more so in the context of the prevalent social order that did not give evidence of concerted attempts to thwart perpetration of hierarchy, inequality and injustice. Consequently, socio-economic develop-ment did not keep pace with political evolution.[1]

Independent India inherited an underdeveloped economy, extraordinary cultural (linguistic, religious and ethnic) divisive-ness, social authoritarianism and injustice, rather than a healthy interacting 'melting pot' of differing races and com-munities. The irrational decaying social forms and traditions, suppression of women, imbalances in agricultural and in-dustrial set-up and the dilemmas inherent in an effort to synthesize democracy and socialism in order to combat these ills, would make the picture all the more grim. It was, indeed, the most challenging proposition to innovate a social structure resisting change, to secularize a cultural milieu steeped into religiosity, to seek egalitarianism in an economy thriving on exploitation, and also to build a united, strong and democratic state on the basis of unity in diversity.[2]

True, as Apter said, "it was easier to transfer the concrete structures, such as parliamentary institutions, than the attitudes which went along with the operation of these structures in the West".[3] However, looking back critically, it would appear that only half-way-house structural provisions had been permitted by the British in India, which were at best an exercize in ambiguities. In fact, democracy formed a part of the legacy of pre-independence India, only in terms of what the British 'preached', not what they 'practised'. People at large were, therefore, not expected to grasp fully the dynamics of change following the transfer of power from alien to Indian hands and its implications for socio-economic environment in an ideological sense. Democratic experiment in independent India proved that democracy was not a matter of pre-existing conditions, but a matter of political will to create and maintain proper conditions for its survival.[4]

The political structure was thus conceived as the central instrument, and not merely a super-structural edifice, of socio-economic renovation, by both challenging and changing the complex hegemonic processes of existing social traditions and economic structures. This is not to suggest that traditional structures were totally sterile, stagnant or devoid of potential. The richness, intensity and variety of traditional structures have always been venerated by Indian intellectuals and political leaders ever since the socio-religious reform movements.[5] At the same time, there has also been a parallel stream of renouncing undesirable aspects of the hegemonic process.[6] As long back as the medieval period, the *bhakti* movement revolted not only against the highly intellectualized path (*tapa*) of salvation (*moksha*) but also against rigid social forms, represented by caste distinctions and hierarchy. Caste system, a perverted interpolation of the ancient *chaturvarnya* system (functional division of society, for which the west, from Plato to Marx, has been aspiring) was, however, originally conceived as an institutional mechanism to ensure compassionate interdependence in a pluralistic culture.[7] Over the centuries, the social structure working through caste system became ossified as orthodox, hierarchical and rigid.[8] M.N. Srinivas identifies *Sanskritization* as the earliest form of change in India's social system, later followed by westernization, modernization and politicization.[9] Implicit in the urge to elevation and egalitarianism among castes is the search for justice. With growing westernization, advent of modern technology, ideology and politicization, this urge got collectivized. Sanskritization was not enough, for it did not substantially affect structural deficiencies.[10]

As economic incompatibilities came to be understood as pernicious follow-up of injurious caste discriminations, the need for structural innovations began to be felt keenly. In view of pervasive illiteracy, poverty, low level of awareness, fatalism and misplaced contentment, the strategy of directed, engineered or induced structural change appeared to hold attractive promise. The preamble and part IV of the Constitution (incorporating Directive Principles of State Policy), were designed as indices of the objectives of socio-economic transformation in India. In keeping with the general concern for an egalitarian and a just society, the Directive Principles emphasized the principle of 'progressive discrimination' in favour of economic interests of weaker sections of society, identified as Scheduled Castes and Scheduled Tribes. The crux of the Directive Principles was unambiguous as far as it was stated that the largest share of societal acquisitions should go to the people at large as against confining benefits to a particular segment of beneficiaries, political, social or economic. The Directive Principles were thus conceived as 'fundamental' to socio-economic renovation.[11]

In practice, however, as Raymond Williams states, in another contezt, relations between social, economic and political institutions are very complex. The substance of these relations is a "direct indication of the character of the culture of the given society".[12] The national experience in India confirms this and points to the limits of political democracy in bringing about socio-economic transformation. The mechanics of procedural, that is, electoral democracy, has relegated the imperatives of

justice to a secondary reckoning. Quest for egalitarianism has
not gone beyond an over-enthusiasm to extend reservations for
the scheduled castes and tribes. Even in this limited sphere,
actual dividends have not reached all sections of the backward
castes.[13] Although politicization should be taken as the corners-
tone of collective consciousness, especially among the affected
sections of the society, the growing incidence of caste violence,
in spite of the statutory safeguards, might make politics itself
an alienating process. Populist policies in this regard are likely
to prove an inconsequential exercise.

The anticipated shift "from programmatic ambivalence to a
politics of programmatic commitment" following the Congress
split in 1969,[14] did result in several radical constitutional and
legislative enactments in the subsequent decade.[15] In most
cases, however, these enactments hardly moved beyond theoretical commitments; partly owing to vacillation and irresolution
regarding implementation of reforms and partly owing to
strong resistance put up by powerful vested interests, who could
not be annoyed by the ruling authorities for reasons of political
expediency. The recurring failure of measures of land reforms
or ceiling on urban property proved the extent to which
collusion between economic elite, bureaucracy and political
power contributed to thwarting of progressive ideals.

Later, the experiment of emergency embodying a coercive
strategy of change, was rejected by popular verdict as being
antithetical to democratic ideals. The alternative concept of
"total revolution" visualized by Jaya Prakash Narayan also
proved fragile[16] as confirmed by the Janata phase during
1977-80.[17] As a result, the political ethos in the 1980s, once
again, seems to be in favour of stability and gradual, orderly
change. It is often argued that gradual change is an ideal
strategy in view of the extraordinary cultural pluralism, where
diversity rather than identity of interests is a dominant feature
and where frequent compromises among contending interests
is a pragmatic necessity.[18] Political beliefs, attitudes and
ideologies in such a politico-cultural milieu, often tend to be
flexible, adaptive and ambivalent. The resultant politics of
caution, compromise and reconciliation basically concerned
with electoral objectives, finds itself seriously inhibited in

performing the fundamental task of restructuring the existing socio-economic pattern.

It is to be conceded that the socio-economic history of post-independence India has not been a trek of stagnation, stasis or instability. The nexus between inequality and backwardness, however, remains unbroken, notwithstanding the repeated radical pronouncements of the ruling authorities.[19] Despite impressive record, in cumulative terms, of upward trends in industrial and agricultural output and of expanding horizons of modernization, the democratic-socialist structure has accomplished marginal distributive justice and segmented social development. Whereas the political structure is endowed with special responsibility of socio-economic restructuring, the other extreme of power needs to be tamed and regulated, as Palme Dutt said: "Just as imperialism has produced its mythology to cover-up its real predatory record with the conventional picture of its "civilizing mission", so we need to be on guard against corresponding presuppositions and conventional mythologies in the opposite direction".[20] In fact, the missing link in the process of change in India's transition seems to have been a reorientation of tradition toward change and of change toward progress at the social base. Instead of emphasizing upon the commonly conceived consensual bases of India's culture, an exploration of tension areas in this process of change, might aid in delineating the emerging challenges facing the socio-economic infrastructure. Then alone can these be faced squarely.

II

Major Indo-Anglian Novels: Themes and Issues

It is an historical coincidence that Indian novel in English was acknowledged as 'mature' with the inception of progressive consciousness in Mulk Raj Anand's writings during the 1930s. Quest for qualitative renovation and renewal of social world has been persisting thereafter in strands of Indo-Anglian fiction. The protest novel as developed by Mulk Raj Anand, K.A. Abbas and Bhabani Bhattacharya exhibits faith in the historical creativity of the common man, an irreconcilability to hind-rances in his advancement and a striving to make life better, richer and more purposive. That resulted in the introduction of the suppressed-protestant, the fighter and the innovator in concrete Indian situations, hitherto neglected in the Indo-Anglian fiction. A continuity from pre-independence period is visible, so far as critical unmasking of antagonisms of socio-economic infrastructure and the political regime is concerned, for similar kind of incompatibilities continue to characterize Indian life in one form or the other. However, the Indo-Anglian novel has fallen short of evolving a 'tradition' of social protest novel, working through revolutionary consciousness, with the exception of Mulk Raj Anand and Bhabani Bhattacharya, to whose contributions we now turn.

For more than half a century now, Mulk Raj Anand stands out as a colossus dominating the scene of aesthetic political criticism in Indian fiction in English, in the tradition of Rabindranath Tagore, Sarat Chandra and Bibhuti Bhushan, and Prem Chand (his predecessors in Bengali and Hindi, res-pectively). The first novel of Anand, *Untouchable* (1935), rightly characterized as "a minor classic",[21] heralded both revolution-ary consciousness and the coming of age of the Indo-Anglian novel.

Mulk Raj Anand has prolific contributions to his credit and has enquired into broad range of ideas and issues in his fiction, encompassing the whole process of resurgence in India.[22] To begin with, the autobiographical novels, *Seven Summers*,[23] *Morning Face*[24] and *Confession of a Lover*,[25] and the 'Lal Singh Trilogy' comprising *The Village, Across the Black Waters* and *The Sword and the Sickle*,[26] present an overview of the phase of pervasive crises in pre-independence India. These novels expose the prevailing social orthodoxy, religious obscurantism, and economic plight of the average Indian, compounded through political repression by the British. The 'trilogy' specifically portrays the evolution of rising socio-political consciousness in rural India, with embryonic optimism about salvation in political action.

The autobiographical novels, read with *Apology for Heroism*,[27] (Anand's autobiography of ideas) give significant clues to the evolution of his revolutionary consciousness. These novels reveal how a sensitive and inquisitive child, braving the challenging enviornment, grows into a rebellious youth. The death of his innocent cousin and his uncle shatter the adolescent's faith in omnipotent and benevolent God. Fraternizing with a Muslim household, results in social humiliation of his aunt, who commits suicide. The death of the Muslim girl, he had fallen in love with, widens the void. Thus he acquires an early awareness of socio-religious formalism and its tragic consequences in India. The police assault on him as a child, when caught for breaking the curfew imposed after the Jallianwalla bagh massacre, adds a political dimension to his consciousness. Later, when he comes in contact with freedom fighters, Gandhians as well as terrorists, his conviction is confirmed that individual dignity was incompatible with colonial rule. The autobiographical novels thus identify the formative initiation of Anand as a youth to an aesthetics of protest.

The impact-imprint was further etched in sharper contours during Mulk Raj Anand's stay in Europe in the crucial decades, 1924-1945, as recorded in *Apology for Heroism*. It was the period which witnessed "political, social and human causes as genuine impulses for the novel and poetry".[28] Anand experienced the revealing confrontation of 'old fates', god and evil in man and nature, with 'new fates', economics and politics, pervasively affecting the common man.[29] He began a serious process of introspection concerning validity of idealism and organized religion, including Hinduism, and realized the futility of rituals, social hierarchy, mysticism and obscurantism. The 1926 general strike in England came to him as an evidence of inadequacy of democracy as an answer to social inequality. The undemocratic British rule in India further exposed the deliberate imposition of subhumanity on the people.

About this time, Anand was also drawn to Marxism, not as an intellectual doctrine, but more as a convincingly humane, rational, scientific and historically reliable explanation of human suffering. He imbibed the call for transformation. His difficulty, like that of Jean Paul Sartre, was where to begin from. And the beginning he devised for himself was "to study the causes of one's frustration, the reasons of one's failure to get to grips with realities", compounded by the nation's "failure to know, failure to dream and failure to get hold of one's

destiny".[30] It was an experience of shame and humiliation
through denial of fundamentals of human dignity. Like
Jawaharlal Nehru, Anand envisioned for India a new kind of
social democracy, other than capitalist democracy, because the
latter meant no more than "a fraudulent use of the word democracy . . . to cover all the defaults of reaction".[31] Political
independence was visualised by Anand as an immediate,
not an ultimate goal. It was for him, as Gandhi had repeatedly
asserted, a means to ensure "freedom from ignorance, freedom
from caste, freedom from slavery to custom".[32] His vision of 'a
far reaching social revolution' came very close to Nehru's
call for 'Destination man' as the goal of the advance of
democracy in India.[33]

The overview of the socio-political upheaval in pre-independence India, as outlined in the Lal Singh trilogy and the
autobiographical novels, gets supplemented by the dated political novels dealing with specific political events in post-independence India mentioned earlier (such as integration of
princely states in the Indian federation and the incidents of
Indo-Pak confrontation in Kashmir, in novels like *Private Life
of an Indian Prince*[34] and *Death of a Hero*).[35] Anand, however,
attains a genuine breakthrough in novels, where he strikes at
the entrenched socio-economic and political ills and indicates
his faith in innovative democracy as India's only hope. These
novels— *Untouchable* (1935), *Coolie* (1936), *Two Leaves and a
Bud* (1937), *The Big Heart* (1945), *The Old Woman and the Cow*
(1960), *The Road* (1961)—genuinely portray archetypes of revolutionary consciousness,[36] nowhere else available in Indo-
Anglian fiction.

Untouchables, Mulk Raj Anand's first and most popular
novel, is a powerful indictment of Hindu religion and social
hierarchy. It is a rejection of impositions, by the so-called
privileged and 'the pure' on the outcastes in Indian society. It
is a revealing narration of man's cruelty against man and cal-
lous disregard for human dignity. *Untouchable* is a record of
the events of a single day in the life of an eighteen-year-old
sweeper boy, Bakha. As on any other day, the sweeper boy
keeps to his assigned job of sweeping, cleaning lavatories,
market place and the temple courtyard, but as the day comes
to an end, the sweeper boy has undergone "a spiritual crisis of

such breadth that it seems to encompass the whole of India".[37] The sweeper boy, as it turned out, accidentally 'touched' a caste Hindu, which was considered sacrilegious, for in the process the caste Hindu had been polluted. On the other hand, the temple priest's attempt to molest the sweeper boy's sister (Sohini) went unpunished, as usual. Reprimanding the priest was unthinkable. The sordid aspects in the intent and misdemeanour of the 'man of god' were simply ignored. Subsequent events of the day—a hockey match and a wedding were also robbed of their thrill for the sweeper boy by the poison of prejudice and hatred. The rebel in him was pining for retribution and justice which, he knew, had for long been denied to his class.

An evolving awareness enables Bakha to question subhuman degradation and strengthens his resolve to revolt. Personal cleanliness and sportsmanship distinguish him from the general community of sweepers in India as an intelligent and determined person. Anand, however, does not portray him as a pioneer of violent protest. He realizes the futility of such an alternative in view of the organized power of the high castes compounded by the frustrating despair, almost immobilizing the depressed classes. The sweeper boy, therefore, is confined to ideational protest and, in his failure to act, one might discern the fidelity if not the strength of the novel, as a noted critic observes.[38]

True, individual protest, even an act of indiscretion prompted by frustration and anger, might have been of no consequence. Anand, therefore, suggests three possible solutions in the novel. First, there was the option to get converted to the casteless order of Christianity, a bait offered by Colonel Hutchinson, a missionary, and rejected by Bakha because the step would have meant acceptance of the pessimistic notion of man being born in sin and giving credibility to an unscientific notion akin to myth. The second alternative, most appealing in the thirties, was the Gandhian ideal of integrating the untouchables, the Harijans as he called them, with the Hindu social order and thereby seeking to rekindle humane values of the past. Gandhi appealed to the conscience of the people and said that "while we are asking for freedom from the grip of a foreign nation, we have ourselves, for centuries, trampled underfoot millions of human beings without feeling the slightest remorse

for our iniquity" (p. 160). Anand also notes appropriately how
the British rulers tried 'to alienate the untouchables from
Hinduism by giving them a separate legal and political status'
under the Communal Award of Ramsay MacDonald (August
1932). There is also mention of Gandhi's fast unto death
against the Communal Award and the eventual conclusion of
the Poona Pact (September 1932), resulting in joint electorate.
However, Anand is not convinced of the efficacy of Gandhi's
moral approach resting on faith in transmutation of people's
conscience.   The novel, therefore, offers a third alternative
through a young poet, Iqbal Nath Sarshar, who visualizes a
casteless society for India, based on scientific-technological
advancement, as if in anticipation of the critique of Gandhi's
anti-industrial philosophy in *The Sword and the Sickle* and *The
Big Heart*. Through the poet, Anand seems to be suggesting a
preference in *Untouchable* for an organic, not merely mechanical
change.
     One might note in passing that India has come a long way
since 1935 when *Untouchable* was first published, yet it would
be a tall claim to suggest that resistance against change in
social outlook has been entirely eradicated. Untouchability
persists in free India, despite statutory provisions to safeguard
the interests of scheduled castes and tribes. It is a matter of
concern that the process of social integration, time and again,
has been subjected to strain by forces which have vested
interest in caste and communal factionalism.
     Perhaps that explains Anand's returning to the same theme
in his novel, *The Road*, twenty-eight years later. There is agonizing realization of the persisting misery of the so-called lowly
born. The central character, Bhikhu, is more confident and
resolute than Bakha, the sweeper boy in *Untouchable.* Unlike
Bakha, who had resigned himself to await the dawn of the
future, Bhikhu chooses to take the road to Delhi, the national
capital, "where no one knew who he was and where there
would be no caste or out-caste" (p. 111) and, where, according
to an articulate character in the novel, Thakur Singh (the
Sarpanch) "they do nothing else but discuss the constitution
and how the Harijans must be protected against the higher
castes" (p. 103).
     Anand, thus, seems to accept the centrality of politics in

the developmental process of social re-organization in post-independence India. The anticipation emerges out of the restricted potential of self-generated change in the given social milieu, although Anand takes cognizance of the immediacy of synchronization of political initiative and a corresponding consciousness for change. Anand believes that the new political structure has the potential of bringing about changes conducive to secularization, notwithstanding its sustenance with the help of traditional forces. With concerted efforts, the primordial identities in India could ultimately be made to yield a culturally viable national psyche and a legitimate forum for change.

Unlike Anand's emphasis on political initiative, Bhabani Bhattacharya, another veteran critic of the decaying socio-political order in India, explores the potential and the possibility of *sanskritization*[39] as a strategy of inter-caste integration and social change. In turn, however, he ends up by satirizing the whole process. Bhattacharya's *He Who Rides a Tiger* is an exposure of hypocrisy, ritualism and degeneration of Hindu society into an unjust syndrome of caste polarization, inequality and cultural stagnation. More than this, it is a bold protest against the socio-cultural determination of the personality.

He Who Rides a Tiger is the story of a skilled blacksmith, Kalo, initially deep-rooted in his own caste, yet always urging to move ahead, thwarting the fetters imposed by his caste and class. The urge finds an outlet when he christens his daughter as Chandra Lekha, a name unknown in his caste. The urge gets stronger when he succeeds in sending Chandra Lekha to an English Convent school, much against the wishes of the upper classes and his own brotherhood. The girl shows brilliance by winning the Ashoka memorial medal in an all-Bengal essay competition, thus attaining a status otherwise denied to her caste. Meanwhile, the plague of hunger overtakes Bengal, and Kalo, like millions of others, has to leave for Calcutta in search of job. While travelling on the footboard of the train and unable to control his hunger, Kalo steals three bananas. He is penalized with three months' rigorous imprisonment. In Jail he meets a young revolutionary who sparks off his subdued urge to seek parity with the so-called upper castes/classes and not to dilute the urge. The young man (Bikash Mukherjee, known as B-10 and Biten throughout the narrative) makes Kalo realize, "We are the scum of the earth. The boss people scorn us because they fear us. They hit us where it hurts badly—in the pit of the belly. We've got to hit back".[40] Frustrated and desperate to earn a living, Kalo is offered a suggestion by B-10: "Can you wear a saffron loin cloth, smear your body with ashes and mark a red-paste trident of Shiva on your forehead . ... the temple is a market and the priest a dealer. People are always ready to pay well for feeding the inner man" (pp. 42-43). What is implied is that only Brahmins possess the exclusive and authoritative right to do as suggested by B-10. Since one is a Brahmin only by birth, it is sacrilegious for the low-born even to think of such a transformation. Out of jail, and without means, Kalo accepts the job of a procurer for a brothel, where one day he finds to his horror, his own daughter. Utterly dejected, Kalo resolves to have his revenge.

With two seers of dried grams and a proper Shiva stone, Kalo ultimately succeeded in performing the magic trick of creating a God, became a twice-born and "flouted the three thousand years of his yesterdays . . . (and) transcended the station that birth and blood had assigned him" (p. 81). He was scum no longer. Master of the newly founded temple, he was now a pillar of society (a pillar created by two seers of gram). A blacksmith, re-incarnated as a Brahmin, he took on the name, Mangal Adhikari and vaulted class boundaries, however, soon to move only among the so-called high-caste, for whom he felt no warmth. The myth of caste superiority lay exposed. Yet he was upholding that same myth, turning it into a leverage for his strength. At a certain point, he submerged himself so completely in his new role that he became as rigid as the Brahmins themselves. His daughter, however, kept reminding him of the reality he had conveniently chosen to ignore.

Some explanation could be seen in Meenakshi Mukherjee's view that the uneducated blacksmith could not be expected to possess the intellectual strength to accept his rootlessness,[41] as did Biten (B-10) who had renounced his Brahmanism in order to belong to the down-trodden. Kalo had upset and challenged the old social order by investing himself with Brahminhood and rising to the top. Instead of undermining society, he had become a part of it. Kalo as Mangal Adhikari, rode the tiger of lie, to dismount or to continue the ride was not easy, either way. Uneasy on the tiger's back, the urge to kill the tiger growing ever stronger, Kalo came face to face with the dreadful eventuality of his daughter being sacrificed at the altar of his ambition. Lekha, with no will Left to protest, had accepted her installation as the 'Mother of sevenfold Bliss', (a living goddess) following the mortification of being proposed by one of the old, but rich trustees (already having four wives). Kalo retrieved his senses and was reminded of the initial obligation to seek revenge. He decided to confess his fraud to a large congregation gathered to witness installation of the Mother of Sevenfold Bliss and, thus, ultimately killed the 'Tiger'.

Bhattacharya gives as interesting an overview of the reactions of dismay and disbelief among the audience over the unvarnished truth, as of the variety of selfish, hypocritical and ignorant worshippers, given earlier in the novel. A lawyer and a judge wanted the freak to be brought to law. A secretariat official suggested recourse to preventive detention. The politician brooded over the possibility of direct action by the masses to deal with the enemies of society. The chairman of the board of trustees, and a business tycoon, Sir Abalabandhu marvelled at the blacksmith's "business sense" and wished he had one or two men like him in his office. The down-trodden, sitting removed from the main throng, cheered the victory of their brother. The scum of the earth had hit back, and had done so where it hurt most.

It is a point of dispute among literary critics whether the final 'outburst' should have come from Chandra Lekha or from Kalo himself.[42] It is true that Kalo is made to escape the consequences of his act in the novel, which is an unrealistic lapse, in the sense that the vicious circle of power, money and greed is unlikely to condone such adventure. However, the final outburst appropriately, not unexpectedly, ought to have come from Kalo (as it does in the novel), for logically speaking it was his battle; it was his initiative and it was his resolve to take revenge. It was he who had created the tiger, mounted it and, therefore, it was he who had to kill it.

The icon of tiger is suggestive of the magnitude of the challenge of economic exploitation and social stasis. The categories of caste and class, therefore, inadvertently get mixed up at every level, for the stakes are both social (status) and economic (power). However, Bhattacharya exposes the constraints of *sanskritization*, as a strategy of 'positional', not 'structural' change, through satirizing the process of mounting and then killing the tiger of hypocrisy by matching violence. The conclusive act of defiance on the part of the blacksmith is also an indication of Bhattacharya's embryonic optimism about possibilities of self-generated change in India's social system.

Dimensions of economic crudities and injustice, however, attain authentic pinnacle in Mulk Raj Anand's *Coolie* and *The Big Heart* (and to a lesser extent in *Two Leaves and a Bud*), matchless for their incisiveness. The journey from *Untouchable* to *Coolie* is a transportation "from microcosm to macrocosm" as K.R.S. Iyengar puts it.[43] *Coolie*, as popular as *Untouchable*, is regarded by some critics as the most satisfying political novel.[44] It exposes the evils of emerging dehumanized economic system, decaying social order and repressive political authority. The story is woven around the wanderings of a hill urchin, Munno, moving in desperation from village to town, to city, and, finally, back to the hills. Munno acquires, in the process, chilling experiences of ruthless urban expanse, who is condemned and denigrated as rustic, abject and worth no reckoning. In fact, another ugly facet of social determinism is exposed as Munno bemoans: "I am a Kshatriya and I am poor, and Varma, a Brahmin, is a servant boy, a menial, because he is poor. No, caste does not matter . . . all servants look alike . . . there must, only be two kinds of people in the world, the rich and the poor" (p. 69).

Munno's varied experiences include his employment as a domestic servant, as a worker in a pickle factory, a street coolie, a cotton-mill worker and, lastly, a household helper-cum-rikshaw-puller. It is in Bombay at the cotton-mill, that he is rudely awakened to harsh machinations of imperialist-capitalist combine. Complete disdain by the British management of the mill for minimum welfare needs of workers; the British foreman, at once a recruiting authority and high-handed task-master, the mill door-keeper-cum-soulless-money-lender; and the grocer in the workers' colony, fleecing and bleeding the helpless workers, all combine into an unholy alliance against workers, whose despair is of no concern to anyone. When a handful of conscious workers manage to organize a strike in protest, the management injects the venom of communal hatred. Communal riot breaks out and the cause of the strike is lost as retribution gets the better of sensitivity to shared suffering. With government intervention, concern for law and order takes precedence over the now forgotten cause of the workers. The young Munno is absolutely bewildered. He is knocked down by an Anglo-Indian lady's car. Out of pity, she takes him along to distant Simla, where he dies prematurely of consumption.

Yet another coolie meets his end, without causing concern to society or government, to pause and enquire into the causes of pervasive insensitivity. Anand's empathy for the cause of workers in industrial complexes or rural areas or on plantations, is comprehensive as he unfolds the sordid sequence of individuals metamorphosed into clods. Socio-economic renovation becomes a transparent myth, if political democracy continues to connive at the denial of fundamental human rights.

Anand's quest for radical consciousness emerges with greater clarity in his powerful novel, *The Big Heart*, where he attempts an illuminating synthesis of the macro-concern of *Coolie* with the micro-intensity of *Untouchable*. *The Big Heart* elucidates and stresses the point that caste and class are no longer separable in India; especially after the introduction of industrialization, (understood as *Kalyug*—the age of machine, in common parlance in India) an inescapable fact of modern civilization. The novel encapsulates the tensions resulting from innovative technology and the displacement of artisans. It is, in fact, an elaboration of the resolve earlier stated in *Untouchable*, explaining India's suffering for not accepting the machine: " . . . we must, of course, remedy that . . . I shall go against Gandhi there and accept it" (p. 167).

Ananta, the principal character, returns from Bombay to his home-town, Amritsar, and resumes his hereditary job as a coppersmith. He finds to his dismay that the new industrial establishment, owned by a couple of rich dealers in finished metal vessels has thrown the artisans into disarray. He also finds himself pitted against disdainful disapproval of his own community as he had brought along a widow-companion without marrying her. Gandhi's word of caution against machines and the fact that machines were already there, installed by powerful dealers, leaves the artisans in confusion and indecision. The predicament of impotent fury only hurts them much worse. Forgetting his own problems, Ananta comes to the resuce of fellow-artisans and chooses to implement his experiences of Bombay. He urges them to get organized into a trade union: "though it is good to live on doubt, one must believe in something, specially at moments when it is necessary to act" (p. 91). Ananta echoes Anand's concern to rise against superstition, fatalism, fear and inaction and resolves to take them out of their dwarfed existence: "to courage of manhood . . . to believe in Revolution as a new kind of religion" (p. 139). Through a poet, Puran Singh Bhagat (like poet Iqbal Nath Sarshar in *Untouchable*) Anand seems to be indicating an intellectual justification for Ananta's resolution. The poet, further explaining Ananta's idea of revolution, warns the people to be "on guard against those . . . who substitute Brown rule instead of the white" (p. 149). He also assails Gandhi for defending the vicious circle of the old order, that is the institution of private property in India.

Anand's portrayal of Ananta is neither of a dreamer nor a rabble rouser, but of a pragmatic rationalist and sober idealist, committed through and through to action, not to abstractions. He realizes that "the revolution is not yet. . . . It is only through a great many conflicts between the employers, authorities and the workers, in a whole number of battles, which as comrades elsewhere are fighting, that there will come the final overthrow of the bosses" (p. 209). Ananta, however, falls victim to the fury and violence of one of his own colleagues and gets killed in the end. The finale seems to suggest the pivotal necessity of conviction and revolutionary consciousness preceding actual revolution.

The Big Heart confirms Anand's faith in progress through industrialization, although he is aware of the cultural strains and economic antagonisms involved in the process. He is nearer Nehru's vision than either the Russian, Chinese or even Gandhian visions of revolution. Anand is reported to have stated that *The Big Heart* agglomerated the "picture of India ten years ahead".[45] The relevance of the theme, for many more years to come, is vindicated by Bhabani Bhattacharya's *Shadow from Ladakh*[46] which appeared twentyone years later.

Bhattacharya's *Shadow from Ladakh* further probes the twilight zone of India's transition from agriculture, small-industry-based economy to heavy industrialization, anticipated in Anand's *The Big Heart*, long before India actually embarked upon planned industrialization. Whereas, given the ambivalent situation of pre-independence India, Anand could only suggest possible areas of conflict likely to emerge in the developmental syndrome, Bhattacharya had before him the actual and ideological experience of three decades of independence. *Shadow from Ladakh*, therefore, is an expression of the compelling need of rapid industrialization for "development plus defence — a compulsion of our current history" (p. 30). However, Bhattacharya would like to see the ill-effects of mechanization and industrialism counter-balanced by the ethical discipline of Gandhi and the aesthetic harmony of Tagore.

In portraying the antagonisms of Gandhigram and Lohapur (steel-town) as two nodal extremities in India's contemporary ethos, the novelist highlights the presence of crossroads, ambivalence of alternatives and irresolution in policies, conceived as inevitable stages of development, (not as perennial irreconcilables) in a nation's maturing into a viable political identity.

The theme is artistically brought out through powerful characterization. Satyajit, an ex-teacher at Shantiniketan, disciple and associate of Tagore, and later, founder of Gandhigram (at the behest of Gandhi himself), personifies Gandhian ideals of austerity, simplicity and sacrifice. On the other hand, Bhaskar Roy, an engineer, trained in the USA, brilliant and equally dedicated to his vocation, represents the opposing ideals of rapid progress, big organization, powerful state and a natural, worldly conception of happiness. Satyajit, for instance, persists with Gandhi's '*Sarvodaya*' logic that "the factory or the mill was ugly, repressive. It uprooted the masses of people from a healthy rural environment. . . . India could not afford to wait until large scale industry absorbed her enormous manpower. Small, hand-worked machines such

as the spinning wheel, available to all, had to be the answer"
(p. 73). Bhaskar Roy, on the other hand, is insistent on acknow-
ledging the forces of change, lest India should be left behind
on the global map of progress : "India needed the big
machines, not spinning wheels, change not tradition. Not the
heritage of philosophic inanity, but the dynamism of technological progress even with all its inevitable chaos" (p. 155).

The fervour of dissonance, however, is not constantly
sustained but decisively moderated and mediated by Tagorean
image of harmony. The quest for harmony and synchronization
is realized at one level through the aesthetic perceptions of
Suruchi (Satyajit's wife) and the intellectual, pragmatic logic
of Bireswar (Satyajit's close friend and M.P.) and at another
level, through symbolic growth of love between Sumita
(Satyajit's daughter) and Bhaskar Roy. Later, in the novel,
Satyajit is disallowed to go forward with his peace-mission to
the Sino-Indian borders (a utopian-Gandhian ideal in 1962);
Sumita is exposed to the changing realities of expansive
development, war, violence, aesthetics and natural impulses of
life; and Bhaskar Roy is drawn to alternative plans of
expansion of the steel-town.

Toward the end of the novel, Bireswar stresses the
current context: "This hour in India's national life has to be
one of *conscious amalgam*. It's the hour of both dawn and
twilight, the two are alike in content" (p. 344). Spurred by the
mill-workers' strike against plans of expansion of steel town,
in the direction of Gandhigram, in order to save Satyajit's life
(who goes on an indefinite hunger strike), Bhaskar Roy with-
draws his original plan and proposes to the Central government
an alternative site. Satyajit, too, realizes that Suruchi "was
now leading him *forward* to Shantiniketan" (p. 212). Thus
the circle is complete and replete with the aesthetic ideal of
harmony.

The final image that emerges is one of symphony, collective
goodness and cooperative progressivism, despite the undercurrent of discordance in the face of the lurking humiliation at
the Sino-Indian border. Although Bhattacharya is conscious of
the challenge of nation-building and socio-economic transformation, his complacency and hesitation to go in for unpleasant

alternatives, turns his presentation into a sort of utopian socialist vision of a post-industrial society (in a not yet industrialized
situation). Thus, for the novelist, if "steel town belongs to the
present, Gandhigram to the future" (p. 156). The symbol of
Gandhigram might turn out to be a beacon for future
generations as a reference point of glorious ideals of the past;
however, such idealization is a poor consolation in the larger
context of contemporary challenges.

Moving on to another travesty of India's socio-economic
life, namely, desecration, subjection and exploitation of women,
one comes across several notable Indo-Anglian novels, such as:
R.K. Narayan's *The Dark Room*, B. Bhattacharya's *Music for
Mohini*, M.R. Anand's *Gauri* and Nayantara Sahgal's *The Day
in Shadow*. All these novels, with varying emphases, explore
aspects of injustice perpetrated on Indian women, notwithstanding the statutory penal provisions. The novelists are not
unaware of the contributions of various social and political
reform movements, incorporating concern for the rights of
women. The exertions, for instance, of Ram Mohan Roy,
Ishwar Chandra Vidyasagar, Dayanand, Ranade and Gandhi
formed the cognitive backdrop of statutory sanction provided
for women's rights in post-independence India under the
stewardship of Jawaharlal Nehru. Emancipation of women,
however, has remained largely a matter of scratching the
surface. It is suspected that the male-dominated society, cognizant of possible changes in the social structure, consequent
upon awareness among women, might renew its repressiveness
in other forms and reverse the accomplishments of hard-won
identity. The sort of deception often seen, sermonizing about
women's emancipation, without accepting their equality, has
indeed made a mockery of statutory provisions. Freedom continues to remain a mirage for women in India. In their aesthetic
perceptions, the Indo-Anglian novelists, however, transcend
nihilism and indicate an emergence (howsoever slow) of consciousness of individuality and selfhood among contemporary
Indian women and gradually, possibly marginally, changing
corresponding attitudes in society.

Whereas R.K. Narayan and Bhabani Bhattacharya explore
the ethical and attitudinal dimensions of exploitation of women,
Mulk Raj Anand and Nayantara Sahgal probe the economic,

legal and institutional ramifications of the problem. Unlike Raja Rao, who idealizes womanhood in spiritual, metaphysical sense (which is hypocritical), all these four novelists portray women as role-performers; aspiring, suffering, protesting and reconciling as mothers, wives, sisters and mistresses. When role-expectation and role-performance come to be at cross purposes, emotional isolation, crisis of values and clash of tradition with modernity threatens to ruin the family world of 'order', 'discipline' and 'harmony'. The novelists, however, do not accept ignorance as bliss. The simmering discontent, the awakening consciousness and purposive determination are depicted favourably. In the novelists' perception, this might prove to be an antidote to the emerging negative tendencies of apathy and alienation.

It is important to bear in mind that the traditional basis of social life in India has been the institution of marriage. Despite reservations on its modus operandi, the Indo-Anglian novelists, by and large, accept the sanctity of marriage as a social institution. There are, however, instances of condemnation and defiance of conventions that are contaminating the institution. For instance, Bhattacharya ridicules the current practice of matrimonial advertisements, which has degraded marriage into a commercial transaction. R.K. Narayan highlights the dark contours of relationship in an arranged marriage. Nayantara Sahgal explodes the myth of 'marriage-happiness' equation. For Mulk Raj Anand, marriage is a linear extension of the social structure and its contradictions. All the four novelists are critical of the oppressive tensions of the ethos of Indian marriage. Whereas Anand and Nayantara Sahgal are not hesitant in suggesting separation, in cases of discord, Narayan and Bhattacharya are still convinced of the efficacy of moral approach based on faith in ethical discipline and cultural resilience. The ideal image of woman for Bhattacharya and Narayan remains one of symphony, goodness and cooperation, despite the undercurrent of ever lurking dissonance and humiliation. A sort of complacency and hesitation to go for unpleasant alternatives is visible in Narayan and Bhattacharya. Anand and Sahgal, on the contrary, are vociferous in their condemnation of injustice.

Of all the Indo-Anglian novels, it is in Mulk Raj Anand's

Gauri and Nayantara Sahgal's *The Day in Shadow* that the emergence of independent womanhood is perceived to have attained a level of reckoning. The two novels, therefore, might be taken as instances of emerging innovative feminine consciousness, in the positive sense, in post-independence India. Whereas Anand explores the rural setting reeling under superstition, irrationalism, ignorance and male chauvinism, graphically indicating the helplessness of uneducated or semi-educated women, Nayantara portrays the upper crust glitter in metropolitan India and the fraudulent core beneath the superficial glamorous trappings, reducing woman to an object of exhibition and a commodity. The issue is whether in a remote innocuous village or in metropolitan complex, Indian woman, by and large, is involved in a fundamental quest for self-identity.

Mulk Raj Anand's *Gauri* is inspired, as the author himself says, partly by "the peasant woman", an epic poem by the nineteenth century poet, Nicholai-Nekrasov, and partly by the Indian epic *Ramayana*. Despite the imagery of divinity of Sita, Gauri, the principal character in the novel, grimly portrays perpetration of feminine repression through the ages. The story rings a bell of familiarity as Gauri, in her innocence, is married to an idler, Panchi. Condemned to eking out survival in penury and humiliation, Gauri's conscience is burdened with instructions usually handed out to girls, fashioning out unquestioning obedience and subservience at the in-laws' place. Gauri is in a quandary. Family tensions are aggravated by severe drought. Inevitably, as it were, she is cursed and blamed for the natural calamity. Abuse, physical assault and humiliation become the order of the day and crush her spirits. She is branded an adulteress. She is sent back to her mother's place, where worse fate awaits her. The mother, poor as she is, has to make a choice between the household cow and the daughter and decides to sell off the latter to a 'respectable old man'. Gauri manages to escape from her tormentor and is given shelter by a humane physician, Colonel Mahindra. She is employed as a nurse. Later, the penitent mother of Gauri, finally restores her daughter to her husband. The husband is coerced by village gossip and barbed homilies into asking Gauri to prove her 'purity'. Her outburst is painful though courageous: "Rama turned out Sita because everyone doubted her chastity during her stay with Ravana.

I am not Sita that the earth will open up and swallow me. I shall go out and be forgotten of him" (p. 244). Gauri chooses the dignity of self-assertion, walks out of her husband's place and returns to Mahindra's clinic.

Thus, unlike Savitri (in R.K. Narayan's *The Dark Room*) and Mohini (in Bhattachary's *Music for Mohini*),[47] who re-concile themselves to their fate and choose to stay at home and suffer so as to preserve harmony and familial happiness, Gauri takes the bold step of leaving home, "transfigured from the gentle cow's acquiescent visage of the time when she had arrived in Panchi's house, to that of a woman with a will of her own" (p. 244). For a brief moment, the thought that the earth might open up to rescue her as it had opened up to receive Sita, came as an echo from some distant memory. But the ground was hard and solid under her feet and showed no sign of opening up to prove her innocence. She waved her head to forget Sita and thought of the road to the town" (p. 245).

One might recall, in this context, Meenakshi Mukherjee's comment that, in *Gauri*, "the Sita myth is introduced only to be exploded at the climactic point".[48] Rejecting, rather than extol-ling, the time-honoured ideals of meek suffering by women, Anand, in fact "re-enacts" the Sita myth effectively, the con-textual difference, notwithstanding.[49]

Anand seems to believe that to an extent, myth and religion may provide sustaining power to the suffering individual. How-ever, one has to devise means for oneself, as the reality dawns with a vengeance, as it were. The road that Gauri takes, there-fore, may not be the road to comfort, success or even assured happiness, an avenue for "progress", as Anand would perceive it.

Nayantara Sahgal's *The Day in Shadow*[50] examines and stresses the urban, affluent-class milieu in a metropolitan situa-tion, only to bring home an equally grim reality of Indian women's plight. It is the story of an educated, thinking woman, Simrit, who values scholarship, commitment and ethical integrity, as opposed to her enterprising, ambitious and selfish husband, Som, for whom 'business' is the supreme ethics. The gulf between discordant values increasingly widens, leading to their separation. Som's world of commerce, ambition and power has no room for qualms about norms, values and friendships. For instance, caught up in a spiralling mania for affluence" (p. 87), Som finalizes a deal with a German industrialist, Rudy Vetter, to manufacture armaments. For Simrit, it is the final breaking point, for she considers it to be an absolutely inhuman proposal. "Children in their cradles should fear men like you" (p. 87), she tells him in anger. Being a sensitive writer, Simrit craves for "a clear cold atmosphere, where there was some goal beyond self-advancement" (p. 89).

But, divorce, as it becomes inevitable, also entails conditions, imposed by Som and foolishly approved by Simrit in her ignorance, resulting in a virtual monetary killing—"a sort of Hiroshima" (p. 138), as it is described by Raj Garg (a sympathiser of Simrit and an M.P.) in the novel. The heavy tax-payments—imposed on Simrit owing to inordinately exaggerated obligations shown in their son's name—leave her no more than a pauper. Legally speaking, it was true that "the only thing you could get without a hitch was a divorce" (p. 45), yet in society, age-old perceptions and attitudes regarding women's independent identity had not changed. Legal provisions were no solace, nor compensation for social frigidity. Simrit, therefore, "feels uprooted and abandoned in a husband-centred world".[51] The divorce settlement continues to weigh heavy on her, not only in socio-economic, but also psychological, terms: "The tissue of marriage could be dissolved by human acts, but its anatomy went on and on" (p. 64). Simrit herself, it seems, is unable to transcend the middle class sensibility of Indian women ingrained over time. Interestingly, however, a critic, Irene Gilbert, comments that "perhaps it is only a difference of degree, but many independent women in the West would insist their situations were similar".[52] Ultimately, however, Simrit does emerge as an individual asserting her distinct identity but she also realizes the limits of isolated individual efforts in a nefarious social web: "Life was never long enough to overthrow all the tyrants" (p. 236). However, she hopes: "May be the question would be different in the twenty-first century" (p. 6).

Nayantara's aesthetic optimism notwithstanding, nothing short of structural changes is likely to alter the situation qualitatively. Nayantara Sahgal, ideologically a liberal reformist, envisages and emphasizes the need of adequate legal-structural protection. The novel forcefully exposes and criticizes the inadequacy of present legal provisions in India, regarding status of women. The novelist's insistence on inception of protest consciousness among women is, therefore, as imperative as the corresponding necessity of social sanctions and legal protection.

The Day in Shadow has been considered by some critics "as an adult novel, which concerns itself with the twin problems of rootlessness and restlessness".[53] In addition, and more importantly, it is also a tragedy of lawlessness in social perceptions of wamanhood in India. True, political democracy has enfranchised women in India, yet this political status has been ineffective in social terms, beyond a marginal point even for the educated elite, as Sahgal demonstrates. Liberation, total and final, is still a mere ideal, so far as social perspectives of democracy are concerned.[54] The quantitative perceptions of political democracy, unfortunately, have also denuded the qualitative prospects of social equality.

III

The Emerging Perspective

The Indo-Anglian novel, broadly speaking, has fallen short of evolving a 'tradition' of protest novel, working through revolutionary consciousness. The protest novels of Mulk Raj Anand, Bhabani Bhattacharya and to a lesser extent, Nayanatra Sahgal, nevertheless, can be taken as significant contributions, exploring dimensions of estrangement, confrontation and conflict, characterizing the process of transformation, from one socio-economic formation to another. In this sense, quest for qualitative renovation of art gets interwoven with that of reconstruction of 'quality of life' as a precondition for the visualized egalitarian order. The aesthetic experiments of Anand, Sahgal and Bhattacharya succeed, to an extent, in creating historically possible innovative literature, involving a sort of creative programme, cutting through perceived complacencies of social consciousness in India.

For both Anand and Bhattacharya, the twin goals of social liberation and economic development are supreme obligations of the political structure. In exposing the limitations of political democracy, Mulk Raj Anand explodes the myth of capitalist growth and visualizes a socialist utopia for India's down-trodden. Bhattacharya's fiction, not particularly enamoured of capitalist abundance, tempers the socialist vision by Gandhian precept of non-violence and Tagorean ideal of harmony. Whereas Anand is unsparing in his denunciations of hypocritical stances, vitiating India's socio-economic climate, Bhattacharya defies injustice mildly. For Anand, nothing short of structural transformation would alleviate India's social decadence and economic backwardness. For Bhattacharya, reconciliation could still be an alternative. Anand views class conflict as an inevitability in a society on the verge of industrialization. Caste configurations are, in fact, sustained as natural concomitant, in turn, aggravating class tensions. In Bhattacharya's perception, class and caste conflicts are not actuely configurated. They, rather, work through 'conflict within consensus'. Thus, Anand's radical consciousness, visualizing fundamental change through conflict, get chastened by the ideal of cultural consensus in Bhattacharya. Empathy for insensitiveness to basic human issues, nevertheless, remains a common denominator for both.

In their fiction, both Anand and Bhattacharya confront squarely paradoxes, dilemmas and challenges of the socio-economic order in India, rather than falling for metaphysical idealistic or complacent alternatives. As analysts of contemporary society, they cover a broad range of characters in a variety of situations, usually transforming alienated existences on the periphery into itinerant protestants. They move beyond chronicle of events in search of perspective. Bhattacharya, for instance, says: " . . . facts never tell much unless they are seen in terms of human experience".[55] Contemporary facts attain representative significance with the qualifying adjective "human" to which Anand and Bhattacharya consistently adhere. 'Quality of Life' remains their central concern.

Echoing Protagoras, Anand states: "Men make of their own deeds, they make of their own character, good or bad, and they shape of their own destiny".[56] So does Bhattacharya. They are convinced, like Nehru, of the immanence of man's power to master nature through rationalism, science and technology and visualize a renovated social order for India based on reason and faith in human capacity. The traditional

attitude of India, Anand explains, is essentially non-human,
even superhuman.[57] Both, Anand and Bhattacharya have,
therefore, consciously created characters who protest against
conformism and alleged cultural resilience pervasive in India.
These characters also expose aspects of ambivalence regarding
mute suffering and rebellion, resignation and hope, compliance
and visionary emancipation. Comprehensive social change will
be possible, when this ambivalence is eradicated through a
change-oriented progressive consciousness,

More than Bhattacharya, Mulk Raj Anand has been un-
justly accused of conformism[58] by some critics, of exhibiting
lack of confidence in revolutionary forces,[59] by others, and of
propaganda by still others.[60] Their critical value notwithstanding, these accusations fail to note the relevance of purposive art,[61] reconciling "an intellectual desire for objectivity
with an emotional urge for commitment.[62] In fact, the portrayal of all the major characters of Anand is rooted in radical
consciousness, even when they are trapped in the cruel web of
adversity.[63] They aspire for some way out of their respective
predicament to what D. Riemenschneider calls "the individual
self-realization".[64] To expect them to be revolutionary intellectuals or leaders would be unfair as well as unrealistic in
the context of the socio-economic and political ethos they are
meant to represent. The ethos is, no doubt, frustrating and
requires total effort. Anand's characters (partly also of
Bhattacharya's), are, however, not defeatist. They fulfil their
respective roles fully cognizant of the numerous constraints,
without camouflaging or idealizing. Struggle for survival keeps
them so hopelessly engaged that ideological or conceptual
sophistication seems a dishonest expectation. They, nevertheless, remain sensitive to their surroundings and question
the questionable. It is in their awareness of fundamental
rights as human beings and their refusal to suffer injustice and
repression that the foundations of radical culture actually lie.
That also dispels the myth of 'contentment', 'mystical silence'
and spiritual attainments, built around the Indian character.[65]

Impervious to the luxury of introspective, conformist,
urban-centred or even spiritual fiction, Mulk Raj Anand, more
than Bhabani Bhattacharya, has chosen to move beyond the
middle-class milieu and assailed the roots of prevalent norm

structure in Indian society. Bhattacharya, however, follows Anand in his commitment to resurrect human dignity, as a prelude to genuine and comprehensive democracy in India, social, political, and economic. Anand's aesthetic political criticism is thus a constant reminder of the need to ensure freedom and dignity. Bhattacharya follows this closely. This would, in other words, mean sustenance of the ever-expanding areas of human consciousness to make man truly "human".

It is true that in their politico-aesthetic vision, Anand and Bhattacharya do not fully overcome the hazards of applying definitive theories of social change to vacillating human situations. Nevertheless, they create modes in which the creative mind is portrayed in its determined and determining relationship to social actuality. In the ultimate analysis, the voice of protest in these critics of Indian society does not remain the voice of despair, (as in their counterparts in the West) but is distinguishable as an affirmative cognition of life in the light of the progressive ideals disseminated in their aesthetic consciousness.

References

1. See Jawaharlal Nehru, *An Autobiography* (New Delhi, Allied, 1962), pp. 529-536. Also see B.M. Bhatia, *History of Social Development* Vol. II (New Delhi, Vikas, 1977), pp. 216-257.
2. See Rajani Palme Dutt, *India Today* (Calcutta, Manisha, 1970), pp. 15-18.
3. David E. Apter, *Political Change – Collected Essays* (London, Frank Cass, 1973), p. 216. Also see N. Maxwell, *Woman on a White Horse* (Oxford, Institute of Commonwealth Studies, 1975), p. 366.
4. M. Seliger, *Ideology and Politics* (New York, Free Press, (1976), p. 275.Also see Charles F. Andrain's valuable distinction of democratic "spirit" and "institutions" in the context of third world democratic experiments. "Democracy and Socialism—Ideologies of African Leaders", in David E. Apter, *Ideology and Discontent* (New York, Free Press, 1964), p. 157.
5. See G.C. Pandey, *The Meaning and Process of Culture* (Agra, Shiva Lal Agarawala and Co., 1972), pp. 81-100; and S. Radhakrishnan, *Religion and Culture* (New Delhi, Orient Paperbacks, 1968), pp. 22-50.

6. See for instance, Nehru's categorical emphasis: "We have too much of the past about us and have ignored the present. We have to get rid of that narrowing religious outlook, that obsession with the supernatural and metaphysical speculations, that loosening of the mind's discipline in religious, ceremonial and mystical emotionalism which came in the way of our understanding of ourselves and the world". *The Discovery of India* (New Delhi, Oxford University Press, 1980), pp. 519-520. Also see Nirad C. Chaudhari's cryptic satire in *To Live or Not to Live* (New Delhi, Orient Paperbacks, 1970), pp. 70-90.

7. M.N. Srinivas *Social Change in Modern India* (New Delhi, Orient Longman, 1972), p. 75.

8. For instance, Karl Marx commented in 1853 that "India was one of the cradles of civilization more ancient than Greece but . . . the ancient civilization of India came to stagnate failing to catch up with the Greek and Roman in ancient Europe, from which through the Middle Ages developed the modern bourgeois Europe". Quoted in E.M.S. Namboodiripad, "Class Struggle in India", *The Marxist*, 1, 2 (Oct.-Dec. 1983), 7.

9. *n.* 7.

10. L.I. Rudolph and S.H. Rudolph point out the parallel tendency of 'negative identity', that is, rejecting Hinduism in favour of Buddhism, Christianity or Islam. *The Modernity of Tradition— Political Development in India* (New Delhi, Orient Longman, 1969), pp. 135-154.

11. 'Fundamental' not is the juristic sense, as stated by Articale 37 of the Constitution. In fact, the controversy regarding the primacy of Fundamental Rights or the Directive Principles, dates back to the Golak Nath Judgment of 1967 and continues to linger on even after the Keshvanand Bharthi Judgment of 1973, aggravating the larger issues of confrontation of 'liberty' and 'justice' on the one hand, and of contention for supremacy of Parliament and Judiciary on the other.

12. Raymond Williams, *Marxism and Literature* (Oxford, Oxford University Press, 1977), p. 117.

13. *n.* 10, pp. 146-152.

14. See Iqbal Narain, "Ideology and Political Development—Battle for Issues in Indian Politics", *Asian Survey*, XI, 2 (Feb. 1971), 185-196.

15. For instance, the Constitution Amendments, 24th, 25th, 26th, 29th and 30th of 1971 and parts of 42nd Amendment of 1976.

16. It is interesting to note V.S. Naipaul's psycho-cultural interpretation of J.P.'s Movement: "It is like going back to the solace of incantation and back to Gandhi as to the only Indian truth, as though Britain still ruled in India; as though the Indian political situation remains unchanging, as eternal as India itself, requiring the same ideal solution". *India: A Wounded Civilization* (Harmondsworth, Penguin Books, 1979), p. 145. For an antipodal interpretation see

David Selbourne, *An Eye to India—the Unmasking of A Tyranny* (Harmondsworth, Penguine Books, 1977), p. 25.

17. See Iqbal Narain, "Politics of Non-Issues", *Asian Survey*, 19, 2, (Feb. 1979), 165-177.
18. See for instance, Taya Zinkin, *India Changes* (New York, Oxford University Press, 1958), pp. 119-122.
19. See David Selbourne's candid comment: "India's is a political economy in which the poor are (not unusually) held in a vice-like grip; held not only by the exigencies of poverty and structural destitution, but by functional political necessity". *n.* 16, p. 11.
20. *n.* 2, p. 16.
21. T.D. Brunton, "The Heritage of Indianness" in M.K. Naik *et al.* (ed.), *Critical Essays on Indian Writing in English* (Dharwar, Karnataka University Press, 1968), p. 218.
22. Anand has to his credit fifteen novels, ten collections of short stories, apart from twenty-four non-fiction books and approximately thirty critical papers.
23. *Seven Summers* (London, Hutchinson, 1951).
24. *Morning Face* (Bombay, Kutub, 1968).
25. *Confession of a Lover* (New Delhi, Arnold Heinemann, 1976).
26. London, Jonathan Cape, 1939, 1940 and 1942.
27. *Apology for Heroism* (1946), (New Delhi, Arnold Heinemann, 1975).
28. Saros Cowasjee (ed.), *Author to Critic: Letters of Mulk Raj Anand to Saros Cowasjee* (Calcutta, Writers Workshop, 1973), p. 1.
29. *n.* 27, p. 125.
30. *n.* 27, p. 113.
31. *n.* 27, p. 134.
32. *n.* 25, p. 251.
33. See M.R. Anand, "The Writer's Role in National Integration: A Discussion", *Indian Literature*, V, 1 (1962), 58.
34. London, Hutchinson, 1953.
35. Bombay, Kutub, 1963.
36. All these novels have been published by Kutub Popular, Bombay, though first four novels were originally published in London. The years in parentheses are the original years of publication.
37. Saros Cowasjee, *So Many Freedoms* (Delhi, Oxford University Press, 1977) p. 45.
38. *n.* 37, p. 54.
39. 'Sanskritization', as defined by M.N. Srinivas and as used here "is the process by which a "low" Hindu caste, or tribal or other group, changes its customs, ritual, ideology and way of life in the direction of a high and frequently "twice-born" caste. Generally such changes are followed by a claim to a higher position in the caste hierarchy than that traditionally conceded to the claimant caste by the local community . . . but all this takes place in an essentially stable hierarchical order. The system itself does not change". *Social Change in Modern India* (Delhi, Orient Longman, 1972), pp. 6-7.

40. *He Who Rides a Tiger* (1955), (Delhi, Hind Pocket Books, n.d.), p. 39.

41. *The Twice Born Fiction* (Delhi, Arnold Heinemann, 1971), p. 115.

42. See for instance, Meenakshi Mukherjee, *n.* 41, p. 117, and K.R. Chandrasekharan, *Bhabani Bhattacharya* (Delhi, Arnold Heinemann, 1974), pp. 82-83.

43. *Indian Writing in English* (Bombay, Asia, 1962), p. 265.

44. For instance, V.S. Pritchett, quoted by S. Cowasjee, *n.* 37, p. 63.

45. Jack Lindsay, *The Elephant and the Lotus* (Bombay, Kutub, 1965), p. 18.

46. *Shadow from Ladakh* (Delhi, Hind Pocket Books, 1966).

47. *The Dark Room* (Bombay, Pearl Publications, 1960). *Music for Mohini* (New Delhi, Orient Paperbacks, 1952).

48. *n.* 41, p. 159.

49. See S. Cowasjee, *n.* 37, p. 155 and *n.* 28, p. 29.

50. *The Day in Shadow* (Delhi, Vikas, 1971).

51. Jasbir Jain, *Nayantara Sahgal* (New Delhi, Arnold-Heinemann, 1978), p. 58.

52. Irene A. Gilbert, Review of *The Day in Shadow, Journal of South Asian Literature*, X, 1 (Fall, 1974), 187.

53. A.V. Krishna Rao, *Nayantara Sahgal: A Study of Her Fiction and Non-Fiction*, 1954-1974, (Madras, M. Seshachalam and Co., 1976), p. 69.

54. See Nayantara Sahgal, "Adultery in Life and Literature", *The Sunday Standard* (28 Sept. 1975), 6, and "An India beyond Politics", *The Sunday Standard* (28 Jan. 1970), p. 6.

55. *So Many Hungers* (Delhi, Orient Paperbacks, 1978), p. 22.

56. *The Big Heart, n.* 36, p. 210.

57. *Apology for Heroism, n.* 27, p. 95.

58. H.M. Williams, "English Writing in Free India", *Twentieth Century Literature*, 16 (Jan. 1970), 5.

59. Y. Tupikova, "Mulk Raj Anand", *Soviet Literature* (1953), 161. and, S.R. Bald, "Politics of a Revolutionary Elite: A Study of Mulk Raj Anand's Novels", *Modern Asian Studies* 8, 4, (1974), 483.

60. Khushwant Singh, "After the Raj", *New Statesman* (10 Sept. 1960), 348. Also see M.K. Naik, *Mulk Raj Anand* (New Delhi, Arnold Heinemann, 1973), p. 7 and H.H. Anniah Gowda, "Mulk Raj Anand", *The Literary Half-yearly*, VI, (1 Jan. 1965), 51-60.

61. See Bhattacharya's defence statement in this regard, Sudhakar Joshi, "An Evening With Bhabani", *The Sunday Standard* (7 April 1969), VII.

62. Alastair Niven, *The Yoke of Pity* (New Delhi, Arnold Hienemann, 1978), p. 119.

63. See, for instance, Darshan Singh Maini's comment: . . . "there is something in the pith and grain of his work, something in its tenor and texture that defies the Critical *pundits* . . . Anand has the ability

to translate into fictive forms the vague fears and urges and aspirations of that mass of bewildered humanity, we call *Bharat*, and for this purpose he has fashioned a poetic realism of his own with a corresponding idiom". "The Aging Lions", *Gentleman* (July 1984), 84.

64. *An Ideal of Man in Anand's Novels* (Bombay, Kutub, n. d.) p. 1.
65. See S. Cowasjee, "Mulk Raj Anand: Princes and Proletarians", *The Journal of Commonwealth Literature*, 5 (July, 1968), 64.

6

The Emerging Politico-Aesthetic Vision: Innovative Affirmation

"The amalgam of progressivism, conservatism, prejudice, courage and fear that is in the make-up of most intellectuals is an inevitable pre-condition of clear and intelligent thought".

—*Mulk Raj Anand*

The emerging politico-aesthetic vision is an affirmation of cognate viewpoints of novelists on politico-cultural life in India. The spectrum of the vision encompasses various levels of awareness, cognitive, affective, evaluative, as constitutive parts of practical consciousness, in response to major forms of hegemony in India, identified in the preceding chapters as historical antecedents, political institutions and socio-economic infrastructure. By virtue of artistic mediation and selection, the creative writers also move ahead of the prevailing socio-political assumptions in quest of innovative consciousness, which may ultimately prove to be of lasting relevance. At that level of creative realization, politico-aesthetic vision is, indeed, capable of paving the way for an active, protesting and liberating role of political imagination in society.

Quest for innovative consciousness constitutes a departure from the existing patterns and norms and aspires for an ideal arrangement of structures, morals and opportunities. This invites a vital question of defining and determining the nature and limits of freedom of political imagination.[1] However, since imagination is not outside the cognitive process, it cannot be conceived as being free of the object and constraints of that process. This question, related to the question of 'typicality' and 'universalism', therefore, involves another question of interpretation and evaluation of the idea, ideal and ideological content of art.

The very appeal to imagination as a political category links culture as a creative activity and its role in relation to the socio-political structure in a non-conformist fashion. Each sub-system of ideas contained in an art work, therefore, is a significant strand of an organic vision, expressing aspects of possibility or reality of the socio-political universe. This dispels the myths of monolithic or static opinions erroneously identified with conscious works of art. Discernment of identifiable sub-system of ideas and ideological orientations, is helpful in further distinguishing fundamental orientations from transient opinions, regarding political institutions and processes. Politico-aesthetic vision, in this sense, incorporates both an organic totality of perspective and a specific point of view for an aspired political future.[2]

I

Themes and Concerns: A Panorama

Notwithstanding the rich heritage of Sanskrit classics,[3] novel in India, including the Indian novel in English, owed its genesis to the politico-cultural interaction of India with the west in the nineteenth century. In the twentieth century, especially during the crucial decades from the 1920s to the 1940s, Indian literature witnessed evolution of a new content as the movement for political freedom began to take shape and aggregate mass consciousness. The ethical imperatives of Gandhian politics remained a central concern of the artists, even by the end of the 1950s. Whether accepted or rejected on the anvil of creative and political practice, they still continue to revel as vital catalysts of the national movement.

Among the major political novels of pre-independence India, Raja Rao's *Kanthapura* stands out as the most profound and authentic, prolific and accurate presentation of the Gandhian creed. Among post-independence novels, Manohar Malgonkar's

A Bend in the Ganges is outstanding for its authenticity and depth as a critique of Gandhian politics. B. Rajan and R.K. Narayan could further be singled out for contrasting interpretations of Gandhian ideology and charisma, usually misconceived as identical.

It is relevant to keep in view the emergence of the parallel movement of progressivism in India in the 1930s, rightly identified with Mulk Raj Anand. Anand's fiction enunciated and projected humanistic socialism as an effective corrective to the ethical politics of Gandhi. It was perhaps a fitting extension of Anand's commitment that critical appreciation of the turbulent epoch was undertaken by several notable novelists such as K.A. Abbas, B. Bhattacharya, M. Malgonkar and Chaman Nahal, among others, who also sought to probe comprehensively into the mythical aura attributed to Gandhism. In totality, the Indo-Anglian novelists have discerned history as a conglomerate of causal factors and factual interactions and processes, except for Malgonkar and Rushdie who are distinguishable for their extreme stances of penchant for accuracy and elusion, respectively.

Spiritualization of politics, in terms of non-violence, has been another pertinent concern of the novelists. Although there is no Indo-Anglian novel which justifies or glorifies violence *per se*, it is possible, however, to perceive differences in degree to which novelists accept non-violence as an ennobling philosophy or as a prime strategy in politics. In a way, these differences in degree may also be ascribed to the confusion between Gandhian charisma and politics, resulting in a blurring of critical edges. Except for Mulk Raj Anand and Raja Rao (who are committed in their preferences for socialism and Gandhism respectively), other novelists are ideologically ambiguous. In this context, Manohar Malgonkar deserves notice, when he categorically denounces spiritualization of politics as a myth. Whereas Anand is not averse to revolutionary violence, if it is imperative, Malgonkar conceives of it as an actuality, whether one likes it or not.

Several historical novels of the Gandhian era exhibit an urge for an egalitarian utopia. It is strange that political experience of domination, denial and persecution in colonial India should have invited consternation and defiance, but what has finally emerged is a comforting recourse to an idealism, visualizing harmony and peace amidst the chaotic reality of discord. Probably, this shows an anxiety for continuity with the past and acceptance of incremental change, rather than a predisposition toward revolutionary structural change, threatening a break with the past. Although positive in the sense of providing sustenance and resilience to the social structure, such a strand has not proved particularly conducive to the growth of innovative political consciousness in India. However, the novelists seem to be deeply concerned about the form, purpose and extent to which the legacy of the past is likely to be transmitted to posterity, for the desired national edifice would largely depend on such efforts.

The hiatus between social and political worlds, sought to be bridged by the unifying ethos of nationalism, re-emerged in more aggravating form soon after independence. In addition, the creative artists were faced with the challenge of comprehending as well as validating the enormous phenomenon of change in totality, encompassing all spheres of life. During the 1950s, the socio-political optimism and aesthetic rebellion of progressive fiction of pre-independence era seemed to be giving way to the politics of despair, flowing largely from the west. The Indo-Anglian political novel, however, did not degenerate into nihilistic fiction.

Although beginning on a low key, the novelists began to discern a more comprehensive appreciation of the political reality during the 1960s, 1970s and the 1980s. The novelists are aware of the ambivalence resultant from induction of democratic structures in a society for long inhibited by feudal, obscurantist and imperialist structures and processes, compounded by veneration for the bequest which precluded inquisitiveness to question and to make informal enquiries. Mulk Raj Anand, Nayantara Sahgal, Bhabani Bhattacharya and Salman Rushdie have been consciously concerned with renouncing that obsession. Malgonkar and Sheorey also attempt critical examination of the initial trials of a nascent democracy.

Whereas Mulk Raj Anand (and to a lesser extent Malgonkar) advocates annihilation of feudal anachronisms as a prerequisite for social democracy, Raja Rao proudly affirms his

faith in monarchical form of government. For Nayantara
Sahgal, the 'middle road between capitalism and communism'
is an efficacious alternative for India's liberal democracy,
provided the norms of consensual politics of Nehru are
scrupulously followed. Raja Rao, on the contrary, believes
that Nehru's prescriptions in that regard are no more than a
utopian liberal's priority. A.G. Sheorey assails erosion of
public ethics and believes it to be a divisive tendency. For him,
revival of Gandhian norms of public conduct alone could
consolidate democratic structures in India. Of all the Indo-
Anglian political novelists, Nayantara Sahgal is the most
vociferous in exposing and condemning the creeping politico-
cultural conformism and loyalism in contemporary India.
Salman Rushdie is a notable exception, as he moves beyond
conventional politico-aesthetic idioms and projects immediacy
of innovative political imagination to face squarely the
paradoxes of liberty and authority, charisma and democracy,
revivalism and progress. For Rushdie, India's tryst with
destiny is perpetual.

By and large, the novelists are favourably predisposed
toward the politics of reform in post-independence India,[4] with
the exception of Mulk Raj Anand. Nayantara Sahgal is particularly sceptical about the potential efficacy of the hitherto
successful strategy of non-violent and incremental change in
the larger context of the politics of violence currently gaining
ground in India. Sahgal's *A Situation in New Delhi* is a valuable
interpretation of the changing political ethos in the country.

Variants of analysis notwithstanding, political novelists,
dealing with the dynamics of democratic political structure in
India, seem to agree on the continued relevance of the core
democratic values, transmitted through the nationalist movement and incorporated in India's constitution, namely, liberty,
equality and justice. In a substantial way, it is an extension
of the pre-independence ideals for an egalitarian utopia in
free India. Further, interesting enough, the novelists almost
consensually prescribe an active role for intellectuals.[5] There
is an assertion of a specific regimen for intellectuals to act
before it is too late, so as to avert ensuing national crises.

Acceptance of socio-economic renovation as the corresponding imperative of political democracy remains the central

tenet of progressive political novels. Mulk Raj Anand stands out almost as an aesthetic titan whose fiction consistently and categoricatly upholds that democracy is a way of life, ensuring recognition and realization of the dignity, freedom and fulfilment of man. In Anand's view, quest for socio-economic transformation is likely to remain a mythical mirage, unless political democracy is purposively and progressively oriented toward genuine incorporation of justice and equality in the socio-cultural fabric of India.[6] Purposive politics is capable of becoming a synonym of creative action, if pursued as a vocation, in full awareness of its implications for the society at large. Such a sense of vocation is born out of a passionate commitment to and conviction of causes, visualized by Anand through his romantic, pragmatic and revolutionary characters in his fiction.

Bhabani Bhattacharya's social realism has acquired a hue different from Anand in ideological terms, though he shares the central concerns of Anand's aesthetics. Bhattacharya visualizes an egalitarian order wherein caste and class no longer inhibit cultivation of a truly 'human' personality and positive aspects of the cultural heritage of the past are rehabilitated. India's cultural plurality notwithstanding, Bhattacharya's fiction evinces a sort of embryonic optimism for spontaneous and self-generated social change in contradiction to Anand's persistent advocacy of directed change. Bhattacharya's notion is thus closer to Nayantara Sahgal's perception of politics of gradual reform than to Anand and Rushdie who perceive structural changes as conducive to erasing the socio-economic fragmentation in India. Though subscribing to different ideological priorities, Anand, Bhattacharya, Sahgal and Rushdie do not compromise on the fundamentals of 'quality of life' and liberty of thought, conscience and action.

Thus the preceding illustrative panorama of the thematic concerns would bring out that the Indo-Anglian political novelists present a wide-ranging spectrum. What could be identified as their crowning concern is the unfailing quest for identity—individual and national, which transcends political confines and moves into the realm of a total psycho-cultural personality. In this quest, the Indo-Anglian political novel has come full circle, beginning with Mulk Raj Anand and culminating in Salman Rushdie.

II

Dilemmas of Evolution: Tradition, Change and Ideology

The Indian novel in English represents not only the panoramic setting of the socio-political ethos but also the aspirations, limitations and dilemmas of evolution from tradition to modernity, experienced by a nation which is complex, heterogeneous and plural in its socio-cultural character.[7] These dilemmas as creative challenge to the writers have distinctly influenced the nature and direction of their perceptions. This is evidenced by the novelists' aesthetic exploration of the variety and complexity of the process of socio-political evolution in India, notwithstanding, the inclusive sense of unity inherent in this evolution.[8] Raja Rao has responded to the traditional moorings of Indian culture, affirming the reconciliation of matter and spirit, the temporal and the eternal, the physical and the metaphysical into a harmonious synthesis in terms of orthodox cultural revivalism. Mulk Raj Anand, on the contrary, has responded to the historical and the contemporary socio-cultural anachronisms that have hampered the growth of an equitable socio-political order in terms of progressive social realism. R.K. Narayan, Nayantara Sahgal, Bhabani Bhattacharya and Manohar Malgonkar, with differing emphases, have responded to the situational flux and aberrations, creeping in the socio-cultural milieu from time to time in an open-ended dialogue with new pragmatic orientations.

The tension areas perceptible in the interactive evolution of politics and culture in India seem to flow from the dichotomized and rigid compartmentalization of tradition, change and ideology. In the Indo-Anglian perspective, the point could be illustrated through the aforesaid aesthetic schools. Raja Rao interprets tradition as a value system and norm structure, emanating from the rich cultural heritage of classical Indian philosophy. In this context, notions of change (and modernity), perceived as intrusions from the west, do not find favour with Raja Rao's antiquarian ideal of aesthetics. His interpretation of tradition is coupled with a cyclical view of history which undermines the dynamics of historical forces and mythicizes socio-cultural evolution. Raja Rao's *brahminic* elitism, Hindu orthodoxy and intellectual arrogance overwhelmingly pervasive in *The Serpent and the Rope*, turns his creative vision into reticent and backward-looking aesthetics.

The progressive political vision of Raja Rao, discernible in *Kanthapura*, seems to have returned in *Comrade Kirillov*, where he attempts a synthesis of *vedanta* and Gandhism.[9] In politico-cultural terms the synthesis is unique both for its freshness of perspective and rooted orthodoxy. Although *Comrade Kirillov* presents an 'affectionate criticism of Gandhism', from the Marxist point of view as Rao himself puts it, what finally emerges is a reversion to *Vedanta*: "*Vedanta* alone has the courage of the ultimate—it longingly uncovers the limits of your own ignorant authority and asks for more inquiry into your biological, psychological and psychic self".[10] The progressive vision, thus, gets blinkered by a sort of metaphysical autocracy which covertly justifies social stagnation, moral resignation and cultural hierarchy. Raja Rao's interpretation of culture as tradition, beyond and in contravention of history, makes his vision retrogressive in political terms.[11] Raja Rao. however, is not apologetic. Instead, he seems to come out with gospel truth in a dogmatic manner: "Either you believe the world exists—and so you. Or you believe that you exist—and so the world. . . . The first is the vedantin's position—the second is the Marxist's and they are irreconcilable".[12]

True, Raja Rao's *Vedantic* etymology is irreconcilable with Marxist analysis, as represented by Mulk Raj Anand in Indo-Anglian fiction. Anand interprets culture in material terms and tradition as the significant past. By virtue of the simple laws of evolution in Anand's view, tradition needs to be continually examined and questioned in the light of stages of historical growth. Anand does not denounce the perennial aspects of the cultural heritage in terms of the foundational values, which provide resistance to the social universe. However, when cultural heritage overtly or covertly becomes an instrument of social stasis, moral degeneration and repression, it needs to be revaluated and reoriented toward norms of progressive evolution. In fact, Anand's progressive consciousness has its genesis in his condemnation of the decaying morality of Hindu/Brahmin hegemony (so gloriously upheld by Raja Rao) in the *Untouchable*, which becomes more and more inclusive in his subsequent fiction.

Tradition, in Anand's view, is not incompatible with ideology. Both are amenable to the dynamics of change. Since change is an imminent logic of progress, both tradition and ideology have to be dialectically interactive. Anand's aesthetics could thus be termed as "cultural materialism" (to use the expression of Raymond Williams) as opposed to cultural revivalism of Raja Rao. In politico-cultural terms, Anand's cultural materialism strikes a balance between the ideas of innovation devoid of roots and of tradition bereft of dynamism, the former being the danger of mechanistic Marxism and the latter of orthodox revivalism. Anand's humanistic Marxism is thus a quest for a progressive re-orientation of the past in order to make it relevant to the present.

Bhattacharya, Narayan, Sahgal and Malgonkar subscribe to none of the aforesaid interpretations. Bhattacharya seeks to synthesize norms of conventional cultural resilience with the changing ethos of political transformation and technological advance, in the tradition of Tagore. His *Music for Mohini* is a valuable illustration of this synthesis. R.K. Narayan has attempted to adapt puranic myths to contemporary social problems with a tragi-comic irony, so characteristic of Narayan's literary style. His *Maneater of Malgudi* deserves an especial mention in this regard. Nayantara Sahgal's exploration of cultural sanctions of social interaction results in a contextual questioning of conventional morality. More than any other Indo-Anglian novelist, Sahgal has attempted a persistent revaluation of conventional morality in her major fiction, especially in regard to man-women relationship in India. Her *The Day in Shadow* is, particularly identifiable as an epitomization of innovative consciousness in this regard. Malgonkar, like Raja Rao, is a strange blend of progressive political awareness and dogmatic social ethics. His *Combat of Shadows*, however, attempts a synthesis of ideas of conventional morality on the one hand and modernity on the other.

Exploration of culture as tradition has involved employment of myths as major icons of explanation in all the political
novelists in Indian English. For instance, Raja Rao's extensive
use of myths from *Ramayana, Mahabharata* (and *Sthala
Purana*, as he terms the local myths) gives his *Kanthapura* an
aura of profound authenticity and rootedness, along with
renovative Gandhian vision. B. Rajan in *The Dark Dancer* has
most effectively employed myths of *Nataraja* and *Karna* as
symbols in the language of politics. R.K. Narayan and
Bhattacharya have also gone back to *puranic* myths. It is,
however, Mulk Raj Anand who has attempted a re-enactment
of a cultural myth, the Sita myth, in purely contemporary
terms, in *Gauri*. Nayantara Sahgal, like Anand, is progressively
oriented toward classical myths. On the whole, myths as
symbols of heritage, form part of the politico-aesthetic vision
of the Indo-Anglian novelists. The relevance of such psycho-
cultural orientation lies in relating the present with the
perennial in the past.

Conceptualization of political change in terms of ideology,
in contradistinction to tradition, distinguishes other novelists
from Mulk Raj Anand and Raja Rao, who are committed to
socialism and Gandhism respectively in their own deterministic
ways. Nayantara Sahgal is also identifiable for her ideological
primacy of liberal democracy. Other Indo-Anglian novelists
exhibit ideological ambivalence. Bhabani Bhattacharya's
syncretic politics and harmonious aesthetics are, in essence, a
synthesis of progressivism, Gandhism and Tagorean ideals.
Manohar Malgonkar's politico-cultural universe is a dwindling
balance between aristocratic grandeur and commonplace life.

Ideological commitment or its absence explains the novelist's worldview, as also his perception of the dialectics of
change in society. Thus it is not hard to perceive that an
ideologically conservative Raja Rao is suspect of all change in
Indian society, whereas Anand does not hesitate in visualizing
radical changes in the social order. Similarly, it is possible to
explain Bhattacharya's and Sahgal's preference for incremental
change, as rooted in their conviction in the politics of reform.
The ideological ambivalence of the majority of the political
novelists may be interpreted as an inclination toward the

traditional norms of accommodation, consensus and compromise, instead of rejection, defiance or revolutionary
choice. It is pertinent to note that beneath the seemingly
stable social universe, an uneasy tension of traditional moorings and the changing ethos is invariably present in a society
in transition. The writers on the fence have explored this
dimension best.

Quest for comprehension of tradition in face of change takes
one back to a quest of identity. A noted aesthetician explains
that identity as the focal point of creativity has been a long
tradition in India, serving two ends: a return to Indianness and
a return to critical spirit.[13] In their attempts at innovative
consciousness, the novelists have also visualized culturally
cohesive units which transcend the stereotype of contemporary
experience.

Whether in philosophical, ideological or pragmatic terms,
the Indo-Anglian novelists' explanation of the dilemmas of
evolution with reference to tradition and change in Indian
society is essentially concerned with the normative content of
transformation. However, their politico-aesthetic vision is not
confined to "an information theory of value" or a "cognitariat" perception, as Alvin Toffler would say. On the contrary, it is a sort of a Socratic quest for self-comprehension, at
the cultural level. In this explanation, the novelists have
invariably perceived politics and ethics as inseparable and
inalienable, as opposed to the amoral conception of politics.

B. Rajan aptly puts the whole issue in perspective. "The
question to be answered is whether the Indian tradition with
its capacity for assimilation and its unique power of synthesis
can come to terms with the new (and the new is inevitable)
without deep erosions in its fundamental character".[14] The
novelists are conscious of the normative inheritance and cultural
continuity, and yet an open-ended quest, cognizant of the inevitability of change and development, is perceptible in their
syncretic awareness. The aesthetic ideal of infinity of improvement of human destiny makes the quest politically perpetual.[15]
However, paradoxical as it might sound, the unity of politics
and aesthetics is conceivable in all the major political novelists.

Thus the Indo-Anglian novel does not propose to live

purely off the ethical past or deny or reject the philosophic-
cultural moorings from which politics is also derived. What is
sought is a reinterpretation and a re-valuation of the past
vis-a-vis the changing ethos. For living art does not flourish in
a static society which threatens to affront the artist's values at
every turn.

III

Quest for Indigenization: Innovation and Affirmation

Progressive aesthetic culture does not emerge in a vacuum
or away from the political civilization, but as a natural result
of socio-cultural and political evolution. As a culture
evolves, the aesthetic vision absorbs the achievement of the
previous epochs and develops them on a new basis which is
conducive to innovative consciousness. The Indian political
novel in English, critically assimilating the legacy of the past,
in both political and cultural terms, has evolved a politico-
aesthetic vision which is innovative as well as affirmative in
content, as if genuinely in quest of indigenization.

It is often argued that the intellectual genesis of the Indo-
Anglian novel is traceable to the ambivalent circumstances of
its birth in the politico-cultural interaction of two divergent
civilizations, resulting in an aesthetics of ambiguity. However,
as B. Rajan explains, "the man with mixed allegiances is contemporary Everyman and that to shut one's self off from the
challenge of the 'non-Indian' betrays not a sense of nationality
but an obsession with insularity".[16] The Indo-Anglian political
novel has communicated the complexity and variety of socio-
political experience to an extent that does not betray the curse
of either cultural rootlessness or political schizophrenia. Dilemmas of evolution notwithstanding, the Indo-Anglian novelist
does not exhibit an aesthetic confusion on issues concerning
socio-political primacy. In full awareness of the frustrating
ethos of his aesthetics, the novelist seems to be sure of his
bearings. The political idioms, he has used, vary from revivalism to revolution, romanticism to reform, conservatism to
innovation. Yet, beneath this creative abundance of complexity
and variety, is perceptible an inclusive unity of innovation and

affirmation. The point becomes pertinent, if the Indo-Anglian endeavours are perceived in the context of world aesthetics of the past half century. Whereas in the western social-aesthetics a move from social realism (of the 1930s) toward an aesthetics of alienation (during the 1960s and the 1970s) is prominently perceptible, such a move has been kept within aesthetic limits in India, probably through conscious, purposive protest and an ultimate affirmation of the relevant past as well as the desired future.

Quest for politico-cultural renaissance inadvertently or otherwise, forms part of the renovative-affirmative idiom of the Indo-Anglian political novel. Political acculturation is interpreted as a corollary of national identity. Vision of egalitarian democracy is sustained by exertions of secularization, nonviolence and justice. Individual dignity and national inviolability remain unexceptionable objectives. Also, an exploration and rejuvenation of core politico-cultural values remains a precondition as well as the ultimate objective of the novelists for indigenization. In other words, the novelists offer an explanation and interpretation of India's political reality *on its own terms.*

Two popular misinterpretations of the interactive continuum of politics and culture in India need to be examined at this point: first, the myth of two political cultures and secondly, the myth of misplaced evasive withdrawal. The myth of two political cultures has been enunciated by Myron Weiner on the basis of a dichotomized view of elite (national level) and mass (local level) political cultures in India.[17] Whereas it is true that there are significant differences between the national-level and local-level leadership and their orientations towards basic politico-cultural processes in the polity, the differences however, do not qualify to be diagnosed as dichotomous. The characterization of local-level politics as 'mass' politics is also misleading It is, indeed, uncharitable to impose ideational formats out of context, as Weiner has done. Besides, the issue at stake is not so much the polarities of the local and the national politics, as the exploration of the possibilities of interplay between the two as between the political structure and its social base.

The Indian novel in English has attempted this exploration to a considerable extent and has brought out an inclusive vision of politics, culture and society in India. Although inadequate attention has been addressed to ethnic loyalty-structures, the novelists have consciously and successfully exposed the conflictual contours of collective entities like caste, class and community in contradistinction to the social scientists who tend to homogenize collective entities and shared attitudes and sentiments.

V.S. Naipaul has propagated another myth—the myth of "the Indian ability to retreat, the ability genuinely not to see what was obvious: with others a foundation of neurosis, but with Indians, only part of a greater philosophy of despair, leading to passivity, detachment, acceptance".[18] Committed to such a blinkered assumption, Naipaul indulges in self-righteous verdict on Indian literature: "Indian attempts at the novel further reveal the Indian confusion. . . . In India, thoughtful men have preferred to turn their backs on the here and now and to satisfy what President Radhakrishnan calls 'the basic human hunger for the unseen'. It is not a good qualification for the writing or reading of novels".[19]

However, the preceding discussion of the socio-political concerns of the novelists shows, in ample measure, the Indian novelists' concern with the *here and now*. That should be an adequate argument to dispel the so-called mythicization of Indian character. Even a casual look at the progressive fiction of Anand, Bhattacharya, Sahgal and Nahal would expose the hollowness and deceptive unidimensionality of Naipaul's pronouncements. Whereas one might sympathize with Naipaul for his superficial acquaintance with the complex Indian reality, it needs to be reasserted that, even as novelists like Raja Rao and Sudhin Ghose might betray exaggerated concern for 'the basic human hunger for the unseen', they distinctly possess a social vision, though it might be classified as revivalistic. Naipaul's quick dismissal of the possibilities of creation of good novels is certainly not borne out by the discussion of the creative writings in the present study.

Moreover, if the novel 'belongs' to the west, so do so many other things—ideas, ideals, structures and ideologies. If Indo-Anglian endeavours were inherently incompetent, one would gladly accept that as a fact. But to assail honest endeavours and competent creativity with a bias against a country *per se* is not a legitimate exercize in literary criticism. The element of exaggeration and bravado in Naipaul's otherwise brilliant assertions notwithstanding, the fact is that Indo-Anglian novel seeks to interpret Indian reality, through an Indian perspective, not necessarily cut off from the outside world. That alone places this branch of Indian literature as a serious endeavour for intellectual reassessment of society, culture and politics in India. Further, an urge for relevance has not deteriorated Indian novels in English to the status of cultural determinants of Indian politics or *vice versa*. Although stopping short of a full-fledged creative programme of political engineering, the novels, nevertheless, have explored the dynamics of political order and chaos against a socio-cultural perspective. The novelists have also taken cognizance of the role politics has played in mobilizing and stirring cultural consciousness in India. The dilemmas of creative writers, inhibiting incessant process of exploration, are indeed, the dilemmas of the entire community of intellectuals in India, caught between the dialectics of tradition and change in a world of transition.

It may not be presumptuous at this stage to state that, in the given socio-political totality in India, there should have been more political novels imbued with intensity than are available at present, sustaining the tradition initiated by Mulk Raj Anand and further enriched by Bhattacharya and Sahgal. As mentioned earlier, several significant political concepts and formulations in evidence during different phases of the nationalist movement have not been comprehensively explored as psycho-social bases of nationalism in India. For instance, pacifism, politics of renunciation and compassion, militant nationalism and deification of the nation could be cited in this regard. Similarly, in response to challenges flowing from induction of democratic structures in a social system weighed down by hierarchy and injustice, the Indo-Anglian political novel, by and large, shows no overriding urgency to move beyond enunciations which had been discerned earlier and were very much part of the contemporary idiom of protest and national aspirations. On the other hand, considerable anxiety and consternation are manifest at the erosion of Gandhian values and Nehruvian vision of nation-building. The intensity of protest, however, is not consistent or total with regard to the inhibiting constraints and paradoxes in India's socio-political life.

Indeed, there are numerous instances of brilliant flashes of creative analysis and sensitized projection. These flashes, however, fall short of constituting a living and vibrant tradition. For instance, M. Malgonkar, C. Nahal and B. Rajan come up with insightful interpretations of Gandhian politics, but fail to sustain the ingenious edge on other themes. This applies to other novelists as well. It is with Salman Rushdie's *Midnight's Children*, that a distinctive departure and a breakthrough affirming the novelist's capacity to evolve and go beyond conventional idiom is perceptible. That, however, needs to be sustained with consistent aesthetic and political commitment.

Limitations, notwithstanding, the Indo-Anglian political novel has served as a valuable point of confluence of main-streams representing India's antiquity and the present (and also probably the imminent future) manifesting an urge to discern and unravel the many splendoured socio-political reality. In this context, it is relevant to recall V.K. Gokak's observation: ". . . the Indian writer with an olympian vision does contemplate the tragicomic panorama that is India—the glory, jest, and riddle of the world. . . . Imagine the magic mirror of this olympian vision splintered into a million fragments and that will give good idea of the contemporary republic of letters in India."[20] It is also possible to envision through the splintered million fragments of political imagination, a multi-dimensional prism of integrated vision. For ultimately, the salience of political fiction lies in its architechtonic perception of the socio-political reality, in contrast to the polarized specialization of the social sciences.

It would be presumptuous to believe that discovery of India, in an all-inclusive sense, is possible at a given point of time. However, during the preceding half a century, the Indo-Anglian political novel has assiduously undertaken an aesthetic journey with a mission, as it were, to re-discover aspects of the composite macrocosm of the Indian Self. In the process, it has attributed meaning, content and orientation to the mosaic of the complex socio-political reality. The aesthetic journey has been, in essence, characterized by an ongoing movement, from

cultural erudition to politico-cultural critique. The politico-
aesthetic vision of the Indo-Anglian novelist has, however,
remained imperatively affirmative even in its quest of innovation, as it has not lost sight of its Indian identity.

References

1. See, for instance, Herbert Marcuse's argument: "The political
   protest, assuming a total character, reaches into a dimension, which,
   as aesthetic dimension, has been essentially apolitical. And the
   political protest activates in this dimension precisely the foundational organic elements: the human sensibility which rebels against
   the dictates of repressive reason and, in doing so, invokes the
   sensuous power of imagination". *An Essay on Liberation* (Boston,
   Beacon, 1969), p. 30.
2. See, for instance, Rabindranath Tagore's assertion: "All our poetry,
   philosophy, science, art and religion are serving to extend the scope
   of our consciousness towards higher and larger spheres. Man does
   not acquire rights through occupation of larger space, nor through
   external conduct, but the rights extend only so far as he is real, and
   his reality is measured by the scope of his consciousness." *Sadhana*
   (London, Macmillan, 1913), pp. 18-19.
3. Attempts have been made to trace the origins of fictional form in
   India to Sanskrit classics—in the *Katha* and cluster stories in *Jataka*
   and chain stories in *Panchtantra*, developed into longer and sustained
   prose narratives in the sixth and seventh centuries in such works as
   Banabhatta's *Harscharita* and *Kadambari*, Subandhu's *Vasavdutta*
   and Dandini's *Dasa Kumaracharita*, among others. For details see
   T.W. Clark, *The Novel in India—Its Birth and Development* (Berkeley,
   University of California Press, 1970), and C.D. Narasimhaiah,
   (ed.), *Literary Criticism—European and Indian Traditions* (Mysore,
   University of Mysore, n. d.).
4. For an interesting comparison, see Thomas Pantham, "On the
   Reformation of Political Culture in India; Participatory and Egalitarian values among Political Elites; *The Journal of Commonwealth
   and Comparative Politics*, XVIII, 2(July 1980), 172-189.
5. It is relevant to recall that several political analysts have also
   reacted in a similar vein. For instance see Yogendra K. Malik (ed.),
   South Asian Intellectuals and Social Change (New Delhi, Heritage,
   1982) and S.H. Rudolph and C.I. Rudolph (eds.), *Education and
   Politics in India* (Cambridge, Mass, Harvard University, 1972).
6. Tagore made an identical exhortation:
   "Those of us in India who have come under the delusion that mere
   political freedom will make us free have accepted their lessons from
   the west as the gospel truth and lost their faith in humanity. We

must remember whatever weakness we cherish in our society will become the source of danger in politics." *Nationalism* (Madras, Macmillan, 1976), p. 74.

7. For an interesting theoretical comparison see M.D. Sahlins and E.R. Service (eds.), *Evolution and Culture* (Ann Arbor, MI, University of Michigan, 1970).

8. It is pertinent to recall V.K. Gokak's assertion that modern Indian literature has been shaped by three distinct traditions—the mystical, the humanist and the socialist: see *English in India: Its Present and Future* (Bombay, Asia, 1965), pp. 175-8.

9. See Asha Kaushik, "Meeting Raja Rao", *The Literary Criterion*, XVIII, 3 (1983), 33-38.

10. *Comrade Kirillov* (New Delhi, Orient Paperbacks, 1976), p. 73.

11. See, for instance, his repetitive refrain: "I am a monarchist" in *The Serpent and the Rope* (New Delhi, Orient Paperbacks, 1968), p. 102.

12. *n.* 11, p. 333.

13. S. Mokashi-Punekar, *The Indo-Anglian Creed* (Calcutta, Writers Workshop, 1972), p. 60.

14. B. Rajan, "Identity and Nationality", in John Press (ed.), *Commonwealth Literature—Unity and Diversity in a Common Culture*, (London, Heinemann, 1965), p. 108.

15. The apprehension of many as voiced by one of the characters of Nayantara Sahgal, stands negated: ". . . between Marx and anti-Marx what India stands for may get drowned out in confusion". *The Day in Shadow* (Delhi, Vikas, 1971) p. 158. The allusion to confusion, even if accepted, may prove another step in search of perspectival clarity'.

16. *n.* 14, p. 108.

17. Myron Weiner, "India: Two Political Cultures" in L.W. Pye and S. Verba (eds.), *Political Culture and Political Development* (Princeton, Princeton University, 1965), pp. 199-244.

18. V.S. Naipaul, *An Area of Darkness* (Harmondsworth, Penguine Books, 1968), p. 188.

19. *n.* 18, p. 214.

20. V.K. Gokak, *India and World Culture* (Delhi, Vikas, 1972), p. 118.

Select Bibliography

I

PRIMARY SOURCES

Indo-Anglian Novels*

Abbas, K.A., *Tomorrow is Ours*, Bombay, Popular Book Depot, 1943.

——, *Defeat for Death*, Bombay, Padmaja, 1944.

——, *Inquilab*, Bombay, Jaico, 1955.

Ali, Aamir, *Conflict*, Bombay, National Information and Publications, 1947.

Ali Ahmed, *Twilight in Delhi* (*1940*), Bombay, Oxford, 1966.

Anand, Mulk Raj, *Across the Black Waters* (1940), Bombay, Kutub-Popular, 1955.

——, *The Big Heart* (1945), Bombay, Kutub-Popular, n.d.

——, *Two Leaves and a Bud* (1937), Bombay, Kutub-Popular, 1966.

——, *Untouchable* (1935), Bombay, Kutub-Popular, n.d.

——, *The Village* (1939), Bombay, Kutub-Popular, 1954.

——, *Private Life of an Indian Prince* (1953), Delhi, Hind Pocket Books, 1970.

——, *The Road*, Bombay, Kutub-Popular, 1961.

——, *The Sword and the Sickle* (1942), Bombay, Kutub-Popular 1955.

——, *Coolie* (1936), Bombay, Kutub-Popular, n.d.

——, *Morning Face*, Bombay, Kutub-Popular, 1968.

——, *Gauri* (1960), Delhi, Orient Paperbacks, 1976.

*Date within brackets indicates original publication.

——, *Seven Summers*, Bombay, Kutub-Popular, 1963.

——, *Death of a Hero*, Bombay, Kutub-Popular, 1963.

——, *Confession of a Lover*, New Delhi, Arnold-Heinemann, 1976.

Bawa, P.S., *Memories of the Raj*, Delhi, Hind Pocket Books, 1981.

Bhattacharya, Bhabani, *So Many Hungers* (1947), Delhi, Orient Paperbacks, 1978.

——, *A Goddess Named Gold*, Delhi, Hind Pocket Books, 1960.

——, *Music for Mohini*, New Delhi, Orient Paperbacks, 1952.

——, *He Who Rides A Tiger* (1955), Delhi, Hind Pocket Books, n.d.

——, *Shadow From Ladakh*, Delhi, Hind Pocket Books, 1966.

Chitale, Venu, *In Transit*, Bombay, Hind Kitabs, 1950.

Das, Kamala, *Alphabet of Lust*, New Delhi, Orient Paperbacks, 1976.

Day, Lal Behari, *Govind Samanta or History of a Bengal Raiyat*, London, Macmillan, 1874.

Dutt, S.C., *Shunkur: A Tale of the Indian Mutiny of 1857*, London, Lovell Reeve & Co., 1885.

Futehally, Zeenuth, *Zohra*, Bombay, Hind Kitabs, 1951.

Gargi, Balwant, *The Naked Triangle*, Ghaziabad, Vikas, 1980.

Hiro, Dilip, *A Triangular View*, London, Dobson, 1969.

Hosain, Attia, *Sunlight on a Broken Column*, London, Chatto & Windus, 1961.

Karaka, D.F., *We Never Die*, Bombay, Thacker & Co., 1944.

——, *There Lay the City*, Bombay, Thacker & Co., 1942.

Malgonkar, Manohar, *A Bend in the Ganges*, London, Hamish Hamilton, 1964.

——, *The Devil's Wind*, Delhi, Orient Paperbacks, 1972.

——, *Princes* (1963), New Delhi, Orient Paperbacks, 1970.

——, *Distant Drum*, Bombay, Asia Publishing House, 1960.

——, *Combat of Shadows*, London, Hamish Hamilton, 1963.

Marath, S.M., *The Wound of Spring*, London, Dennis Dobson, 1960.

Markandaya, Kamala, *The Golden Honeycomb*, London, Chatto & Windus, 1977.

——, *Some Inner Fury*, London, Putnam 1955.

——, *A Handful of Rice*, Delhi, Hind Pocket Books, 1966.

Mascarenhas, L., *Sorrowing Lies My Land*, Bombay, Hind Kitabs, 1955.

Nahal, Chaman, *Azadi*, New Delhi, Orient Paperbacks, 1975.

——, *The Crown and the Loincloth*, New Delhi, Vikas, 1982.

Narayan, R.K., *Waiting for the Mahatma* (1955), Mysore, Indian Thought, 1967.

——, *The Dark Room*, Bombay, Pearl, 1960.

——, *The Man-Eater of Malgudi*, London, William Heinemann, 1962.

Nagarajan, K., *Chronicles of Kedaram*, Bombay, Asia, 1961.

——, *Athawar House*, Madras, Higginbotham's, 1939.

Rajan, Balachandra, *The Dark Dancer*, London, Heinemann, 1959.

Rao, Raja, *Kanthapura* (1938), New Delhi, Orient Paperbacks, 1971.

——, *The Serpent and the Rope* (1960), New Delhi, Orient Paperbacks, 1968.

——, *Comrade Kirillov*, New Delhi, Orient Paperbacks, 1976.

Rushdie, Salman, *Midnight's Children* (1981), London, Picador, 1982.

Sahgal, Nayantara, *A Time to be Happy* (1958), Bombay, Jaico, 1963.

——, *This Time of Morning* (1965), New Delhi, Orient Paperbacks, n.d.

——, *Storm in Chandigarh*, Delhi, Hind Pocket Books, 1969.

——, *The Day in Shadow*, Delhi, Vikas, 1971.

——, *A Situation in New Delhi*, London Magazine edition, 1977.

Sheorey, Anand Gopal, *Dusk Before Dawn—A Novel of Post-Freedom India*, New Delhi, Vikas, 1978.

Singh, Khushwant, *Train to Pakistan* (1955), Bombay, Pearl, 1957.

——, *I shall not Hear the Nightingale*, London, John Calder, 1959.

Venkataramani, K.S., *Murugan, The Tiller* (1927), Madras, Svetaranya Ashram, 1929.

——, *Kandan, The Patriot*, Madras, Svetaranya Ashram, 1932.

Zutshi, C.M., *Motherland*, Lahore, Hero Publications, 1944.

II

SECONDARY SOURCES

Books

Almond, G.A. and Verba, Sidney, *The Civic Culture*, Princeton, Princeton University Press, 1963.

Amur, G.S., *Manohar Malgonkar*, New Delhi, Arnold Heinemann, 1973.

Anand, Mulk Raj, *Apology for Heroism*, (1946), New Delhi, Arnold Heinemann, 1975.

——, *Is there an Indian Culture?* Bombay, Asia, 1963.

——, *The King-Emperor's English: Or the Role of the English Language in Free India*, Bombay, Hind Kitabs, 1948.

Apter, David E., *Political Change: Collected Essays*, London, Frank Cass, 1973.

Azam, Kousar J., *Political Aspects of National Integration*, Meerut, Meenakshi, 1981.

Bald, S.R., *Novelists and Political Consciousness*, New Delhi, Chanakya, 1983.

Bakhtiyar, Iqbal (ed.), *The Novel in Modern India*, Bombay, The P.E.N. All India Centre, 1964.

Bary, W.T. *et al.* (eds.), *Sources of Indian Tradition*, New York, Columbia University Press, 1958.

Barry, Brian, *Sociologists, Economists and Democracy*, London, Collier-Macmillan, 1970.

Becker, George J., *Documents of Modern Literary Realism*, Princeton University Press, 1963.

Beer, Samuel and Ulam, Adam, (eds.), *Patterns of Government* New York, Random House, 1958.

Benjamin, Walter, *Illuminations: Essays and Reflections*, London, Jonathan Cape, 1970.

——, *Understanding Brecht*, London, New Left Books, 1973.

Berger, Morroe, *Real and Imagined Worlds: The Novel and Social Science*, Combridge, Mass, Harvard University Press, 1977.

Bhatia, B.M., *History of Social Development*, Vol. II, New Delhi Vikas, 1977.

Bhatnagar, K.C., *Realism in Major Indo-Anglian Fiction*, Bareilly, Prakash Book Depot, 1980.

Bill, James A., and Hardgrave, R.L., *Comparative Politics—The Quest For Theory*, Columbus, Ohio, Charles E. Merill, 1973.

Blotner, Joseph L., *The Political Novel*, New York, Doubley & Co., Inc., 1965.

Bluhm W.T., *Ideologies and Attitudes: Modern Political Culture*, New Jersey, Prentice-Hall, Inc., 1974.

Bombwall, K.R., *The Foundations of Indian Federalism*, Bombay, Asia, 1967.

Bondurant, J.V., *Conquest of Violence—The Gandhian Philosophy of Conflict*, Bombay, Oxford University Press, 1959.

Borenstein, Audrey, *Redeeming the Sin: Social Sciences and Literature*, New York, Columbia University Press, 1978.

Brecher, Michael, *Nehru—A Political Biography*, London, Oxford University Press, 1959.

Brockway, Thomas P. (ed.), *Language and Politics*, Boston, D.C. Health & Co., 1965.

Brown, Archie and Gray, Jack, (eds.), *Political Culture and Political Change in Communist States*, London, Macmillan, 1977.

Brown, Norman, *The United States and India and Pakistan*, Cambridge, Harvard University Press, 1953.

Camus, Albert, *The Rebel*, Harmondsworth, Penguin Books, 1977.

Carras, Mary C., *Indira Gandhi: In the Crucible of Leadership*, Bombay, Jaico, 1980.

Cary, Joyce, *Art and Reality*, London, Cambridge, 1957.

Caudwell, Christopher, *Illusion and Reality. A Study of the Sources of Poetry*, London, Lawrence and Wishart, 1946.

Caute, David, *The Illusion: An Essay on Politics, Theatre and the Novel*, New York, Harper & Row, 1972.

Chandrashekharan, K.R., *Bhabani Bhattacharya*, Delhi, Arnold Heinemann, 1974.

Chaudhary, Nirad C., *The Autobiography of an Unknown Indian*, New York, Macmillan, 1951.

——, *To Live or not to Live*, New Delhi, Orient Paperbacks, 1970.

Clark, T.W., *The Novel in India—Its Birth and Development*, Berkeley, University of California, 1970.

Collingwood, R.G., *The Principles of Art*, Oxford, Oxford University Press, 1947.

——, *The Idea of History*, Oxford, Oxford University, 1961.

Coupland, R., *The Indian Problem*, London, Oxford University Press, 1944.

Cowasjee, Saros, (ed.), *Author to Critic: Letters of Mulk Raj Anand to Saros Cowasjee*, Calcutta, Writers Workshop, 1973.

——, *So Many Freedoms*, Delhi, Oxford University Press, 1977.

Dahl, Robert, *Political Opposition in Western Democracies*, New Haven, Yale University Press, 1966.

Daniel, Thorner, *The Shaping of Modern India*, New Delhi, Allied, 1980.

De, S.K., *Studies in the History of Sanskrit Poetics*, London, Luzac & Co., 1923.

Dolan, Paul J., *Of War and War's Alarms—Fiction and Politics in the Modern World*, New York, The Free Press, 1976.

Dorsch, T.S. (Trans), *Classical Literary Criticism*, Harmondsworth, Penguine Books, 1965.

Dutt, Rajani Palme, *India Today* (1946), Calcutta, Manisha, 1979.

Eagleton, Terry, *Criticism and Ideology*, London, New Left Books, 1976.

——, *Marxism and Literary Criticism*, London, Methuen & Co., 1976.

Eagleton, Terry and Wicker, Brian, *From Culture to Revolution*, London, Sheed & Ward, 1968.

Easton, David, *A Systems Analysis of Political Life*, New York, John Wiley & Sons, 1965.

Eliot, T.S., *To Criticize the Critic and Other Writings*, London, Faber & Faber, 1965.

Emerson, Rupert, *From Empire to Nation*, Boston, Beacon, 1960.

Erikson, E.H., *Gandhi's Truth: On Origins of Militant Nationalism*, London, Faber & Faber, 1970.

Fanon, Frantz, *The Wretched of the Earth* (Trans: C. Farington) New York, Grove Press, Inc., 1963.

Finer, S.E., *The Man on Horseback*: *The Role of the Military in Politics*, London, Pall Mall Press, 1962.

Gandhi, M.K., *Cent Percent Swadeshi*, Ahmedabad, Navjivan, 1948.

Geertz, Clifford (ed.), *Old Societies and New States*: *The Quest For Modernity in Asia and Africa*, New Delhi, Amerind, 1971.

Gokak, V.K., *English in India*: *Its Present and Future*, Bombay, Asia, 1965.

———, *India and World Culture*, Delhi, Vikas, 1972.

Goldmann, Lucian, *Towards a Sociology of the Novel* (Trans. A. Sheridan), London, Tavistock, 1975.

Goodwin, K.L. (ed.), *National Identity*, London, Heinemann, 1970.

Gorky, Maxim, *On Literature*, Seatle, University of Washington Press, 1973.

Green, Philip and Walzer, Michael, *The Political Imagination in Literature—A Reader*, New York, The Free Press, 1967.

Harrex, S.C., *The Fire and the Offering*: *The English-Language Novel of India 1935-1970*, Calcutta, Writers Workshop, 1977.

Hemenway, S., *The Novel of India* Vol. 2: *The Indo-Anglian Novel*, Calcutta, Writers Workshop, 1975.

Holland, Henry H. Jr. (ed.), *Politics Through Literature*, New Jersey, Prentice Hall, Inc., 1968.

Hook, Sidney, *Towards an Understanding of Karl Marx*, New York, John Day, 1933.

———, *Marx and the Marxists—The Ambiguous Legacy*, N.J., D. Van Nostrand Co. Inc., 1955.

Howe, Irwing, *Politics and the Novel*, New York, Horizon Press, 1957.

Iyengar, K.R.S., *Indian Writing in English*, Bombay, Asia, (1962), 1973.

Jameson, Fredrick, *Marxism and Form*: *Twentieth Century Dialectical Theories of Literature*, New Jersey, Princeton University Press, 1971.

Jain, Jasbir, *Nayantara Sahgal*, New Delhi, Arnold Heinemann, 1978.

Jay, Martin, *The Dialectical Imagination*, Boston, Little Brown & Co., 1973.

Jotwani, Motilal, *Contemporary Indian Literature and Society*, New Delhi, Heritage, 1979.

Kavanagh, Dennis, *Political Culture*, London, Macmillan, 1972.

Kermode, Frank, *The Sense of an Ending: Studies in the Theory of Fiction*, Oxford, Oxford University Press, 1967.

Kothari, Rajni, *Democratic Polity and Social Change in India*, New Delhi, Allied, 1976.

Kriplani, Krishna, *Modern Indian Literature: A Panoramic Glimpse*, Bombay, Nirmala Sadanand, 1968.

Kroeber, Alfred, L. and Klukhohn, *Culture: A Critical Review of Concepts and Definitions*, New York, Vintage Books, 1963.

Lal, P., *The Alien Insiders: Indian Writing in English*, Calcutta, Writers Workshop, 1982.

Lane, Robert, E., *Political Ideology*, New York, Free Press, 1962.

Lawrenson, D.T. and Swingewood, A., *The Sociology of Literature*, New York, Shocker Books, 1972.

Leavis, F.R. and Thompson, Denys, *Culture and Environment*, London, Chatto & Windus, 1960.

Leighton, Alexander, *My Name is Legion: Foundations for a Theory of Man in Relation to Culture*, New York, Basic Books, 1959.

Lerner, Daniel, *The Passing of Traditional Society*, Glencoe III, The Free Press, 1958.

Lindsay, Jack, *The Elephant and the Lotus: A Study of the Novels of Mulk Raj Anand*, Bombay, Kutub, 1965.

Lipset, S.M., *Political Man—The Social Bases of Politics*, New York, Doubleday, 1960.

Lowenthal, Leo, *Literature and the Image of Man*, Boston, Beacon, 1957.

Lukacs, George, *The Historical Novel*, Boston, Beacon, 1963.

——, *The Meaning of Contemporary Realism*, London, Merlin Press, 1963.

——, *Studies in European Realism*, New York, Gosset & Dunlop, 1964.

Majumdar, R.C., *British Paramountcy and Indian Renaissance*, Bombay, Bhartiya Vidya Bhavan, 1961.

——, *The History and Culture of the Indian People*, 11 Vols. Bombay, Bhartiya Vidya Bhavan, 1964-77.

Malik, Yogendra K. (Ed.), *Politics and the Novel in India*, New Delhi, Orient Longman, 1978.

South Asian Intellectuals and Social Change, New Delhi, Heritage, 1982.

Marcuse, Herbert, *Eros and Civilization*, New York, Random House, 1955.

——, *Negations: Essays in Critical Theory*, (Trans. Spino J.J.) Boston, Beacon, 1968.

——, *An Essay on Liberation*, Harmondsworth, Penguin Books, 1969.

——, *The Aesthetic Dimension*, Boston, Beacon, 1977.

Margolies, David N., *The Function of Literature—A Study of Christopher Caudwell's Aesthetics*, New York, International Publishers, 1969.

Maxwell, N., *Woman on a White Horse*, Oxford, Institute of Commonwealth Studies, 1975.

Marx, Karl, *Economic and Philosophic Manuscripts of 1844*, Moscow, Progress, 1974.

——, *Articles on India*, Bombay, People's Publishing House, 1951.

Marx, Karl and Engels, Frederick, *On Literature and Art*, Moscow, Progress, 1976.

Mathur, P.C., *Social Bases of Indian Politics*, Jaipur, Aalekh, 1984.

McCutchion, David, *Indian Writing in English: Critical Essays*, Calcutta, Writers Workshop, 1969.

Medden, David, (ed.), *Proletarian Writers of the Thirties*, Southern Illinois University Press, 1968.

Mehta, P.P., *Indo-English Fiction: An Assessment*, Bareilly, Prakash Book Depot, 1968.

Mehta, V.R., *Ideology, Modernization and Politics in India*, New Delhi, Manohar, 1983.

Mehta, Ved, *Portrait of India*, New York, Farrar, Strauss and Giroux, 1970.

Menon, V.P., *Transfer of Power In India*, Calcutta, Orient Longmans, 1957.

——, *The Story of the Integration of the Indian States*, Bombay, Orient Longmans, 1956.

Mohan, Ramesh (ed.), *Indian Writing in English*, New Delhi, Orient Longman, 1978.

Mokashi-Punekar, S., *The Indo-Anglian Creed*, Calcutta, Writers Workshop, 1972.

Montgomery, J.D. and Hirschman, A.O. (eds.), *Public Policy*, Vol. 17, Cambridge, Mass, Harvard University, 1968.

Moore, Barrington Jr., *Social Origins of Dictatorship and Democracy*, Harmondsworth, Penguine, 1969.

Morawski, Stefan, *Inquiries into the Fundamentals of Aesthetics*, Cambridge, The MIT Press, 1974.

Mukherjee, Meenakshi, *The Twice Born Fiction*, Delhi, Arnold Heinemann, 1971.

Mukherjee, Radhakamal, *The Culture and Art of India*, London, Allen & Unwin, 1959.

Mukherjee, Sujit, *Towards a Literary History of India*, Simla, Indian Institute of Advanced Study, 1975.

Nahal, Chaman, *The New Literature in English*, New Delhi, Allied, 1985.

Naik, M.K., (*et al.*), *Critical Essays on Indian Writing in English*, Dharwar, Karnatak University, 1968.

— —, *Mulk Raj Anand*, New Delhi, Arnold Heinemann, 1973.

— —, *Aspects of Indian Writing in English*, Madras, Macmillan, 1979.

Naipaul, V.S., *An Area of Darkness*, London, Andre Deutsch, 1964.

— —, *India: A Wounded Civilization*, Harmondsworth, Penguine, 1979.

Nandi, Sudhir Kumar, *Studies in Modern Indian Aesthetics*, 2 Vols. Simla, IIAS, 1975-77.

Narain, Iqbal, *Twilight or Dawn: Political Change in India*, Agra, Shiva Lal Agarwala & Co., 1972.

Narasimhaiah, C.D. (ed.), *Literary Criticism: European and Indian Traditions*, Mysore, University of Mysore, n.d.

— —, *Raja Rao*, New Delhi, Arnold Heinemann, n.d.

— —, *The Writer's Gandhi*, Patiala, Punjabi University of Patiala, 1967.

— —, *The Swan and the Eagle*, Simla, IIAS, 1969.

— —, *Awakened Conscience—Studies in Commonwealth Literature*, New Delhi, Sterling, 1968.

Nayar, Kuldeep, *India After Nehru*, New Delhi, Vikas, 1975.

Nehru, Jawaharlal, *Independence and After—A Collection of Speeches*: September 1946-May 1949, Delhi, Publications Division, Govt. of India, 1949.

——, *The Discovery of India* (1946), New Delhi, Oxford University Press, 1981.

——, *An Autobiography*, New Delhi, Allied, 1962.

Nicholson, Kai, *A Presentation of Social Problems in Indo-Anglian and Anglo-Indian Novel*, Bombay, Jaico, 1972.

Nisbet, Robert A., *Sociology as an Art Form*, Oxford, Oxford University Press, 1976.

Niven, Alaistair, *The Commonwealth Writers Overseas*, Brussels, Didier, 1976.

——, *The Yoke of Pity*, New Delhi, Arnold-Heinemann, 1978.

Orwell, George, *A Collection of Essays*, Garden City, Doubley & Co., 1957.

Palma, Guiseppe Di, *Apathy and Participation: Mass Politics in Western Societies*, New York, Free Press, 1970.

Pande, G.C., *The Meaning and Process of Culture*, Agra, Shiva Lal Agarwala & Co., 1972.

Parkin, Frank, *Class Inequality and Political Order: Social Stratification in Capitalist and Communist Societies*, London, Mac Gribbon & Kee, 1971.

Parmeswaran, Uma, *A Study of Representative Indo-Anglian Novelists*, New Delhi, Vikas, 1976.

Parsons, Talcott and Shils, Edward, *Toward a General Theory of Action*, Cambridge, Harvard University Press, 1951.

Plekhanov, George, *Art and Social Life*, London, Lawrence & Wishart, 1953.

Podar, A. (ed.), *Indian Literature*, Simla, Indian Institute of Advanced Study, 1972.

Prawar, S.S. *Karl Marx and World Literature*, London, Oxford University Press, 1978.

Press, John (ed.), *Commonwealth Literature—Unity and Diversity in a Common Culture*, London, Heinemann, 1965.

Punnose, K.P. (ed.), *Contemporary Indian Novelists*, New Delhi, Literary Market Review, 1975.

Pye, Lucian W., *Politics, Personality and Nation-Building*, New Haven, Yale University Press, 1962.

——, *Communications and Political Development*, New Delhi, Radha Krishna Prakashan (Indian Edition), 1972.

Pye, L.W. and Verba, S. (eds.), [*Political Culture and Political Development*, Princeton, Princeton University Press, 1965.

Radhakrishnan, S., *Religion and Culture*, New Delhi, Orient Paperbacks, 1968.

Rana, A.P., *The Imperatives of Non-Alignment*, New Delhi, Macmillan, 1976.

Rao, A.V.K., *Nayantara Sahgal: A Study of Her Fiction and Non-Fiction 1954-1974*, Madras, M. Seshachalam & Co., 1976.

Rao, T.V.S., *Indian Writing in English: Is there any worth to it?* Madurai, Kodal, 1976.

Riemenschneider, D., *An Ideal of Man in Mulk Raj Anand's Novels*, Bombay, Kutub, n.d.

Rolland, Romain (trans. C.D. Groth), *Mahatma Gandhi*, New York, The Century Co., 1924.

Rosenbaum, Walter A., *Political Culture*, London, Thomas Nelson & Sons, 1975.

Roy, M.N., *Gandhism, Nationalism, Socialism*, Calcutta, Bengal Radical Club, 1940.

Rudolph L.I. and Rudolph, S.H. *Modernity of Tradition*, Chicago, Chicago University Press, 1967.

——, *Education and Politics in India*, Cambridge, Mass, Harvard University Press, 1972.

Sahlins, M.D. and Service, E.R. (eds.), *Evolution and Culture*, Ann Arbor, MI, University of Michigan, 1970.

Sarkar, Benoy Kumar, *The Aesthetics of Young India*, Calcutta, Kar, Majumdar & Co., 1922.

Sarma, G.P. *Nationalism in Indo-Anglian Fiction*, New Delhi, Sterling, 1978.

Sartre, Jean Paul, *Between Existentialism and Marxism*, New York, William Morrow and Co., 1974.

Savarkar, V.D., *The Indian War of Independence, 1857*, Bombay, Phoenix, 1947.

Selbourne, David, *An Eye to India—The Unmasking of a Tyranny*, Harmondsworth, Penguin Books, 1977.

Seliger, M., *Ideology and Politics*, New York, Free Press, 1976.

182   *Politics, Aesthetics and Culture*

Sen, S.P. (ed.), *History in Modern Indian Literature*, Calcutta, Institute of Historical Studies, 1975.

Shafer, Boyd C., *Nationalism—Myth and Reality*, New York, Harcourt, Brace and World, 1955.

Shahane, V.A., *Khushwant Singh*, New York, Twayne, 1972.

Sharma, K.S., *Indo-English Literature: A Collection of Critical Essays*, Ghaziabad, Vimal Prakashan, 1977.

Shils, Edward, *The Intellectual Between Tradition and Modernity: The Indian Situation*, The Hague, Mouton & Co., 1961.

Slaughter, Cliff, *Marxism, Ideology and Literature*, London, Macmillan, 1980.

Speare, Morris Edmund, *The Political Novel*, New York, Russell & Russell, 1966.

Spearman, Diana, *The Novel and Society*, London, Routledge and Kegan Paul, 1966.

Spencer, M. Dorothy, *Indian Fiction in English: An Annotated Bibliography*, Philadelphia, University of Pennsylvania, 1960.

Srivastava, A.K., *Alien Voice—Perspectives on Commonwealth Literature*, Lucknow, Print House, 1981.

Steinvorth, Krans, *The Indo-English Novel: The Impact of the West on Literature in a Developing Country*, Wiesbaden, Franz Steiner Verlag, 1975.

Tagore, Rabindranath, *Nationalism*, Madras, Macmillan, 1976.
——, *Sadhana*, London, Macmillan, 1913.

Taylor, Ronald (trans, ed.), *Aesthetics and Politics*, London, NLB, 1977.

Trilling, Lionel, *The Liberal Imagination—Essays on Literature and Society*, New York, The Viking Press, 1951.

Trotsky, Leon, *Literature and Revolution*, Ann Arbor, University of Michigan Press, 1960.

Vazquez, Adolfo Sanchez, *Art and Society—Essays in Marxist Aesthetics* (trans. by Maro Riofrancos), London, Monthly Review Press, 1973.

Verghese, C.P., *Essays on Indian Writing in English*, New Delhi, V.N. Publications, 1975.

Walsh, William, *R.K. Narayan—A Critical Appreciation*, London, Heinemann, 1982.
——, *A Manifold Voice—Studies in Commonwealth Literature*, London, Chatto and Windus, 1970.

——, *A Human Idiom: Literature and Humanity*, London, Chatto and Windus, 1964.

Watkins, Evan, *The Critical Act—Criticism and Community*, New Haven, Yale University Press, 1978.

Webster, John C.B. (ed.), *History and Contemporary India*, Bombay, Asia, 1971.

Wellek, Rene, *The Later Nineteenth Century*, London, Jonathan Cape, 1966.

——, *The Later Eighteenth Century*, London, Jonathan Cape, 1955.

——, *The Rise of English Literary History*, Chapel Hill, University of North Carolina Press, 1941.

Williams, H.M., *Studies in Modern Indian Fiction in English*, 2 Vols., Calcutta, Writers Workshop, 1973.

——, *Indo-Anglian Literature, 1800-1970: A Survey*, New Delhi, Orient Longman, 1976.

Williams, Raymond, *Marxism and Literature*, London, Oxford University Press, 1977.

——, *Communications*, Harmondsworth, Penguine, 1971.

——, *The Long Revolution*, Harmondsworth, Penguine Books, 1965.

——, *Culture and Society: 1780-1950*, London, Harper and Row, 1958.

Wilson, Robert N., *Man Made Plain*, Cleveland, Howard Allen, 1958.

Wood, Neal, *Communism and British Intellectuals*, New York, Columbia University Press, 1959.

Young, Crawford, *The Politics of Cultural Pluralism*, Wisconsin, University of Wisconsin Press, 1976.

Zinkin, Taya, *India Changes*, New York, Oxford University Press, 1958.

Zwick, Edward (ed.), *Literature and Liberalism*, Washington, D.C., The New Republic Book Co., 1970.

Articles

Achebe, C., "Novelist as Teacher", *New Statesman*, 69 (29 January 1965), 161-62.

Adkins, J.F., "History as Art Form: Khushwant Singh's Train

To Pakistan", *The Journal of Indian Writing in English*, 2, 2 (July 1974), 1-12.

Almond, G., "Comparative Political Systems", *Journal of Politics*, 18 (1956), 391-409.

Anand, Mulk Raj, "Tradition and Modernity in Literature", *Journal of South Asian Literature*, XI (Fall 1974), 45-50.

——, "Trends in Modern Indian Novel", *The Journal of Indian Writing in English* (January 1973), 1-6.

Asnani, S.M., "Towards a Closer Understanding of the Indo-English Novel", *Journal of South Asian Literature*, XVI, 2 S-F, 1981), 153-158.

Bantock, G.H., "Literature and the Social Sciences", *Critical Quarterly*, 17, 2, (Summer 1975), 99-127.

Bellapa, K.C., "The Elusive Classic: Khushwant Singh's *Train to Pakistan* and Chaman Nahal's *Azadi*", *Literary Criterion*, 15, 2 (1980), 62-73.

Bhatnagar, O.P., "Feminine Fiction In India", *Commonwealth Quarterly*, 8-9, (December 1978), 73-80.

Bhattacharya, Bhabani, "Literature and Social Reality", *The Aryan Path*, 9 (September 1955), 392-96.

Blaise, Clark, "A Novel of India's Coming of Age: *Midnight's Children*", *The New York Times Books Review* (9 April, 1981), 19.

Caute, D., "Realism and Commitment", *Times Literary Supplement*, 70 (26 March 1971), 347-8.

Chatterjee, Kalyan, "The Scientific Method and the Literary Culture", *Quest*, 93 (January-February 1975), 49-53.

Church, Richard, (et al.), "Claims of Politics", *Scrutiny*, 8, 2 (September 1939), 130-167.

Cowasji, Saros, "Mulk Raj Anand and His Critics", *Banasthali Patrika*, 12 (1969), 57-63.

——, "Princes and Politics", *The Literary Criterion*, VII, 4, (Summer 1969), 10-18.

Crick, Bernard, "Writers and Politics", *Critical Quarterly*, 22, 2 (Summer, 1980), 63-73.

Davidson, J.F., "Political Science and Political Fiction", *The American Political Science Review*, LV, 4 (December 1961), 851-860.

Dayananda, James Y., "Manohar Malgonkar on His Novel *The Princes*: An Interview", *Journal of Commonwealth Literature*, 9, 3 (April 1975), 21-28.

———, "The Novelist As Historian: Manohar Malgonkar's *The Devil's Wind* and the 1857 Rebellion", *Journal of South Asian Literature*, X, 1 (Fall 1974), 55-67.

Dey, Esha, "Raja Rao's India: The Axis of *Comrade Kirillov*— An Anti-Novel", *Commonwealth Quarterly*, 5, 20 (September 1981), 24-43.

Dubey, Rani, "Salman Rushdie's Interview with Rani Dubey", *Debonair* (June 1982), 56.

Eagleton, Terry, "Literature and Politics Now", *Critical Quarterly*, 20, 3 (Autumn 1978), 65-69.

Elliot, R.C., "Literature and Good Life: A Dilemma", *Yale Review*, 65 (Autumn 1975), 24-37.

Enzensberger, H.M., "Writer and Politics", *Times Literary Supplement*, 3422 (1967), 857-8.

Epps, Garrett, "Politics As Metaphor", *The Virginia Quarterly Review*, (Winter 1979), 75-98.

Ezeloe, Mosso, "Cross-cultural Encounter in Literature", *Indian P.E.N.*, 43 (November-December 1977), 11-12.

Fisch, H., "Sanctification of Literature", *Commentary*, 63, (June 1977) 63-9.

Gilbert, Irene, "Review of *The Day in Shadow*", *The Journal of South Asian Literature*, X, 1, (Fall 1974), 185-188.

Gowda, Anniah H.H., "Mulk Raj Anand", *The Literary Half-Yearly*, VI, 1 (January 1965), 51-60.

———, "Contemporary Creative Writers in English in India", *The Literary Half-Yearly*, 10, 1 (January 1969), 17-39.

Graeme, F., "The Study of Art in a Cultural Context", *The Journal of Aesthetics and Art Criticism*, (*JAAC*), XXXII, 2 (Winter 1973), 249-56.

Guptara, P.S., "The Impact of Europe on the Development of Indian Literature", *Review of National Literatures*, 10 (1979) 18-34.

Guzman, Richard R., "The Fiction of Raja Rao", *The Virginia Quarterly Review*, 56 (Winter 1980), 32-50.

Hall, R.W., "Plato's Theory of Art: A Reassessment", *JAAC*, XXXIII, 1 (1974), 75-82.

Hein, Hilde, "Aesthetic Consciousness: The Ground of Political Experience", *JAAC*, XXXV, 2 (Winter 1976), 143-152.

Hoffman, S.A., "Faction Behaviour and Culture Codes: India and Japan", *Journal of Asian Studies*, XL, 2 (February 1981), 231-254.

Hoggart, R., "Literature and Society", *American Scholar*, 35 (Spring 1966), 277-89.

Jain, Jasbir, "Coming to Terms with Gandhi: *Shadow From Ladakh*", *The Journal of Indian Writing in English*, 3, 2, (July 1975), 20-23.

Jha, Rama, "The Influence of Gandhian Thought on Indo-Anglian Novelists of the Thirties and Forties", *Journal of South Asian Literature*, XVI, 2 (Summer Fall 1981), 163-172.

Joshi, Sudhakar, "An Evening with Bhabani", *The Sunday Standard*, April 7, 1969, p. VII.

Kalinnikova, E.J., "On The National Specificities of the Indian Writers in English", *The Literary Half-Yearly*, XXI, 2 (July 1980), 1-10.

Kantak, V.Y., "Indo-English Fiction and the New Morality", *Indian Literature*, XXI, 5, (1978), 39-45.

Kaushik, Asha, "Meeting Raja Rao", *The Literary Criterion*, 3 (1983), 33-38.

——, "Political and the Literary—A Case Study of Dilip Hiro's *A Triangular View*", *Political Science Review*, 16, 1 (January-March 1977), 70-82.

Kim, Y.C., "The Concept of Political Culture", *Journal of Politics*, 26, 2 (May 1964), 313-336.

Kothari, Rajni, "The Congress System in India", *Asian Survey*, VII, 12 (December 1962), 1161-63.

Krishna, Daya, "Three Myths about Indian Philosophy", *Quest*, LIII, (Spring 1967), 9-16.

Kulshrestha, Chirantan, "Khushwant Singh's Fiction", *Indian Writing Today*, 4, 1 (January-March 1970), 19-26.

Lal, P., "Indian Writing in English", *Harvard Educational Review*, XXXIV, 2 (1964), 316-319.

Leites, Nathan, "Psycho-Cultural Hypotheses About Political Acts", *World Politics*, 1 (1948), 102-119.

Liu, Marcia P., "Continuity and Development in the Novels of Nayantara Sahgal", *Journal of Indian Writing in English*, 8, 1-2 (1980), 45-52.

Malik, Hafiz, "The Marxist Literary Movement in India and Pakistan", *Journal of Asian Studies*, 26 (1967), 649-64.

Malviya, K.D., "The Congress Must be a Cadre-Based Party", *Socialist India* 5, 3 (June 1972), 16.

Maini, Darshan Singh, "The Aging Lions", *Gentleman* (July, 1984), 83-87.

Masud, Iqbal, "Naipaul's Views on the Third World are biased", *Gentleman* (February 1984), 50.

Mathur, P.C., "Indigenization of Pre-existing Intellectual Disciplines: An Enquiry into the Problems and Preconditions of Development of Indian Political Science", *Political Science Review*, 18, 2 (January-March, April-June, 1979), 89-106.

Matts, T. and Barebash Y., "Literature in a Changing World, Literature that changes the world", *Soviet Literature*, 11 (1977), 11-15.

Metscher, Thomas, "Literature and Art as Ideological Form", *New Literary History*, XI, 1 (Antumn 1979), 21-39.

Mitchells, K., The Work of Art in its Social Setting and in its Aesthetic Isolation", *JAAC*, XXV, 4 (Summer 1967), 369-74.

Moraes, Dom, "Can Indians Write in English?" *Onlooker*, (July 15-31, 1976), 66-71.

Morawski, Stephen, "The Aesthetic Views of Marx and Engels", *JAAC*, XXVIII, 3 (Spring 1970), 301-314.

Morton, Frederick, "New Truths, Old Values", *New York Times Book Review*, (29 June 1958), 6.

Mount, F., "Literary Spirit in Politics", *Encounter*, 38 (January 1972), 3-9.

Mukherjee, Meenakshi, "Overkill: The State of Research in Indo-Anglian Fiction", *Journal of Literary Studies*, 2, 2, (December 1979), 1-7.

Namboodiripad, E.M.S., "Class Struggle in India", *The Marxist*, 1, 2 (October-December 1983), 1-8.

Nandkumar, Prema, "The Achievement of the Indo-Anglian Novelist", *The Literary Criterion*, (Winter 1961) 152-165.

Nandy, Ashis, "The Culture of Indian Politics: A Stock Taking", *Journal af Asian Studies*, 30, 1 (November 1970), 55-79.

Narain, Iqbal, "Politics of Non-Issues", *Asian Survey*, 19, 2 (February 1979), 165-177.

—,"Ideology and Political Development—Battle for Issues in Indian Politics", *Asian Survey*, XI, 2 (February 1971), 185-196.

—,"Cultural Pluralism, National Integration and Democracy in India", *Asian Survey*, XVI, 10 (October 1976), 903-911.

Narasimhan, Raji, "Indo-English Literature: Criticism Without Criteria", *Indian Horizons*, 24, 1 (1975), 45-71.

Narasimhaih, C.D., "Criticism and Culture", *The Literary Criterion*, VII, 1 (Winter 1965), 20-38.

Narayan, Dhirendra, "Indian National Character", *The Annals of American Academy of Political and Social Science*, 370 (March 1967), 124-132.

Narayanan, Gomathi, "British Fathers and Indian Sons: Guilt and Pride for the Indian Freedom Movement in the Post-Independence Indian Novel in English", *Journal of South Asian Literature*, XVII, 1 (Winter-Spring 1982), 207-224.

Pantham, Thomas, "On the Reformation of Political Culture in India: Participatory and Egalitarian Values among Political Elites", *The Journal of Commonwealth and Comparative Politics*, XVIII, 2 (July 1980), 172-181.

Paolucci, Anne, "India's Banyan: As many trees as branches", *Review of National Literatures*, 10 (1979), 10-17.

Parameswaran, Uma, "Lest he Returning Chide: Saleem Sinai's Inaction in Salman Rushdie's *Midnight's Children*", *The Literary Criterion*, XVIII, 3 (1983), 57-66.

Putnam, H., "Literature, Science and Reflection", *New Literary History*, 7 (Spring 1976), 483-91.

Raghavan, V., "India: Tradition and non-conformism in creative writing and arts", *Eastern Anthropologist*, 29, 2 (April-June 1976), 189-200.

Rajiva, Stanley F., "Contemporary Indian Writing in English", *Quest*, LX (January-March 1969), 72-75.

Rao, K.S.N., "The Untranslated Translation and Aesthetic Consequences: Indian Fiction in English", *Southern Review*, 8 (1975), 189-204.

Reck, R.D., "The Politics of Literature", *PMLA*, 85 (May 1970), 429-332.

Riemenchneider, D., "The Function of Labour in Mulk Raj Anand's Novels", *The Journal of the School of Languages*, (Monsoon 1976), 1-20.

Rneckert, W., "Literary Criticism and History: The Endless Dialectic", *New Literary History*, 6 (Spring 1975), 491-512.

Sahgal, Nayantara, "Testament of an Indo-Anglian Writer", *Indian and Foreign Review*, X, 4 (December 1972), 17-19.

Shapiro, Gary, "Hegel's Dialectic of Artistic Meaning", *JAAC* XXXV, 1, (Fall 1976), 23-35.

Sharp, Patricia, "The Challenge to the Indian Writer Today", *Quest*. LIX (Autumn 1968), 31-39.

Sherill, Kenneth, "The Attitudes of Modernity", *Comparative Politics*, 1 (January 1969), 184-210.

Singh, Khushwant, "After the Raj", *New Statesman* (September 10, 1960), 348.

Singh, Tavleen, "Magic, Mystery, Madness", *The Sunday Statesman* (13 December 1981), 2.

Spegele, R.D., "Fiction and Political Theory", *Social Research*, 38 (Spring 1971), 108-38.

Spender, Stephen, "Writers and Politics", *Partisan Review*, 34 (Summer 1967), 359-381.

Spitz, David, "Politics and the Critical Imagination", *Review of Politics*, 32 (October 1970), 419-435.

Srinivas, M.N., "Is the Sun Setting?", *Seminar* (February 1967), 12-16.

Sullivan, E.D., "Relevance of Fiction", *Virginia Quarterly Review*, 46 (Summer 1970), 411-32.

Thomas, T.K., "The Hindu Ethos", *Religion and Society*, XX, 4 (December 1973), 56-57.

Towers, Robert, "On the World Mountains", *New York Review of Books*, (September 24, 1981), 28.

Tucker, Robert C., "Culture, Political Culture and Communist Society", *Political Science Quarterly*, 88, 2 (June 1977), 173-90.

Tyrner, A.G., "Indo-Anglian Literature and the Indian Elite", *Cornell Journal of Social Relations*, 1, 1 (1966), 25-32.

Vacha, J.E., "It could Happen Here: The Rise of the Political Scenario Novel", *American Quarterly*, 29 (Summer 1977), 194-206.

Vanderbok, William, "Political Culture and Development: Some Pervasive Themes in the Study of Indian Politics", *Modern Asian Studies*, 12, 1 (February 1978), 145-155.

Verghese, C.P., "The Problem of the Indian Novelist in English", *The Banasthali Patrika*, 13 (January 1969), 83-27.

Waters, Bruce, "Politics and Literature", *The Prarie Schooner*, 25 (Winter 1951), 347-359.

Weaver, P.R.C., "Tyranny of Literature", *Times Literary Supplement*, 3361 (June 28, 1966), 663-4.

Wendt, Allan, "Babu to Sahib: Contemporary Indian Literature", *South Atlantic Quarterly*, 64 (1965), 166-180.

Williams, H.M., "English Writing in Free India", *Twentieth Century Literature*, 16, 1 (January 1970), 3-15.

——, "Indian Literature in English: Social Change and Indian Inwardness", *New Literature Review*, 4 (1978), 11-16.

Zuckerman, R.V.H., "Review of *This Time of Morning and Storm in Chandigarh*", *Mahfil*, VI, 4 (Winter 1970), 81-87.

Zutshi, C.N., "Literature and Politics", *Thought*, 21 (2 August 1969), 15-16.

Index

Sahgal, Nayantara, 7, 51, 53, 89, 94-96, 98, 100, 101, 103, 106, 112-114, 139-144, 155, 156, 158, 160, 161, 165, 166
Sanjogita, 50
Sanskritization, 123, 131
Sartori, G., 82
Sartre, Jean-Paul, 4, 13, 18, 22, 122
Sarvodaya, 137
Satthianandhan Krupabai, 50
Satya, 50
Savarkar, V.D., 71
Schiller, 15
Scrutiny, 23
Serpent and the Rope, The, 159
Seven Summers, 126
Shadow from Ladakh, 137
Shafer, B.C., 47
Sheorey, A.G., 89, 95, 96, 112, 113, 155, 156
Shils, Edward, 28, 29
Sholokhov, 17
Shunkur: A Tale of the Indian Mutiny of 1857, 50
Singh, Jogender, 50
Sinha, K.K., 50
Sita myth, 161
Situation in New Delhi, A, 113, 156, 120
Socialism, Democratic, 121
Socrates, 162
Some Inner Fury, 53
So Many Hungers, 60, 62, 64
Srinivas, M.N., 123
Steinbeck, J., 17
Sthala Purana, The, 161
Storm in Chandigarh, 94, 95
Sunlight on a Broken Column, 63, 67
Sword and The Sickle, The 51, 63, 126, 130

Tagore, Rabindra Nath, 62, 126, 137, 145, 160, 161
Taine, Hyppolyte, 15, 16

Tapa, 122
Tasso, 15
Terrorism, 64, 127
There Lay the City, 51
This Time of Morning, 59, 63, 95, 96, 98, 100
Tilak, B. G., 46, 50, 65, 120
Time to be Happy, A, 53
Toffler, Alvin, 162
Toller, 17
Tolstoy, Alexi, 17
Tolstoy, Leo, 17
Total Revolution, 124
Train to Pakistan, 59, 63, 67
Trotsky, 19, 20
Two Leaves and a Bud, 128, 134
Two Nation Theory, 68

Untouchable 51, 126, 128, 134-136
Vedanta, 159
Venkatramani, 51, 53
Verba, Sidney, 29-31
Vico, 15
Vidyasagar, Ishwar Chandra, 139
Village, The, 51, 126
Vivekanand, 46

Waiting for the Mahatma, 7, 53, 55, 57
Walsb, William, 57
Webb, Beatrice, 27
Weiner, Myron, 164
Williams, Raymond, 12, 13, 15, 18, 19, 22-26, 34, 123, 160
Wound of Spring, The, 53
Wood, Neal, 22

Yashpal, 48, 76
Young Zamindar, The, 50
Yug Samachar, 96, 97

Zohra, 53